Privileged Witness

Air Commodore MK Janjua

Edited by Shahidah Janjua

Published by Geepy Publishing 2013

Geepy Publishing
Ireland
www.geepypublishing.com

ISBN-13: 978-0-9927564-0-6

ACKNOWLEDGEMENTS

I owe a debt of gratitude to my mother who kept my father's memoir safe for all the years after his demise in 1982. My brother Ali Janjua provided me with any additional related papers he could lay his hands on. He was eager for our father's story to be told, as this is what he would have wished for, and as a mark of our respect for him. I am grateful to my cousin Kaleem Janjua for his unfailing encouragement and belief in my ability to get it published. I am grateful to all the other members of my extended family who loved my father dearly; who respected and honoured him. Knowing about their love enabled me to keep going in my efforts to transcribe the memoir.

I want to say a heartfelt thank you to my own family; for the love and support of my daughter Nina who has, over the years, shared many stories and fond memories of her grandfather with me. A heartfelt thank you to my grandson Ramir, for his deep and constant love and support and his desire to know all he can about his great grandfather and his own heritage. I have a special thank you for my sensitive and gracious son Adam who died in 2010. He was always encouraging of my writing.

I could not have done this work without the love and support of my closest friends. They gave me clarity, hope and strength in my darkest times and the amazing gift of belief in me.

But none of this would have been possible without the love of my partner John. I cannot begin to quantify his contribution to the whole process. He nursed me through life threatening illness. He helped me to regain my physical and mental strength; helped me to keep my focus, appreciated any small effort I could make to keep writing, without ever being disappointed when I could not. His primary concern has been for my welfare. Above all he has made the physical entity of this published and printed book a reality, by undertaking all the work that would bring it about. I can safely say that without his diligence and tenacity this work would never have come into being. My thanks to him are immeasurable. I am blessed to have him in my life.

Shahidah Janjua

Air Commodore MK Janjua

.

CONTENTS

Acknowledgments

Foreword   3

Introduction   9

Chapter 1   Metamorphosis   23

Chapter 2   Involvement   43

Chapter 3   Their Clarity, Our Confusion   59

Chapter 4   Rises the Stained Sun   107

Chapter 5   Birth Pangs and More   125

Chapter 6   The Steep Climb   145

Chapter 7   Various and Varied Encountered   171

Chapter 8   Kashmir   191

Chapter 9   Clashes and Intrigues   271

Chapter 10   Coup de Grace   309

Afterword   347

Ghazal

I am being accused of loving you, that is all
It is not an insult, but a praise, that is all

My heart is pleased at the words of the accusers
O my dearest dear, they say your name, that is all

For what I am ridiculed, it is not a crime
My heart's useless playtime, a failed love, that is all

I haven't lost hope, but just a fight, that is all
The night of suffering lengthens, but just a night, that is all

In the hand of time is not the rolling of my fate
In the hand of time roll just the days, that is all

A day will come for sure when I will see the truth
My beautiful beloved is behind a veil, that is all

The night is young, Faiz start saying a Ghazal
A storm of emotions is raging inside, that is all

Faiz Ahmed Faiz
(Prison Journal)

Foreword

My father wrote his memoir in order to document his experiences of the years leading up to and just after the partition of India and the birth of Pakistan. Strictly speaking this is not a historical document. There was no academic research undertaken to back up its claims. However, it is the experience and perspective of a significant individual whose actions made a difference at that time and for a considerable period afterwards. It is a personal record of particular events that took place during those years.

My father was the senior most air force officer in Pakistan when it gained its independence. For this reason he was made Commander-in-Chief of the Pakistan air force for a brief period. He designed the air force crest and selected the motto. My father gives an account of his own background in the introduction to his memoir. For those who are not aware of, or too young to have known of his role at that time, I can say that he does not hold back from sharing what he knew of the events leading up to Pakistan gaining its independence. From what he says it is both evident and tragic that the very foundations of the country, as laid down by the first government, were riddled with corruption and self-interest, a legacy left to it by the colonisers but upheld by the Pakistan government. Subsequently the general population has had little choice but to function within that culture, while political leaders have not had the will to change it, since they clearly benefit. Whatever his faults, my father gave his all for his country. He was a patriot in the best sense of the word and was made to suffer for it by those who put their own interests before those of their country.

It is clear that my father was particularly passionate about what happened in Kashmir. The longest chapter in his memoir deals with this issue. He saw it as the duty of the Pakistani leadership to assist the people of Kashmir against attacks and occupation by the Indian forces. Try as he might to get the government to continue military action in defence of the Kashmiri people, they did not. My father took it upon himself to provide whatever assistance he could in the way of warm clothing, weapons and ammunition. At that time the British held the senior most positions in the forces of both countries, India and Pakistan, and were political advisors to both governments. They worked to their own agenda. My father described the loss of life during the whole period of partition as genocide. He understood that Kashmir was being used as a bone of contention between the two newly independent states, a classic example of divide and rule. However this is only a broad sweep of the context, there were many different aspects to the struggles of the Kashmiri people. I am sure others will bring their own unique experiences to bear on, and have their own interpretation of, those events.

Unfortunately the memoir stops short of recollecting the trial, which was preceded by the arrest and imprisonment of my father and several others on what was later proved to be a false charge of Conspiracy. The charge was only made possible by the passing of a law enacted *after* the arrest of the men, which was used to incriminate them. Again, some readers may remember the Rawalpindi Conspiracy Case which was strenuously fought against by the falsely accused men. The Pakistani government of the time, which served the interests of Britain and the United States, produced an 'intelligence report' to say that the Soviet Union was behind the conspiracy. That information was an invention, based on their fears of where the popularity of some of the more influential men may lead.

My father was incarcerated for a number of years, while the trial took place. During that period I was taken on visits to him by my mother. She supported him throughout when many friends and family were too afraid to acknowledge any connection with him. Inevitably my father's career in the air force ended at the point of his arrest. When he was finally released he was, some time later, able to secure a job with the government owned Pakistan International Airlines (PIA) and was posted to London not long after. He was then promoted to Regional Manager, his responsibility being to oversee the operations of the PIA offices in Europe. The immediate family, my mother, my brother and sister, twins, accompanied him to London. I had been sent ahead with my maternal grandmother.

The post within PIA did not last long due to my father's ill health. Others; friends and family who have outlived my father, may know the circumstances in which he left PIA, better than I. In Pakistan he had become a popular and respected political figure and thereby a threat to the incumbent government. It was evident that my father's activities were monitored and he did not feel it was safe for him to return, even to visit his family. He could never have been accused of being faint-hearted; the threat was palpable. Indeed, his publication 'Democratic Pakistan', was banned from export to Pakistan. My father's military training and innate intelligence had enabled him to be an astute strategist and analyst. His analysis of the events in Palestine, were lauded by members of the Pakistan government who otherwise feared and reviled him.

I would not do my father justice if I gave you a sentimental or mawkish picture of him. He was a political activist from an early age, when he challenged the authority of elders whom he believed to be corrupt or unjust. He remained as such throughout his life. He was also a truly loving father who cared deeply for his two wives and his eight children. He had an equal depth of love for his mother, his siblings and their children. Being the eldest son, he never lost his sense of duty towards them, particularly since the death of his own father.

Included among the many attributes his values demanded of him and which he practiced, were kindness, fairness, courage, loyalty and love. As is the case with all human beings he was also riven by contradictions, torn apart sometimes by his sense of justice on the one hand and some unhelpful traditional values on the other. We fell foul of each other when I gave expression to the need to be an independent woman; the right to make my own decisions and mistakes. Inconceivable for a girl then and often times in the present. I left home and we did not speak for four years until my first child, my daughter Nina, was born, when we were reconciled amidst tears and laughter. Towards the end of his life I remember having a conversation with him while we walked in the back garden when, at his instigation, we talked about the meaning of Taboos and their use by societies as somewhere to hide their deepest and darkest secrets. Increasing weakness and fatigue as a result of a series of strokes, resulting in one which left him partially paralysed, prevented him from completing and publishing further works on the subjects dear to his heart.

It is one of my greatest fortunes to have had a father who taught me about what is most valuable in life; love, courage, tenacity, independence of thought and spirit and a politics that embraced all aspects of social justice. He bore these values with an innocence that belied his age and experience. Any inhumane act could potentially break his heart; he believed in the goodness in every human being which, perhaps, would not have survived in an increasingly cynical and cruel world. His heart had already broken when his younger brother and his eldest son died within months of each other. It was only at that point that he finally let go, the burden of grief being too great to compete with any imperative to live. He died in the autumn of 1982.

This memoir is my father's personal record of the turbulent times resulting in the division of the sub-continent. Although he played an active part in them, he also bore witness to the events surrounding them; the role of the British, the Indian and the Pakistani governments, the role of individuals, the political intrigue, the creeping corruption, the cowardice of those in power and the heroism of ordinary people.

Shahidah Janjua

Air Commodore MK Janjua

Introduction

Pakistan has entered the 34th year of its chequered existence[1]. Born amid possibly the greatest orgy of violence in the history of the Indian sub-continent, its birth was also accompanied by the largest mass migration in the history of mankind. From its inception Pakistan was set on a course which brought neither domestic tranquillity nor meaningful social and economic progress; neither peace nor stability to South Asia as a whole.

Successive regimes embroiled the country in three wars, coming off worse on each occasion and finally losing Pakistan's most populace province in 1971, the result being the emergence of a sovereign Bangladesh. Today Pakistan is experiencing its third Martial Law regime: thus for half its life the nation has been under direct military rule. The periods in between have witnessed the enforcement of measures intended to shackle the domestic process.

---

[1]The Partition of the Indian subcontinent in 1947 into two postcolonial states of India and Pakistan was a cataclysmic event, accompanied by unprecedented genocidal violence and one of the largest displacements of people in the twentieth century. www.globalsecurity.org

I have been a witness to these developments, initially from close quarters in my capacity as the senior most Pakistani Officer in the Pakistan Air Force, including my six-month tenure as its officiating Commander-in-Chief from May to October, 1948. After my retirement I took an active part in politics and became a founder member of the National Awami Party, the principal opposition party in Pakistani politics. But my emotional involvement in political developments associated with the freedom movements of India and Pakistan commenced several years prior to the partition of India in 1947. At first my sympathies lay with the independence movement of India as a whole. At a later stage, as the senior most Muslim Officer in the Indian Air Force, I found myself in a position where the various facets of the independence movement became clearer. It was no longer a matter of obtaining independence through a struggle by a homogeneous national mass movement. Although to me it seemed that there was universal desire for independence, yet there were fundamental differences of goal, mainly between the All India National Congress and the All India Muslim League. The latter purported to represent India's Muslim minority, alleging that the former represented only the Hindu majority, despite the fact that several prominent Muslims belonged to its higher echelons. The demand of the Congress was for 'Akhand Bharat' – United India – while the Muslim League waged a struggle for a homeland for the Muslims comprising the provinces of the north west and the north east of India, where they were in the majority. The argument advanced by the Muslim League was that, under the prevailing conditions, which were themselves the culmination of a historically long and complicated background – especially after the so-called Sepoy Mutiny of 1857 – the Muslim minority in a united India, would be overwhelmed by a more powerful and more advanced Hindu majority in all aspects of life, and would therefore lose their identity.

In the context of the situation as it developed, especially from 1945 onwards, I noticed the rise of intense communal emotions on all sides. I was propelled towards the fight for a Muslim homeland due to my own first hand experiences of, what I deemed to be, unjust discrimination against the Muslim minority community to which I belonged. Since I was by then the senior most Muslim Officer in the Indian Air Force, I was obliged to come into contact with political individuals at the highest level. There was then a coalition government in India, with Jawaharlal Nehru heading it. Nawabzada Liaquat Ali Khan was the Finance Minister, later to become the first Prime Minister of Pakistan and Sardar Abdul Rab Nishtar held another portfolio on behalf of the Muslim League: these two men along with Mr. Mohammad Ali Jinnah, comprised the Pakistan team at the Reconstitution Committee, over which Lord Mountbatten presided.

I was nominated to head the Pakistan Air Force sub-committee of the Armed Forces Reconstitution Committee. In this capacity, and for other reasons mentioned earlier, I became deeply involved in the political developments of the period and later in Pakistan where I became a privileged witness.

My story is, I think, interesting in itself, but more importantly it mirrors the experience of an entire generation. At the time of partition the sub-continent stood at the crossroads of history. The very process had shattered the peace and held grave consequences for the future.

The subsequent national experiences of the peoples of the sub-continent, have been vastly different. The Republic of India has done most to fulfil its potential. Despite glaring social inequalities it ranks amongst the first eight industrial nations, with the third highest pool of scientific and technological personnel in the world; playing also a not insignificant role in international affairs. Whereas, alas, in Pakistan, a void has been created which has yet to be filled. Most political literature, if it can be so termed, derives from non-political sources, with perhaps one exception, no eminent Pakistani political personality has recorded his experiences. A few who have written in recent years have been either heavily biased- having thrown facts and scientific research to the winds – or resorted to pure sycophancy. There has been a great dearth of true historical testimony. It is for this reason that, having had much time to reflect, I wish to record my experience during an immensely crucial period in the history of the sub-continent and of Pakistan: to add something, however modest, to the knowledge and the political understanding of the people of Pakistan and hopefully, of others in the sub-continent.

I was the eldest of nine children, four boys and five girls. In the prevailing social values of the area being the eldest son brought certain advantages. My father was an affectionate, humane person and did not ever deny any of his children love or any of the required social and material needs, but perforce decided to invest more in me than he would have done had the order of my arrival or sex been different. I, therefore, received an education intended not only to enhance the social standing of the family but to provide for its material well being and future security. Although all his other children received an adequate education, including my three elder sisters – probably the first educated Muslim girls in our region – all of them undoubtedly suffered disadvantages because of the relatively high expenditure on my upbringing. The means at my father's disposal were limited considering his aims and ambitions for his children: but his firm determination, immense energy and sharp intellect enabled him to fulfil a minimum programme for his family, enabling us to play a useful role in a rapidly changing society.

I was born on 19th May 1914, in a remote village in the Salt Range of the Jhelum district in the Punjab. The name of this hamlet is Malot, said to be a corruption of Mal-Vet, the home of Mal. When written in Persian characters it is readily pronounced as Malot. It is said to have been the seat of the ruler Raja Mal, a Rajput chieftain of the territory lying between the Jhelum and Indus rivers, including Kashmir, who was a contemporary of William the Conqueror. The village and its two ancient temples preceded him by several centuries.

The Rajput members of this small community, my family among them, claim descent from Raja Mal, who was said to have embraced Islam at the hands of a Muslim missionary. We are therefore known as Muslim Rajputs. Apart from pride in this heritage the people of Malot and its surrounding areas were left with a progressively shrinking means of subsistence. The small land holdings in a mountainous, largely barren area – due to salt deposits – had left people with no alternative but to seek employment in the services of successive rulers or to trade in salt. But during British rule they, together with the other so-called martial or warrior races of the Punjab, found employment in the British Indian Army: and their region became, and to this day remains, among the most heavily recruited.

It was for these reasons that my father found his way into a regiment of Mountain Artillery; even though he acted against the wishes of his parents. Being the only son, and the only literate Muslim young man in a vast area, his father in his customary wish on his death bed had blessed him thus: "As for my son, I place a golden pen in his hand." This was indeed prophetic. My father went on to master at least eight languages, all virtually self-taught, and won high honours. He was also acknowledged as one of the best gunners of his time. He was an expert in Military Law and was conversant with the Indian Penal Code. He was a writer, poet, playwright, composer and actor. His manifold activities in all these fields influenced me more than any other factor: and his liberal, humane nature, completely free of religious or racial prejudice, have been an inspiration to me throughout my working life. My mother, a frail little lady but endowed with great patience and courage, gave him all the support he needed. In an era of almost complete illiteracy even among Muslim males, she was of course, illiterate, but this was in no way a handicap to her as the mother of a large family and the wife of a man with ambitions beyond even the understanding of most of his contemporaries.

My father had enlisted as a mule driver in a Mountain Battery and achieved the rank of Captain before he retired. He had wanted me to start where he had finished, so my education was planned to achieve that goal. English was vital for this and I was enrolled in an English medium school, the Grammar School of Quetta. I took the exams for the Cambridge School Certificate in December, 1932 and passed in all subjects, but before the results had appeared I had already taken the entrance examination of the Public Service Commission to train for a Commission in the Indian Army. I qualified and entered the second term in the Indian Military Academy (IMA), Dehra Dun, in February, 1933: Indians by then were not required to go to Sandhurst but instead went to the IMA. The Indian Commission became a substitute for the earlier King's Commission.

[2]. Burhan-ud-Din was the brother of the Ruler of Chitral. In 1944, he was one of three IOC's of the Indian National Army. The Indian National Army was formed from Indian soldiers who were fighting for the British against the Japanese. They were captured by the Japanese and taken to Singapore. They were given a choice: Join the workers who were building the Death Railway including the Bridge Over the River Kwai, or take up arms and fight against the British on the side of the Japanese. Prince Burhan-ud-Din became one of the commanders of the group who opted not to build the Bridge Over the River Kwai.

When Rangoon fell to the British on May 3, 1945, Prince Burhan-ud-Din was captured the same day and placed under arrest. He was charged with a wartime autrocity. Many men under his command had often left their posts to go into Rangoon in search of women, often not to return for several days. Prince Burhan-ud-Din, a deeply religious man, was offended by this practice, so he had five of his soldiers rounded up in Rangoon, brought back, and flogged as deserters. One of them, whose name was Joga Singh, died during the flogging. When the British captured the Indian National Army they were naturally anxious to put some of their leaders on trial. Prince Burhan-ud-Din was tried, convicted and sentenced to seven years in prison in 1946. Three other members of the Indian National Army were also convicted but they received lesser sentences.

I was eventually commissioned as a 2nd Lieutenant in the Indian Army, but according to practice I was posted for a year's attachment to a British unit in India – second battalion, The Highland Light Infantry (Queen Victoria's own City of Glasgow Regiment). At the end of the attachment in August, 1936 I joined my Indian Army unit, 1st Battalion of the 7th Rajput Regiment. Among others in this battalion who rose to high rank later were General Cariappa, the first Indian Commander-in-Chief of the post-partition Indian Army, and Lieutenant general Moti Sagar who became my closest friend in the services. Not being entirely satisfied in the army, I took the first opportunity to transfer to the Indian Air Force in September, 1938. I did my initial flying training in Delhi and advanced training with the RAF in Egypt, with two other Indian Officers: Lieutenant D.A.R. Nanda who retired as Air Vice Marshall from post-partition I.A.F. and Lieutenant Burhan-ud-Din, a prince from Chitral State, who later reverted to the Indian Army. He was a POW of the Japanese, joined the Indian National Army under Netaji Subhash Chandra Bose, was tried with others after the war and dismissed from service. [2]

The Second World War started soon after we returned to India. I was immediately posted to Coast Defence flight in Karachi; but spent most of the early years of the war on the North West Frontier, on operational flying with its interesting and exciting aspects, further training and conversion to modern aircraft and on Army co-operation detachments. Due to the rapid expansion of the I.A.F, I was given command of a squadron at the end of 1942, and then became staff officer at Group and Air Headquarters from the end of 1944 till 15 August, 1945.

On this date I was appointed Deputy President of 57, Services Selection Board at Dehra Dun with the rank of Wing Commander. With this began the hectic part of my life, the tempo of which mounted ceaselessly. I was always politically inclined and had been writing articles and analyses on social and political subjects for several years, under a pseudonym: as a member of the armed forces I could not use my own name. After the war the demand for independence gathered enormous momentum. The vast background, covering many generations, brought the situation to the point of no return: but the interests of the Hindu and Muslim ruling classes clashed. The interests of the British further complicated the situation and heightened tensions to an unprecedented degree.

By the time I was transferred to Air Headquarters, Delhi, in November, 1946 several communal riots had already taken place, the most notable being those in Calcutta, ostensibly in response to the Muslim League call for a Direct Action Day, 16 August, 1946; closely followed by Bihar and Noakhali in East Bengal. This process continued unabated, enveloped almost the whole of Northern India and culminated in the unprecedented holocaust which accompanied the partition of India and the birth of Pakistan.

I saw evidence of acute communal prejudice in which my community, the Muslims, seemed in danger of being overwhelmed. My heart went out to them, but I had not in any way deviated from the prejudice-free influence of my father. I was for the defence of my endangered community and not for offensive action. My anxiety grew and I plunged into activity. I established contact with the Muslim politicians in the interim cabinet. In due course I found them largely complacent and mindless concerning the defence of their community which, even according to themselves, was threatened with virtual extinction. In my view there was no objective of the Muslim masses which required aggression, but there was every apparent reason to prepare for self-defence. In this regard the Muslim League Leadership seemed to have shunned the latter, relied solely on constitutional methods – as repeatedly proclaimed by Mr. M. A. Jinnah – and insisted that other parties abide by such rules, while the emotions of the people were roused to fever pitch. Slogans called for hand-to-hand fighting but took no account of the tools with which to do this. The Hindu opponents, however, were trained and equipped for the purpose.

In those conditions I found myself working on three fronts, especially after 3 June, 1947 when the decision to partition India was announced: briefing the politicians on the state of Muslim personnel and equipment in the I.A.F, actively engaging in dividing the former for Pakistan, as senior representative on the Air Force sub-committee of the Armed Forces Reconstitution Committee; above all trying to finds weapons for beleaguered Muslims who were under ferocious attack by the Hindu majority, in districts to the west and north west of Delhi. It was a small but dangerous effort, in which at least three of us exposed ourselves to well nigh fatal military charges, by taking out small arms from I.A.F. armouries. A clandestine organisation took these to some of the affected areas.

I had several meetings with Mr. Jinnah, Nawabzada Liaquat Ali Khan, Sardar Abdul Rab Nishtar, Raja Ghanzarfar Ali Khan and other Muslim League politicians. I was generally dismayed at their lack of a concrete programme for setting Pakistan off on a sound footing. The Muslim masses had been asked to support the movement and make sacrifices, which they did. What were their leaders going to do for them now? The people of Pakistan were to discover the answer to this after suffering much pain and tribulation.

There was tremendous enthusiasm to start with. We in the Air Force, having taken into account the number and composition of our personnel and the equipment at our disposal, made our first 'five year plan' – an expansion target to be achieved by 1952. The political decision later was to have British Officers as Commanders-in-Chief of the defence forces. I and certain other officers did not agree, but decided to accept it in the best interests of our country. The British C-in-C of the P.A.F. had had no hand in the preparation of our expansion programme. This fact and the clash of views about our national interests and British interests, led to the most acrimonious relationship between me and my C-in-C, and then to my astonishment, with the Defence Secretary and the Prime Minister as well.

Meanwhile, soon after partition, the Kashmir conflict began. The Muslim people of the south west districts of Jammu and Kashmir State had risen against the Dogra ruler in June, 1947 and were engaged in a limited armed struggle. On the establishment of Pakistan they intensified their efforts. In September, 1947 I was approached by a Major Khurshid Anwar, whom I had known earlier in Delhi (in the clandestine organisation), for help with arms and ammunition but above all for petrol and oil to transport volunteers to Kashmir. I considered it a legitimate act for volunteers to go to the aid of Kashmiri people in their struggle to rid themselves of a tyrannical ruler. I ordered whatever was needed and possible to give, together with professional technical assistance. It transpired later that the organisers of tribal volunteers were Abdul Qayyum Khan, Chief Minister of North West Frontier Province, and Pir Manki Sharif, a prominent and widely respected Muslim League leader. The British C-in-C was not informed. The P.A.F. provided help until the Pakistani Army went in, in response to the landing of the Indian Army. It was no longer a people's war of liberation and I halted the material aid. But flights by P.A.F. and some civilian transport aircraft, taking mainly food, medicines and clothing, continued to Gilgit and Skardu. P.A.F. pilots later flew along the Indus valley by night to avoid I.A.F. fighter interception. I do not believe more hazardous flights have been undertaken by any other air force. A complex, tangled situation eventually emerged, the effects of which are still with us.

In May, 1948 I assumed command of Pakistan Air Force for six months, when the British C-in-C was away on sick leave. I had already been promoted to the rank of Air Commodore. During this period several momentous events took place, which were to lead to my ultimate removal. I had already put our expansion programme into effect, disregarding my C-in-C's wishes to the contrary, and had refused to buy 50 war surplus Spitfires, lying at one of our depots, because they were not in our re-equipment programme. This led to a furious encounter with my C-in-C when he, unbeknownst to me, obtained the Prime

Minister's approval for the release of 37 new Tempest aircraft to India, instead of paying for them and keeping them in Pakistan as part of our re-equipment programme.

Overshadowing all of this, however, was the death of the father of the Nation, M.A. Jinnah, on 11, September 1948, and on the same day, an all day conference or 'War Council' meeting at the Prime Minister's official residence concerning the imminent Indian police action against the Nizam of Hyderabad. Jinnah's demise marked the tragic end of a man who had towered above his political colleagues, yet had become, within a short time of Pakistan's creation, a lonely discarded figure of little use to those who had muscled their way into power and were now unwilling to share it. Whatever he may have had in his mind for the people of Pakistan – and I for one believed he wanted to work for the common good within the limits of a liberal bourgeois system – he was unable to put his plans into practice. He was given neither the time nor the assistance needed for his purposes. Indeed, he came up against stubborn resistance from all the quarters that mattered. In his inaugural speech, Jinnah spoke eloquently of a secular Pakistan, free of religious bigotry or sectarian strife. The subsequent history of Pakistan belied his hopes. If I were to be told he died of a broken heart I would have little difficulty believing it.

After his death it became a free for all for the country's political leadership; degrading norms became the order of the day, and unbridled corruption stunted intellectual growth.

I came into direct conflict with the Defence Secretary and some senior British and Pakistani army officers over defence preparations against a possible Indian attack, after their victory over the Nizam's forces. This in the end led to my removal from the post of Deputy Air Commander and made me a virtual exile in Britain in January, 1949. I was, however, recalled by the new C-in-C P.A.F. but our relationship was uncomfortable because of my alleged anti-British attitude. I was selected on merit I hope, but I suspect also to get me away from Pakistan, by getting me to attend a course at the Imperial Defence College, London in 1950. I returned home in January, 1951. Within seven weeks I was arrested (detained at my residence, under armed guard) for complicity in a conspiracy to overthrow the government. This became known as the Rawalpindi Conspiracy Case. I, and ten other army officers and four civilians, were tried by a special tribunal, under the Rawalpindi Conspiracy Special Tribunal Act. The entire proceedings were held in camera, inside Hyderabad Central Prison. The government alone could publish all or any part of the proceedings, a practice without precedent before or since. The verdict was delivered on 5 January, 1953 and I was sentenced to 7 years imprisonment. Liquat Ali Khan, the Prime Minister, had been assassinated on 16 October, 1951. Had he lived at least four of us would have been executed. There were in fact two conspiracies. The first was serious and an overthrow of the government could have been achieved. The second, for which we were tried, had no earthly chance of success and was in reality an academic discussion with, of course, serious implications. I was not present at either of the conspiracies. I was in Australia during the first and in Karachi, 1000 miles away, when the second occurred. None of us served our full sentences. In 1954 the Governor General, Malik Ghulam Mohammad, dismissed the government, dissolved parliament and abrogated the constitution. The Act which he used in justification had a flaw, just like the one under which we were tried: it was ultra vires. We were released on 12 April, 1955.

I now moved into politics. I became one of the founder members of National Awami Party (NAP) together with Wali Khan and Maulana Bhashani. It was the first secular, democratic, patriotic party with a national programme, and an anti-imperialist, and anti-neo-colonialist orientation. It stood for non-alignment, good neighbourliness, and opposed military alliances, such as the Baghdad Pact (later CENTO) and SEATO (South East Asia Treaties Organisation), as being against our national interests. Our stand has been vindicated over the years.

However, the party's initial life was brief. Ayub Khan imposed Martial Law in October 1958 and banned all political activity and then went into a political limbo for some time.

In September, 1959 I applied to join Pakistan International Airlines and was accepted; a step towards my rehabilitation. I arrived in London on Christmas Eve 1959 to assume charge as P.I.A's District Manager for the U.K. and Ireland – later as Regional Manager for all areas from Iran to the U.S.A. Due to ill health and my inability to take up an appointment at the PIA Head Office in Karachi, I resigned in June 1964.

I have been in the U.K. since, but have retained a close interest in the political developments of Pakistan and, indeed, of the Indian sub-continent as a whole. The fall of Ayub Khan, Yahya Khan, Bhutto – the 1965 Indo-Pakistan war, the emergence of Bangladesh after the 1971 war – these are events which I have followed, analysed and have written about from time to time.

Now General Zia-Ul-Haq rules, again under Martial Law, but is working to establish a fundamentalist Islamic system. Not only Pakistan but the entire South and South West Asia and the Middle East are in a state of flux. One watches with interest, trepidation and some hope at the possible direction of events in this vast and highly sensitive region. When one looks particularly at the 33-year old history of Pakistan, India, Bangladesh one sees the mistakes, the disappointed hopes and the positive achievements with a clearer perspective. The sub-continent may still hold many surprises for the world in the next 25/50 years.

Air Commodore MK Janjua

Chapter One

Metamorphosis

"Over my dead body!" said Flight Lieutenant Varma with a vehemence he was normally able to conceal, but which erupted despite all his efforts to curb it. The reference was to the possibility of the selection of a boy in his group.

Flight Lieutenant Varma and I lived in the same house in Dehra Dun in the United Provinces, now Uttar Pradesh, of India, where I was the Deputy President and he a Group Testing Officer on 57, Services Selection Board for the selection of officers for the Indian Air Force. We were walking back to our house and discussing the day's work, as was our wont, when the conversation turned to the group of candidates being tested by Flight Lieutenant Varma. It was not a very bright group, we both agreed. I however, observed that one boy stood out as a possibility. He showed qualities of leadership and seemed to lead the group through all phases of the tests in and out of doors.

"But he has a very low I.Q." said Flight Lieutenant Varma.
"Is it lower than the minimum requirement?" I asked.
"No" said he, "but it is low. In any case, anyone could lead that group.

They are all so dim."

"Yes, but no one else is leading it" I said, "And there are some with high I.Q's; much higher than this boy's, anyway."

"The I.Q. is terribly important. All these qualities are not worth much without the basic intelligence." said he.

I said "No doubt intelligence is important, but we cannot expect brilliance in every candidate. Indeed, it would be patently unjust to do so. This boy has the requisite I.Q. and is obviously able to put this to the best possible use for our purpose. I am unable to agree that just one factor should be made decisive, especially in a case such as the present one."

There was an uneasy pause. Varma seemed to ponder over what might have been the next move in a game of chess, then he said, "Do you know what this boy did when he met me the day he arrived? He said that Professor A, whom I know, wished his regards to be conveyed to me."

"So?" I asked.

"You know what that means!" he said. "It means that he wants me to be influenced in his favour."

"To me it means no such thing, but only that a gentleman who knows you has taken the opportunity to convey his wish to continue association with you." I said. "I am afraid this is the worst implication to attribute to a natural and normal gesture on the part of one of your acquaintances. Surely you are not going to be influenced against a boy to this extent just because you think that there has been an attempt to influence you in his favour. While judging his suitability for commission, you have to disregard completely any personal prejudices for or against him. All you have to consider is whether the sum total of his performance equals that which makes a potential officer and pilot, with adequate training. I must insist that no extraneous factors are brought into selection methods. If this boy or any other shows the requisite potential, he must be selected."

It was at this point that Varma exploded, quite contrary to his normal behaviour.

"What is the boy's name and where does he come from?" I asked, suppressing my own urge to shout back, "Don't be so bloody unfair!"

Temperamentally I was quite capable of such a violent outburst, but I gave him the benefit of the doubt.

He gave me the name of a Muslim boy and said that he was from the Muslim University of Aligarh. Varma knew a Professor at the University through his wife, who was Indian Christian, but was related to Muslims through both her parents. I had always considered Varma as being completely free of prejudice. We were living together, sharing servants, kitchen and dining table. Indeed, for all such purposes, we lived as one family. This was not strange to me because I lived as a member of the family in at least two Hindu and two Sikh families. As we walked and talked, the monsoon rain poured down. The intensity of the conversation seemed to build up with that of the rain. For the first time ever a vague suspicion crept into my mind. As we approached the house the rain became a drizzle and losing even that force, turned to the finest of sprays, gentle and soothing. By the time we entered the house, even that slight suspicion had faded from my mind.

The boy under discussion was one of the nine candidates selected from the batch. This stands out clearly in my memory because, as it transpired, this was the largest number ever selected from one batch. Even more significant was the fact that five of those selected were Muslims; over 50 per cent! This was unheard of. It had been made possible because the Hindu Officers became increasingly cautious about rejecting suitable non-Hindus. In due course I discovered that the increase in communalism had made all non-Hindu communities, with the possible exception of the Sikhs, a target.

The Muslims were overtly placed at the top of the list; with Anglo-

Indians and Indian Christians a close second: other and smaller communities did not entirely escape from being placed in the hierarchy. My own views regarding completely unbiased and fair treatment were known to these officers. Therefore, for a brief period, my presence served as an umbrella for the non-Hindu candidates. The Sikhs, who are a versatile and vigorous community in any case, enjoyed a position of strength, politically at least. Also inter-marriages with the Hindus brought them almost within the fold of the latter.

I would like to state here that while generally the foregoing had become the pattern of behaviour, there were individual instances of scrupulous honesty, integrity and freedom from prejudice on the part of Hindu officers. The one example which stands out in my mind is that of Flight Lieutenant Ramuny, another Group Testing Officer. This officer surpassed all in these positive qualities. But then it is difficult to find many persons of Ramuny's humanity and compassion. I remember an incident when Ramuny's bicycle was stolen. To this day I am of the opinion that he was aware of the identity of the person who stole it. However, when pressed by his colleagues to report the matter to the police he refused to do so. He said with gentle firmness, "His need was greater than mine."

The Independence Movement in India had been gaining strength, and freedom started becoming visible like the first light of dawn on the horizon. Of course, not everyone could see the impending dangers; the probable bloodshed that would mar this vision. Some did have the ability to perceive it; yet others were fully aware of it, because they had planned, and were planning, to dim the brightness which should follow the dawn of a new era, the era of liberty. The discussion on independence and the shape it would take, intensified immediately after the end of World War 11. India was reluctant to be satisfied with a mere pledge of ultimate emancipation. She was unwilling to accept anything short of immediate independence. Soon the question of whether she was fit to manage her own affairs was left behind.

Whether anyone else agreed or not she had decided that she would prefer to be left alone to shape her own destiny, in a world which was becoming too complex to allow anyone to deny her this right. It was not so much a matter of when but how independence would come. All major parties were agreed that the yoke of imperialism be removed and steps taken towards the attainment of that goal. However, there were acute differences in the aims of the two main bodies, the All India Congress which, in spite of all its professions to the contrary, represented the Hindu view and the Muslim League, which by its very definition, stood for the Muslim stand-point, although it not exclude other minorities and, indeed, welcomed them.

The parallel demands for the attainment of freedom and independence had been pursued by the two major communities for several years. After the passing of the Lahore resolution of the Muslim League on 23 March 1940, which proclaimed the demand for an independent Pakistan, the tempo of the movement increased. It gradually built up during the war years. When the end of the war came it released all energies which were then employed on the struggle for independence. The independence movement reached a crescendo and explosive end. The demand for Akhand Bharat, United India, began to be matched by the demand for the recognition of two nations, Hindu and Muslim respectively, with the consequential and inevitable conclusion that separate homelands should be found for the two nations. Arguments for the retention of one India, as it was under the British rule, and for its partition, to accommodate the two separate nations began to be advanced at all levels. The advocates of Akhand Bharat relied mainly on the geographical unity of India, almost to the total exclusion of all other factors. The protagonists of separate nationhood brought forth the cultural and religious factors, which would become predominant in the affairs of India, when the third force, the British, ceased to play a part.

The experience in many parts of the world throughout history showed that nationhood was not a matter of giving a geographical area a name and nor was it recognition of a single faith. Throughout history nations have been made and remade, sometimes depending on one factor and sometimes upon another and all in entirely different circumstances. A straight line, except where it follows the curves of the lakes and rivers, makes Canada a different nation from the United States of America. There are no religious or cultural reasons for this division. But the Canadians feel rather irritated if they are referred to as Americans. A yet more significant fact is that Alaska, which is contiguous to Canada and is separated from the United States of America by the entire width of Canada, is part of the United States and not of Canada. Northern Ireland stands divided from Eire for a reason which is far narrower than the broader one of religion; it is the result of sectarianism, fostered by colonialism.

Scores of similar examples could be quoted. But for the benefit of those most concerned with the problem of the independence of India, and for those of who were to be affected by the mode of such independence, the basic facts of religion and culture were being emphasized. The inequality in almost all walks of life, which was the outcome of prejudice, favouritism and victimisation on the part of the majority community, was being made increasingly apparent. The attempts on the part of this community to exclude the other majority community, the Muslims, from all fields of progress were being illustrated.

Many of us, who found ourselves in particular circumstances, especially in the armed forces, were nor generally exposed to those prejudices and did not experience them personally. For this and several other reasons, which will be discussed later, I have to admit I was not aware of the biases in the same way as many others were. Even if I witnessed a prejudice or injustice on account of it, I was unable to give it the meaning which some others, who suffered from it, were compelled to do. However, the events were moving fast and the impact, which would have taken months to be felt at other times, now took less than days.

It was in these rapidly changing circumstances that Varma's outburst brought the first vague suspicion in my mind of prejudice in practice. Other instances followed in quick succession.

We sat on the veranda of the Selection Board Officers' mess, sipping hot or cold, intoxicating or non-alcoholic drinks, according to taste, habit or tradition. Near me was the Board Psychiatrist, Major Krishnamurty, a Hindu from Madras, who had recently replaced Major Hugh Miller, a charming and fascinating Scot, whom I have always remembered with warmth. The discussion was about impending independence, and it ultimately transformed into a heated argument. Major Krishnamurty conceded the point that the acceptance of a two-nation theory was not only inevitable but, so far as he was concerned, it was vital. He ended by exposing the state of his own mind, obviously full of hatred, when he imparted what he considered to be, very sound advice, to the British and the Congress: "Give Muslims the homeland they want. Put them in the areas of the North West and the East, build a steel wall around them and let them hang themselves!"

Even if I tried, I could not have digested this or dismissed it as an outburst of an overworked man. The effect of this was not given the time to wear off as I had to be admitted to the Combined Military Hospital with a sore throat. I was put in the charge of a Hindu doctor from the Punjab. We became friendly. One day between checks and tests the inevitable discussion developed. This time it revolved around the narrow confines of personal relationships and contact between Hindus and Muslims. Gradually the doctor built up a case, point by point, for a complete boycott of the Muslims by the Hindus in every sphere where contact was possible. This talk culminated in what may have been the most embarrassing experience for the doctor, perhaps in all his life. While he stressed not only the necessity, but the religious duty of every Hindu to shun a Muslim, I gently disagreed, putting forth the argument that after all we were one nation and an attitude like his could not possibly lead to anything but disharmony.

He said, "But it is inconceivable that a Hindu should sit together at the same table with a Muslim. How is it possible for me to use the utensils which a Muslim has touched? How can any Hindu eat the food prepared by a Muslim? Would you do it?"

I was unable to keep up the pretence and said "Yes, I would, because I am one myself!"

At that moment the lightest of feathers could have crushed him.

He had been deceived by my name, like Major Krishnamurty before him. With the exception of some areas of the Punjab, my name, in those days especially, was taken to be a Hindu name by most people.

These incidents, which arose with greater frequency and increasing intensity, removed the cover from my eyes; removed the dust out of them and not only enabled me to see things as they were, but gave me abundant food for thought. I had been brought up under conditions where religion played an incredibly important role. But the religion which was inculcated into me was that of universal brotherhood, tolerance, sympathy, humanity and complete regard for the faiths and beliefs of my fellow beings, the most dominant feature being to value the humanity of others.

I recollect vividly the days of my childhood. The population of my village was entirely Muslim, with the exception of one shopkeeper, who was Hindu. He controlled the commerce of the community, because tradition had made the Muslim too proud to indulge in this 'low, unmanly and un-warrior-like profession'. The 'business' of the Muslim was to bear the sword and leave all other trades to those whom tradition did not permit to indulge in warfare. This tradition, according to some who pondered on its role in the history of the community, was strengthened by the British, who needed the so-called fighting or martial classes for their native army. The class distinction which already existed was thereby enhanced. But while the Hindu shopkeeper became or remained a low class tradesman in the eyes of the warriors, the Muslim, warrior or not, was worse than an untouchable in the eyes of the Hindu shopkeeper. Ultimately these facets of the community just became a way of life, and were accepted as such by Muslims. While the Muslim contempt for the Hindu shopkeeper, the 'bania', gradually lost its force, the latter's contempt remained and even grew.

During the time of my childhood, youth and early manhood, these conditions prevailed. The Muslims went completely out of their way to ensure that the feelings of the Hindus were not offended. They accepted treatment as untouchables, as if it had been ordained by some higher authority. They would avoid contact with the person of the Hindu at his behest; his clothes, utensils, food and water were untouched by Muslim hands for no other reason than that their very touch made all these things impure, 'malichh', and therefore doomed them to destruction, or to be subjected to a process of purification before they could be of use again. With the exception of some rather naughty children, who delight in the agony and misery they create for others or some moments of anger, deliberate attempts were never made to 'pollute' the person or articles of Hindus.

A transaction in the village shop would follow this pattern. The customer would enter the shop but stop at a low barrier beyond which the merchandise and merchant were located. He would ask for the provisions and wait for them to be found or weighed. The customer would then stretch out a receptacle or spread a cloth to receive them. The Hindu shopkeeper would literally throw the goods at him. The customer would then either throw the money or pour the grain, in the case of barter, into another receptacle. At no time was physical contact allowed between the two human beings, or between the customer and the receptacles, or the goods other than those he had purchased. However, at no time did Muslim customers even remotely feel humiliated. Indeed, he was watchful and took extreme care to see that no offence was caused to the Hindu.

This attitude found its way into major matters such as separate Hindu institutions of all types. For many decades this was accepted in the same manner, by the Muslim community as a whole, as the village 'bania's' sanctity was by his local clients. Anything that the Hindus did as a community was taken for granted as their right; they were, after all, different! They had their own way of life to which they were entitled. Some very far-sighted Muslim leaders, Sir Syed Ahmed[3] foremost among them, saw the dangers and started parallel action for the Muslim community in the late 19th century, but it was indeed a long time, and almost too late, before the Muslims generally recognised this fact. When ultimately the Muslims began to work and act on a Muslim basis, the din from Hindu accusations became deafening. The Muslim University at Aligarh, Islamic Colleges and schools were branded as communal while the more ancient Hindu University at Benares, other Hindu Universities, scores of Hindu colleges under Sanatan Dharam[4], Arya Samaj, and others, was termed as national. Indeed, all other communal institutions like Khalsa (Sikh) colleges, Parsee schools and similar and purely communal organisations were not termed communal.

---

[3] Born on October 17, 1817, Syed Ahmed Khan was an Indian educator, politician and Islamic reformer. He helped pioneer modern education in India's Muslim communities through his foundation of the Aligarh Muslim University. His work inspired a new generation of Muslim reformers and led to the revival of Indian Islam in the late 19th century. Throughout his life, Khan published several scholarly works, most notably the pamphlet "The Causes of the Indian Revolt."

[4] The religion which eternally exists in God, which is revealed by God, which describes the names, forms, virtues and the abodes of God, and which reveals the true path of God realization for all the souls is called Sanatan Dharm, the universal religion for the whole world.

The Muslims alone were accused of communalism and for no other reason than doing precisely what the other communities had been doing for generations before them.

The closer I looked the more obvious the differences became. Memories of the close relationship, which my father and I had enjoyed with some Hindu families, came rushing back to me. The best Hindu friend my father ever had was the head clerk of the Mountain Battery in which my father served. His name was Amin Chand. Their relationship can be described only as that of genuine and profound affection. Idiomatically the term 'the morsel and the cup' applied to them, but as certain memories emerged, I understood that religious tradition did not allow them to give full expression to their deep friendship. They shared thoughts, interests, problems, emotions and even spiritual ecstasies, but never food or water. They had everything in common and indulged to the full in their mutual interests, music and literature in particular, but an invisible barrier remained. At that time nothing seemed to affect the intensity, depth and apparent intimacy of their enjoyment. Now it seems astonishing that such closeness had been possible at all. When Uncle Amin Chand, as we all affectionately called him, or his family came to our house, they were free to roam anywhere within it; they had the freedom of the house. But apart from Uncle Amin Chand, who ventured further, even as far as our kitchen, to snatch a tit bit denied him at home by custom and religion, no one crossed the compound. Conversely we could not cross the compound of his house, because his religion forbade us the freedom of the house. In either case, the line was drawn by them. This was the way of life. No one took the slightest notice of the things which separated us. None of us felt that religion, tradition and custom had found manifestation in such odd behaviour. Indeed the behaviour did not seem odd at all. But while our two families had an imperceptible 'something' drawing them towards each other, and several other families found themselves in similar situations, this happy situation did not and could not apply to the two communities as a whole where the barrier was not only visible but solid. It could not be crossed. It was not possible to even clasp hands across or through it. It was inconceivable with such insurmountable obstacles of religion, caste, creed, tradition and custom, for affection to be developed universally. Only in rare instances was it possible for the physical barrier to be broken; on rather more numerous occasions emotions crossed them; but on the whole there was more to divide than to unite them.

I had also experienced physical and emotional closeness to some other Hindu individuals and families. A 'hakim', locally qualified medical practitioner, Bali, was a dear friend of an uncle of mine in another village in West Pakistan. He actually partook of food with us. But this type of intimacy was confined solely to him because no one else from his family, particularly the women, ever allowed it to develop. In the case of Hakim Bali, I have always found a reason for satisfaction in the fact that I was able to assist him to evacuate his family when the violence occurred and the crimson lava of human blood began to flow across India in August 1947 – freedom and separation came simultaneously. Hakim Bali had tried to stay back and thought that his emotional strings had the strength to keep him there. But the tidal wave of human movement proved irresistible and the ties of emotion snapped. Hakim Bali found himself being borne eastward, regardless of his desire to the contrary. Like many others he could not swim against the current. Each human joined the flow of those who resembled him.

Similar relationships existed between our family and Bhimsen, a Hindu owner of a bookshop. This developed on account of my father's love of reading. Bhimsen had a bookshop in a camp at Razmak, in Waziristan, where my father's Mountain Regiment was stationed. Since Bhimsen suffered from a perpetual cold we affectionately referred to him as the sniffing Bheenim. He was always careful, and I am sure delighted, to bring the latest books to my father. He went the way of Hakim Bali, but I had lost contact with him and was unable to help him and his family on their way east.

More recently, during my years as a young officer in the army and the air force, I was an intimate member of at least two Hindu families. In both these my physical contact with the younger members, both gentleman and ladies, was almost normal; the older members, especially the ladies, kept the cordon drawn around themselves. We were able to sit at the same table or the equivalent of it on the floor, for our meals. On many occasions I stayed with them for long periods and was considered one of them. The most vivid memory, and perhaps one of the most touching I have, is about one small incident during a meal. I was asked to dinner by a Hindu officer, one of my best friends and his wife. The latter was reputed to be orthodox and rigidly adhered to the traditions concerning physical contact with non-Hindus. This tallied with my observations. During the meal I drank water, half of a glass which had been full. As I put it down my hostess picked it up and drank the rest. I was astonished and so were some onlookers; but more than that I was deeply moved by the gesture. I was one of her husband's best friends. She has broken a most rigid customary and personal rule, indeed she had committed sacrilege, to convey to me that I was as close to her as a brother.

When I look back on them, with deep emotion and warmth, I find that those were genuine and sincere relationships. But alas they applied to far too few to make for harmony on a national scale. Like the proverbial solitary swallow, they did not make a summer. While one individual or one family was accepted, literally millions were positively rejected. There seemed to be nothing in common between the two peoples except the fact of being on the same land, which had historically been known by the name of India. All within those boundaries became Indians. Under other circumstances, there would have been nothing wrong with this. But when differences exist; of religion, custom, culture, tradition, dress, food, in short every walk of life, even more so when, for some or several reasons, each one of those differences is widened till a series of gulfs appears between man and man, family and family, and community and community, then the situation becomes untenable.

It is my belief that the ultimate goal of humanity is harmony, unity and equality. This is vital for its survival and continued existence. In this age of nuclear fission the alternative to peace and harmony can be total destruction. Although, due to the complexity of human societies, annihilation has become a possibility, yet the very awareness of this fact should persuade humanity to move away from the course which leads to extinction. Collective wisdom will prevail in the end. Before that goal is reached a great deal of agony and suffering, unfortunately, is likely to be the lot of mankind for a period which cannot yet be defined. The trends are mostly in that direction. Some gaps are widened before they can be sealed and many wounds are inflicted and have to be healed. Harmony should be achieved by common consent. There are still efforts made to force unity. The world will find unity, paradoxically, through division; in other words groups will have to recognise the desires and aspirations of other groups: so long as there is no infringement of the rights of others these groups' wishes must be acknowledged. Unless co-operative coexistence is made possible and practiced, the peace of the world remains in jeopardy. I believe that this situation will not be allowed to continue by the succeeding generations. The dangers will be more apparent to them than they are to us; in any event, they will be far more pronounced because science would have produced the most deadly weapons. Despite the ever-increasing complex problems of man, the human race will wish to continue to exist. I believe that progressively they will work towards the attainment of that aim. But this will be made possible only through the struggle of the peoples of the world against all types of exploitation of man by man. When the peoples succeed in liberating themselves from all the exploiting classes, then the barrier creating divisions will have been removed.

In the India of that day a forced unity was the goal of the majority community. In a sense an accident of history, or as some would prefer to call it, history itself, had placed a large Muslim minority in the sub-continent of India among a Hindu majority. The beliefs, faiths, cultures and almost everything that matters in life was as different as it is possible for it to be. Every effort was being made to ensure that these differences were so pronounced as to make it impossible for them not to be noticed. But although the former historical relationship between the Muslims, who had been the rulers, and Hindus, the subject people, marked Muslims out for special treatment by Hindus during the British rule, yet the orthodox Hindus were too exclusive to accept any non-Hindus as equals. Their attitude towards other communities is identical with that towards the untouchables, the only difference being that the latter are a Hindu caste. Had any other community been placed in a situation similar to that of the Muslims in the process of history; had it ruled India for a few centuries; had it acquired the population and the status of a strong minority; that community would have had to face precisely the same alternatives as the Muslims had to in the 1940's – annihilation, submission and ultimate loss of identity. India's long history had shown that the Hindu religion was all-absorbing. Given the opportunity to be given free expression, it overwhelms other faiths. The religious minorities (such as Buddhists and Jains) which had been there before the period of Muslim and British rules, now enjoyed purely nominal separate entity status. They had become virtually indistinguishable from the Hindu religion and culture. The Muslims and the Christians had been able to retain their individualities. The Muslims because of their large numbers and the British presence; the Christians because of their faith, which was that of the colonialist rulers: and both because of the nature of their beliefs, both being monotheistic. Hinduism had had neither the freedom nor the time to be able to assimilate them. Indeed due to the acute religious, and on the part of the Hindu, pseudo-nationalist prejudices, the very things which were required to facilitate assimilation were forbidden. Nothing could be shared with a Muslim or a Christian, so the most important factor, inter-marriage, became impossible. Therefore, the separation of the two groups from the majority Hindu group, especially in the case of the Muslims, was not only retained but became progressively more marked. It became impossible for them to be absorbed. The alternatives left were assimilation by force, destruction or separation. The first two alternatives had become quite impossible and impracticable in modern times. The only solution lay in separation. No other religious community had the numbers, the strength and above all the peculiar geographical situation to qualify for a separate homeland. The Muslims qualified on all counts and would have to resort to them to be able to survive as a people with a distinct faith, a shared culture and history.

These recollections, thoughts and new facts went through my mind like a slide show. I had not been exposed to prejudices, at least I had not been conscious of them, so far as my person was concerned. I was quite incapable of looking at people in any way except on their own personal and professional merits, but I was no longer able to ignore the opposite attitude on the part of others. As I looked more closely I found prejudice in every area of life. For a while I began to feel that I was reading too much into these events. I checked and re-checked and the deeper I went into it the more prevalent I found the prejudice to be. Events moved at the speed of light. It became quite immaterial as to who started it or whether the British had aggravated matters. The fact remained that a situation had developed which could lead to an initial bloody clash and the ultimate subjugation and submission of the smaller community. Again it became immaterial as to whether the Muslims were in that plight because of their own inadequacies, or whether they were deliberately made weak; the only fact that mattered was that they were at a disadvantage in every walk of life and would inevitably be subsumed into the dominant culture, if the country was handed over to the much lauded Hindu majority.

While the manifestation of communal hatred on the part of the Hindus was being brought home to me in the manner I have already described, my association with the exponents of the opposite view developed almost accidentally. During the war years contact with civilians holding strong political views had not been possible. The nature of my duties and physical location had prevented such associations. As a young Flying Officer and Flight Lieutenant I had been either on detachment duties on the North West Frontier, or on assignments in co-operation with the army in a variety of places throughout India. I performed no less a variety of duties and visited no fewer places in my capacity as Squadron Commander. Training, re-equipment, operations with occasional breaks from staff duties at Group and Air Headquarters, occupied my years of service up to the end of the war. Indeed, it was on the last day of the war, 15 August 1945 that I was transferred to 57, Services Selection Board as its Deputy President. Although the impact of the political developments I have described was being felt by almost all of us, yet our involvement was not direct. We waged parallel and smaller battles within our own organisations. When a whole nation becomes involved in a historical struggle it is not possible for any group of individuals to remain unaffected. In the armed forces of India the participation of many in the endeavours by the officer class followed the pattern set by the politicians. Originally three groupings emerged: one for immediate independence, another for continuance of the British rule and a third, a minute minority, of neutrals. The first group waged a consistent and continuous struggle against the British officers and all other categories of Indian officers for matters of privilege, command, tradition and a host of other issues which, under different circumstances, would be considered to be trivial. The feelings and attitudes were entirely those of broad Indian nationalism. The officers, particularly the non-Hindus, seemed to have no communal biases. I certainly had none. To me all men were equal, regardless of their religion, race, colour or caste. I was the first Indian officer to command a mixed squadron. British Personnel were no less happy under my command than the Indians. This was due to my own attitude to life and people. Therefore, even when an action by a Hindu officer against non-Hindus appeared to be unjust, I attributed to it an error of judgement, a human error.

The quite obvious malicious victimisation and the openly hostile attitude of Hindu officers, which I witnessed in Dehra Dun, shocked me. At the time my political conversion, I cannot use any other term, took place. The Service Selection Boards included civilian members. Amongst those on my Board the civilian member was Doctor Mahmood Ahmed, a professor with a doctorate in philosophy from the Muslim University, Aligarh, who later became an officer in the education branch of Pakistan Army, and yet later Head of Department of Philosophy in Karachi University. The Muslim University was reputed to be a staunch supporter of the Pakistan movement and was, therefore, detested by the Hindus and branded as communal. Dr. Ahmed and I indulged in long and serious discussions on the political situation prevalent in the mid-forties. Of course, the Pakistan movement was always the theme. Dr. Ahmed's views and assertions, at the beginning, appeared to be unduly biased and, to a person of my outlook, they seemed tinged with communalism. Although I accepted the broader concept of anti Muslim bias, I resisted those aspects, which to me at that time seemed coloured. The points which gradually emerged from these discussions soon began to coincide with my own experiences and observations of rabid communalism on the part of Hindu officers. The factors which I considered to be exaggerations on Dr. Ahmed's part began to assume real shape; they began to confirm the facts on the ground. The ultimate aim of the Hindus, as envisaged by the Muslim leadership, and the actions of Hindu officers, with whom I worked on the Selection Board, were a mere reflection of the country-wide pattern. Wherever and whenever possible, communalism was like a dagger, thrust into Muslim hearts. The realisation and awareness of this fact came to me with intense pain, the pain which was being experienced by my own kind all over the vast sub-continent of India. The metamorphosis began, from our previous passive demeanour to that of activity. The transformation took place as rapidly as the sequence of events brought about by communalism unfolded, and as painfully as the wounds being inflicted in the ever-growing communal clashes.

On closer scrutiny I found that I was by no means alone in my experiences and having to undergo change in my attitudes. Hundreds of thousands of my generation and my community shared them. This pattern seemed to have existed for many decades and perhaps a few generations. The Muslim leader who spearheaded the Pakistan movement, Quaid-I-Azam Mohamed Ali Jinnah, had himself been a staunch member of the All India Congress. He broke away from it, obviously disillusioned and sufficiently alarmed to seek a drastic solution, this being dismemberment of the sub-continent, to accommodate the two communities as separate nations. Even earlier Iqbal, the greatest Muslim philosopher poet of this century, had progressively moved from the position of devout Indian nationalism to that of devoted Muslim nationalism. His earlier poetry contained eulogies to India and Indian nationalism. He depicted 'Hindustan as paradise on earth; her civilisation superior to and more lasting than those of Egypt, Greece and Rome; where religion could not and did not teach division and hatred; where all were Hindi (Indian) regardless of the differences in faith, and all this had remained indestructible despite the repeated efforts of history and time to destroy it.' From this position of devotion to Hindustan, the most profound affection for it and unquestionable loyalty to it, Iqbal went over to counsel tolerance and unity among the Hindus and Muslims, addressing himself almost entirely to the former. He seemed ultimately to despair as evidenced in his later poetry when he undertook to arouse the Hindi Muslims from a deep slumber. Iqbal seemed to have become conscious of the brief time available to his fellow Muslims to prepare themselves for a fight for their very existence. He wrote passionately; lauded the glories of the Islamic era; exhorted the Indian Muslims to emulate the example of their vigorous, courageous and all-conquering ancestors. He advocated the universal brotherhood of Islam – the world is a Muslim's country – but turned the Muslim' eyes away from Hindustan towards the source of their inspiration in the Holy Land in the Arabian Peninsular. It was no

41

longer desirable to be a Hindi but more important to be a Muslim. He made them conscious of their identity as a separate people and of their plight in a country, their own country, where the hostility of the majority community threatened to overwhelm them and if possible, to destroy them. He seemed to sense that these exhortations and the subsequent awakening once achieved were insufficient – and certainly lacked the pace – to avert disaster. He found that the evolutionary processes to achieve the aim of equal treatment for the Muslims would not be possible and consequently his community would be in jeopardy. Iqbal, therefore, conceived the idea not only of a separate Hindu and Muslim nationhood, but of a homeland for each in the sub-continent. He, together with other Muslim thinkers, gave birth to the concept of a homeland of Pakistan.

While the Muslim leaders of earlier generations became aware of the ultimate dangers through a slow, life-long process, my generation acquired that awareness within a short space of a few years, through intensity of our first hand experiences.

Chapter Two

Involvement

My nature does not include religious, racial, communal and even personal hatred, but it is capable of fierce rebellion against injustice of any kind. The conscious and unconscious injustice which necessarily and inevitably follows occupation of a country and the subjugation of its people by another people, made me join mentally, and often physically, the ranks of those who sought liberation from British rule. To me the foreign rule of India was as abhorrent as it would be to the British, if they were occupied by another people, quite regardless of the few material benefits which the occupier benevolently bestowed. The greater benefit must go to the occupier and this can take place only at the cost of the indigenous population. The incidental benefits which accrued during the British period are not denied but (it cannot be disputed that) the greater benefits had necessarily to be denied the Indian people. The injustice lies in the fact that the people have no voice in their own affairs and are deprived of opportunities for advancement and progress.

This has been the pattern ever since the inception of exploitation of man by man. The imperialist occupied countries, subjugated the people, exploited the resources; a process which led to incidental and minimal benefits to the occupied countries and peoples whose labours had to be mobilised. In earlier times methods employed by the imperialists were crude and cruel and conditions of mass slavery prevailed. One imperial force was displaced by another greater imperial force. As enlightenment increased and human society became more complex, exploitation became more subtle. The chains of slavery became invisible; the shackles were no longer made of steel; the physical pain was not always felt but the exploitation was no less severe; deprivation of progress by the exploited peoples was no less definite. Just as the pattern of subjugation and exploitation underwent a change, so did the pattern of displacement of power. While the more ancient imperialist powers were ousted by other and stronger similar powers and subjugation succeeded subjugation, the more modern imperialism has had to give way to the forces of liberation from within the subjugated people. Indeed, the struggle for liberty has gone yet further and the battles now raging are against exploitation of man by man without regard to race, nationality, colour, caste or creed. In these processes many nations, races, communities and individuals have participated. Prejudices have developed at all these levels and have played havoc with humanity. Prejudice has replaced prejudice; national, religious and racial being the most dominant, violent and cruel. They have divided and oppressed humanity and caused untold suffering. Injustices perpetrated in the name of religion, race and nationality and committed on account of these prejudices are unsurpassed. It is possible for all these prejudices to run concurrently. My generation experienced all of them.

Racial and national prejudices were felt acutely due to the presence of the British in India and prejudice based on religion; ever present, grew steadily, and later rapidly, and reached its climax in 1947. Injustices accompanied both; in the case of the former the Indians as a whole were the victims: in the latter case the Muslims found themselves at the receiving end. Like millions of others I found myself involved in both.

Although according to my way of thinking my endeavours were devoted to the defence and protection of the victims of injustice in my own limited way, yet there can be no neutral position. If you are not with them you are against them. The demand for legitimate privileges, rights, traditions, appointments and other such matters for and by the Indians were considered as proof of being anti-British; despite there being the greatest regard for the qualities of the British people and for personal friendships. Similar demands for and by the Muslims and their attempts to save their lives, were dubbed as acts of aggression and communalism; despite personal friendships they had had; the scrupulous fairness in all their dealings and respect for the customs and way of life of the majority community.

I recognised the communal injustice quite late in the day and acknowledged it with the greatest personal mental agony. My temperament revolted against the extent and the intensity of the injustice. My reaction to it was rapid, anxious and fierce. In the limited field of work I was involved in, on the Selection Board, I became alert and to the best of my ability, protected the non-Hindu candidates from suffering. While I would never, under any circumstances, consider rejecting a suitable candidate who was Hindu, I would not allow a suitable non-Hindu candidate to be rejected. However, at that time communalism had gripped almost the entire subcontinent. During the preceding decades the communal clashes had been sporadic and seasonal. They coincided with religious festivals and functions and occasional provocative and spontaneous breaches and violations caused incidents. This was the pattern during British rule when the clashes received much publicity and attention. It was put forward as proof of traditional hostility; the inability of two communities to live peacefully together without a third neutral force. While the truth of this assertion may be questionable, the fact remained that communal prejudices gained strength, sharpened and led to frequent and violent clashes.

The violence increased in tempo with the visible approach of independence. It became increasingly apparent that the Hindus were well organised. While their leaders advocated non-violence and generally speaking the masses had practiced non-violence, in the struggle against the British, the opposite seemed to apply when it came to the struggle for Akhand Bharat; for an independent Hindu State. The Hindus had acquired adequate weapons for riots; many paramilitary bodies were formed for this purpose: as a consequence Muslim blood began to flow profusely. The Muslims retaliated but their efforts were confined to the areas where they enjoyed overwhelming numerical superiority and their successes, if such gruesome events can be so termed, were on account of this superiority alone. The Hindus were far more brutal and seemed to move according to a preconceived plan of extermination. They also concentrated their activities in areas where they constituted the majority, but their militant communal bodies existed almost everywhere and did not hesitate to join battle on every possible occasion. Non-violence as advocated by one of its great exponents, Mahatma Gandhi, became meaningless and farcical. I vividly recollect the occasion of Mahatma Gandhi's visit to the province of Bihar in those troubled days. The Muslims had suffered intensely and the massacre and carnage up to that time were unparalleled. Mahatma Gandhi went there to restore peace and communal harmony and, as usual, non-violence was being advocated as the basis. This was farcical enough, because extreme violence had been committed by his own community, despite his life long preaching to the contrary. But the farce became complete when the Mahatmaji received a Muslim delegation and acknowledged that their grievances were substantial and fully justified; that the behaviour of the Hindus had been bestial but that non-violence should continue to be practiced by the Muslims, as this attitude was the only correct one and showed Muslim moral strength as opposed to Hindu moral weakness. The Muslims pointed out that the predominantly Hindu Government of Bihar were freely issuing licences for arms to the Hindus but none to the Muslims for their protection. The Mahatma said that this proved that the Hindus were morally weak. When it was pointed out that he himself was surrounded by well-armed bodyguards he said that this could be attributed to his own moral weakness. The Muslims, throughout India, began to wonder whether the Mahatma was utterly helpless, with no control over his own community so far as their relations with the Muslims were concerned or whether there was no sincerity in his advocacy of non-violence. The moral weakness, (but physical and material strength) of the Hindus, according to one of their greatest leaders, led to massacres and atrocities on an unprecedented scale in other areas, prominent among which was West Bengal, Gash Mukhteshwar, Gurgaon and the States of Bharatpur and Alwar. While these measures by the Hindus for the extermination and subjugation of the Muslims were preconceived, well planned, organised and well led, the defensive measures and reprisals by the Muslims were spontaneous, emotional, lacking in organisation and were completely devoid of leadership. At best they were left to individual effort but in the main they were left to their own fate. The Muslim masses suffered from overconfidence in their majority areas and ignorance of the magnitude of the political upheaval, while the leadership suffered from undue reliance on the ability or desire of the administration to maintain law and order.

I would like to illustrate this point with a concrete example. An interim Government was formed in 1946; Pandit Jawahar Lal Nehru was Prime Minister with appropriate Hindu and so called Nationalist Muslim representation. The Muslim League was represented by Nawabzada Liaquat Ali Khan, Sardar Abdul Rab Nishtar, Raja Ghazanfar Ali, I.I. Chundrigar and a Scheduled Caste member, Mandal. I was quite closely associated with Sardar Nishtar, through his brother, Squadron Leader Ghayyus (then A.G. Kakar) and with Raja Ghazanfar Ali (Minister for Health) who belonged to my part of the Punjab and was a friend of the family. I had many occasions to meet the latter in New Delhi. In early 1947 while discussing Muslim-Sikh riots, Raja Ghanzarfar Ali related an anecdote. In one of the riots, the Sikhs had come off worst in Amritsar, their own stronghold, beaten by the Muslims. The Sikhs blamed it on the Muslim police, who were allegedly in the Majority. So they made representation to the British Deputy Commissioner and asked him to withdraw the Muslim personnel in the police for only two hours. After 'due deliberation' the Deputy Commissioner acceded to this request and for two hours the Sikhs literally ran riot and settled their scores, of course, not so much by their renowned courage, as by the surprise attack and the participation on non-Muslim personnel of police on their behalf.

In about June 1947, when I was in Air Headquarters, there was also Squadron Leader Harjinder Singh in one of the departments. This officer was a close friend. He had risen through the ranks through sheer personal drive and efficiency. He was vigorous and defied almost every convention. He had his hair cut and shaved off his beard. Many young Sikhs in I.A.F. followed him in this. He retired from the Indian Air Force with the rank of Air Vice Marshall, having been at the head of the engineering and maintenance branch. Hajinder Singh gave me information concerning large scale preparations by the Sikhs for an armed reprisal against their defeat in March 1947, in Amritsar. General Mohan Singh, of Indian National Army fame, Colonel Dhillon, amply and enthusiastically aided by the Maharajas of Patiala, Nabha, Farid Kot and others, were collecting arms, through Portuguese Goa, and were mobilising and training the Sikhs for riots, which were to coincide with the reconstitution of the sub-continent.

I conveyed this information to Raja Ghazanfar Ali. He was quite complacent about it. He doubted the ability of the Sikhs to obtain arms on such a large scale. He thought it inconceivable that the Portuguese would allow gun running through Goa. I said that he was being very naïve in this respect. When I met him again a few days later he told me that Mountbatten had promised to place the Boundary Force in the appropriate places and to maintain law and order, so we had no need to worry on that score. I reminded him about his anecdote relating to the Deputy Commissioner of Amritsar. I said that if the latter could allow a town two hours rioting, then it would not be impossible for Mountbatten to give two weeks to a province. In any event, even if Mountbatten were sincere, it may be quite beyond his powers to control events created by a mass uprising over such a large territory, with such a complex composition of forces. I was not asking for insurrection or preparation for any type of aggression, I only sought measures to combat a menace and equip the Muslims of East Punjab for their own defence. As I said this, a distant glassy look came into Raja Ghazanfar Ali's eyes, a shadow crossed his face, a hint of bewilderment, but this was momentary apprehension and it quickly passed. He seemed to shake it off! He reverted to his complacency, and like the ostrich buried his head in the sand. He and others did not see any danger; they just did not want to see it; it was far too much effort: so it seemed better to pretend that it did not exist! Their Pakistan was assured, and since the leadership had decided to act strictly constitutionally, completely unconstitutional means adopted by others, resulting in untold misery, savage loss of life and property, caused them little concern; they rubbed their eyes in amazement and wrung their hands in despair and anguish, in some cases it was sincere, in others, not.

I came across this attitude in a vast majority of our political leaders. I could find no excuse for it. To me it was an utter lack of desire to wage a physical struggle on behalf of and through their own people, should the situation so demand. It was tantamount to an act of negligence and a betrayal of the confidence of the people. To exclude the possibility of an armed struggle was sheer folly, to say the least. There was abundant evidence that an armed defence was vitally necessary. Bestiality and butchery had been practiced on the Muslim minority in many places in the northern and eastern provinces of India. No amount of appeals by leaders could lessen the intensity of these barbaric acts. Only active armed resistance could assure the safety of the minority, who were in such a precarious position. The leadership was not only reluctant to listen, but averse to such a suggestion. I met fearful opposition at the topmost level. Such unconstitutional methods could never be considered! So we were to bind ourselves hand and foot and willingly accept the knife at our throats.

As it transpired, a regular army uprising had been planned by the Sikhs, firstly to avenge the earlier defeat by the Muslims and secondly to wrest by armed force, any part of the Punjab which they considered to be theirs and which may go over to Pakistan in the reconstitution. Their second aim was achieved without any struggle on the part of Muslims. Radcliffe and Mountbatten obliged the Sikhs by giving them more than they had hoped for in their wildest dreams. Therefore, they were able to concentrate on their former aim, extermination of Muslims in East Punjab. They achieved it fully, but like all men blinded by prejudice and personal aggrandisement, they created conditions for their own community to stew in its own juice, exposed it to the pressures of the uncompromising orthodoxy of the majority community, which they would have to resist, with body, soul and blood, for their own survival as an ethnic group.

The pace of events became furious; riots assumed the shape and intensity of civil wars; even though localised. The riots covered vast geographic areas and affected populations larger than some of the countries in other parts of the world. The death toll and loss of property were equal to that of a minor local war. The incidence of injustice in the rejection of candidates on a Selection Board became quite insignificant. These injustices involved the entire community in every walk of life, and now death and destruction were in the forefront; subjugation by all possible means and at all costs was the obvious aim of the majority community.

A combination of all these circumstances led to my identification with the cause of the victim community, to which I belonged. Participation in the defence of its lives and its interests in the face of overwhelming odds was the same as that undertaken in defence of a severely persecuted party or people anywhere. While I was acutely saddened by the physical suffering of all involved, regardless of their community, I was naturally more concerned about my own because of their relatively greater weakness and even greater suffering. At that time I was not in direct contact with any Muslim political leaders. I had assumed that the situation which was rapidly developing all around, found the Muslim leadership well prepared for it. The extent of Muslim loss of life and property caused doubts to arise in my mind regarding their preparedness. At a later date I found these fears to have been well founded. The first remote contact I established with the Muslim leaders is when I prepared a thirty-page leaflet on defensive and counter measures by the Muslims in the riots and sent it by the hand of my younger brother, Ashraf, from Dehra Dun to Delhi, to Nawabzada Liaquat Ali Khan. He was then the Secretary General of the All Muslim League. I had requested to be allowed to remain anonymous. However, in later clashes some of the suggestions and counter measures advocated by me, seemed to have been adopted. But more likely, this was due to local initiative gained through practical experience. What I could see from a distance must have been witnessed at close quarters by those young men actively engaged in a life and death struggle.

In November 1946, I was transferred to Air Headquarters, New Delhi, to take over as head of the Manning Department. Although I performed my duties as an Air Force Staff Officer conscientiously, the hectic pace of political developments involved me deeper and deeper in other activities. The entire country was engaged in extremely heated political discussion and Delhi was the centre of it all. Apart from the reason of my temperament which led to my involvement in the events taking place, I was the most Senior Air Force Officer. This combination necessarily brought me close to those engaged in practical politics at that time; this included participation in measures to minimise Muslim losses. The Muslims had no aims which necessitated taking physical offensive action, therefore they were not organised for such a purpose. But in the event of a civil war, which the riots virtually were, weapons were needed just as much for defence as they were for offence. In their majority areas the Muslims were too complacent to acquire arms and in other parts they were not permitted to do so. This situation was apparent to the Hindus who took full advantage of it. They unleashed the forces of aggression in many areas. Each successive incident was more intense than the previous one. The cry for Akhand Bharat and the unity and solidarity of the sacred Hindu motherland, Hindustan, was used to rouse communal passions. While on the one hand the living body of the Muslim was 'malichh' impure, on the other hand his blood was made to flow for the purification of the soil of Bharat. It was not difficult, indeed it was far too easy, to rouse Hindu passions. All possible steps were taken to isolate the Muslims and to direct universal hatred against them. The 'traditional' enmity between the Muslims and the Sikhs was exaggerated and the militant Sikhs took the bait under misguided leadership. They clashed with Muslims at the most crucial time in the political development of the sub-continent. Old scars and wounds were opened and the Sikh support for the Hindu project was assured. The Sikhs suffered a set back when their leader master Tara Singh impetuously unsheathed his sword – Kirpan – in Lahore in March 1947. In the Sikh – Muslim riots which followed, the Sikhs came off worse in the Punjab. Their defeat in Amritsar was particularly humiliating. Vengeance was wreaked five months later in carnage no less brutal and bestial than any war in modern times; nigh on a million Muslims lost their lives in the space of a few days, under the most gruesome conditions; another nine million were completely uprooted and East Punjab became a location of horror and atrocity. The Sikhs carved out a province where they became a minority community, in due course to be absorbed, become indistinguishable from the majority community, or to have to seek further carving up of the territory to retain their identity as a group.

As I have already stated, I found the policy of the Muslim League leadership to be based on, what was termed as a 'constitutional struggle'! It completely excluded armed defence and took no account of the unconstitutional, aggressive posture and practice of the majority community. This was not acceptable to me. The warning by Squadron Leader Harjinder Singh and the utter lack of interest on the part of Raja Ghazanfar Ali and others strengthened my resolve to take whatever steps I possibly could, to minimise loss of Muslim lives. I proceeded to consult some Muslim officers in the Indian Air Force. There were few of them in any key positions to enable them to render the type of assistance needed. After all we constituted 17% of the total officer and airmen strength of the Indian Air Force. However, prominent among us, at the appropriate time and place, were Flight Lieutenant Ghayyus Kakar (later Squadron Leader and transferred to the Foreign Service, diplomatic corps, who achieved the status of Ambassador) and Flight Lieutenant Allah Dad (later Group Captain in the Pakistan Air Force). They were both at I.A.F. Station, Ambala in East Punjab. In the meantime, I had established contact with, what might easily be termed, a Muslim underground defence organisation, run by Major Khurshid Anwar. This contact came about through Khwaja Abdur Rahim, an Indian Civil Service Officer, later Commissioner, Rawalpindi Division, who was engaged in an exercise on the demarcation of boundaries, almost village by village, of the contiguous Muslim majority areas in the Punjab, to ensure that they conformed to the main terms of reference of the Boundary Commission. Contiguous Muslim majority areas were to go to Pakistan and the contiguous Hindu (and Sikh) majority areas to India. Khwaja Abdul Rahim had a large staff working on large-scale maps of the areas; these were for the benefit of our 'constitutional' team and possibly for the advocates pleading our case with Radcliffe. Of course, these were loves labours which were doomed to be lost in the constitutional farce known as the Radcliffe Award.

Major Khurshid Anwar seemed to have been working almost as a one man set up, a lone wolf among so many sheep. He relied on disguise and mobility to render help to the beleaguered Muslims of Gargaon,

Karnal, Rohtak, Bharatpur and Alwar. We managed to acquire some arms and ammunition. Major Khurshid Anwar took these in the boot of his car to wherever he thought the need was greatest. In all the turmoil this was a meagre contribution, but it was designed to minimise loss and to the best of my belief, in the areas I have already named it did achieve a limited success. The Meos and Raughars of those states and districts were traditionally tenacious fighters. They gave an excellent account of themselves in circumstances and against odds which people of lesser mettle would have found overwhelming, if not crushing. They had against them a well organised majority community. The latter had the unhindered, unqualified, unprecedented but enthusiastic support of the Hindu and Sikh rulers of the states of East Punjab; it had the unwritten, tacit but none the less active and effective support of the political bodies of the majority community and the Sikhs. This was the general pattern in the Hindu majority provinces in the entire northern part of India, but it had the intensity of a boiling cauldron in these parts. The Hindus had managed to whip up communal prejudice and hatred of the Sikhs against the Muslims through their myopic leadership, symbolised in the person of Master Tara Singh. The advantages enjoyed by them could not have been matched by the Muslims, even if their leadership had adopted the ruse of the Hindu leaders: in theory constitutional, in practice virulently aggressive. As matters were, the Muslim masses remained entirely exposed, reduced to a dire state in the minority areas; left to their fate to fend for themselves under exceedingly and desperately heroic local initiatives. In the majority areas Muslims made ill-organised and clumsy attempts at reprisals which did little more than provoke further brutalities against those in the minority areas. Such were the conditions under which some individuals endeavoured to save some Muslim, human, lives. They threw out straws in a virtual torrent so that some may clutch at them. In June and July of 1947, the plight of the Muslims, in the aforementioned states and districts, was indescribable therefore, the first consignment of weapons was sent there. But the warning by

Squadron Leader Harjinder Singh had not been forgotten. Further supplies were acquired from various sources and sent to the districts of East Punjab, where General Mohan Singh with the colleagues of the I.N.A. and others were preparing for the coup de grace.

I must explain here that although Harjinder Singh was very friendly with me and may have given me information to enable us to take some defensive action, yet the underlying reason for his generosity was, I believe, that the Sikhs were absolutely confident of their success. Apart from all the factors in their favour, their intelligence network was highly efficient. I gathered from other talks with Harjunder Singh that Mohan Singh and other Sikh leaders showed no concern about Muslim retaliation and appeared to be aware of the lack of preparation and organisation, particularly on the part of the main Muslim leadership, and generally by the Muslim masses. The events of the second and third weeks of August, 1947, justified the best hopes of the Sikh and Hindu leaders and the worst fears that at least I had.

There was unparalleled destruction of Muslim life on the one hand and peerless deeds of individual valour on the part of some Muslims, on the other. I recall one example with deep emotion. Immediately after Pakistan came into being, systematic extermination of Muslims was in progress in East Punjab. Apart from other events, to be described later, I put Pakistan Air Force transport and other available facilities, at the disposal of officers and airmen who had their families in East Punjab, to enable them to rescue whatever they could with the help of the Boundary Force. One officer who was affected was Squadron Leader (later Group Captain) Fayyaz Mahmood, the Senior Education officer. His brothers and others of the family were in Batala, a town in Gurdaspur district sixty miles from Lahore. Squadron Leader Mahmood asked his brother to evacuate the family and then come over to Lahore. The request was firmly turned down. The Muslims in Batala, and some other towns, were putting up fierce resistance. Courageous, fearless leadership was needed in Batala and Fayyaz Mahmood's brother was providing it. It was a desperate rearguard action. Men with guts and nerves of steel were required to fight it successfully, to enable the main body to withdraw. Fayyaz Mahmood's brother succeeded to an astonishing extent. However, it was not long after this that he fell to a cowardly ruse, with a bullet in his back. The opposing side could not face him and had to debase themselves to remove him from the scene, by shooting him in the back.

Inevitably the coin has another side. Much as we may abhor the hideous other face, it is there and demands to be seen. It would be impossible to find an exception to this rule of there being one face of nobility, valour, honour, trust and the other face of dastardly cowardice, despicable treachery and betrayal. The events which are being described here, whose magnitude in terms of human suffering, sacrifice and misery really begs description, produced their own Judas's. I gathered from fragments of conversation with several people over a period, that some of the arms supplied through sources known to me, found their way into enemy hands. On account of haphazard and nervous efforts to obtain weapons for their defence, at a very late stage, the Muslims of East Punjab entrusted the task to hands which were either completely inexperienced or utterly unscrupulous. They were given some defective weapons for their pains and, I understood later, had paid a prohibitive amount of money for them. For all intents and purposes the Muslims had been abandoned by those on whom they had every reason to depend, and who should have provided a cohesive programme for their defence. It is not surprising that the people were such easy prey to all that is vile in human society; the class which accumulates wealth and thrives on human suffering: the enemy of the people in every land. The Muslims of East Punjab paid with blood, rivers of blood; a cost too high for any type of experience.

I was not able to then, and am far less able now, to track down and pin point the perpetrators of those dastardly acts. Maybe all or some of them perished by the sword which they helped place in the hands of the enemy. A happy, but I fear, vain thought and merely wishful.

Chapter Three

Their Clarity, Our Confusion

It was already abundantly clear that the Muslim defence did not in any way meet the demands of the situation at the time. Its inadequacy glared one in the face; it was indeed a nightmare in every meaning of the word. The situation arose primarily due to the heavy emphasis laid on the constitutional nature of the struggle. It was either never considered, or if considered, it was overlooked or forgotten, that constitutional methods can be adhered to only if all the parties, and a majority of the people involved, were to abide by them. In a multi-party agreement, unilateral adherence cannot succeed. This becomes even more acute and impracticable if the majority not only decide not to adhere to the constitution, but go on to violate it by every means at their disposal and with all their vigour. To overlook this factor is to court disaster; and this is precisely what the Muslims faced in the weeks, months, and even years preceding independence. Had the leadership backed its constitutional demand by a strong armed defence, the boundaries of Pakistan would have followed the demarcation lines set in the Muslim League Resolution in Lahore on 23 March 1940. Whether they liked it or not, whether they advocated it or not, whether they practiced it or not, the conflict was an armed one. While the

Muslims did not use arms for their defence, the others used them for their aggression. The rivers of the Punjab ran crimson with blood. The 'constitution' was ripped to pieces; proverbially the pieces should have been scattered to the winds but now they were soaked in blood.

While the blood flowed on the ground, it influenced the hand which was drawing a line on the map. As the districts of East Punjab were cleared of the Muslims, Radcliffe's hand moved further and further west to draw the boundary line. The terms of reference were forgotten. The words 'contiguous majority areas' ceased to exist; were erased from memory, although they remained on paper, twisted, distorted, defying recognition. It was a logical, natural outcome of the situation. How could areas be included in Pakistan; the Muslim homeland, when no Muslims, Pakistanis, existed in them? The hand may well have strayed farther west, but it would have been too obviously farcical. Radcliffe's hand reached out east and applied the surgeon's knife to create an East Pakistan without fear of contradiction, let alone resistance. A cry of anguish rose from the lips which had cried hoarse in defence of constitutional methods. We had been given a truncated Pakistan. Indeed, we had. Under circumstances which we had allowed to be created, how could it be otherwise? How different the outcome would have been if the Muslims, throughout India in general and in the Northern provinces in particular, had been fully prepared, organised and armed for their defence! Consider seriously the consequences if Muslims could not have been dislodged from their homes in East Punjab alone; if the massacre and the exodus had not been possible: ten million Muslims would have remained to ensure the inclusion of the Punjab in the Pakistan of the Muslim League resolution, a legitimate demand – the Punjab being a Muslim majority province. Its repercussions would have reached out into the east and Bengal and Assam, the two Muslim majority provinces, would have been in Pakistan as a whole, as demanded and envisaged in the resolution of 1940. Many tragedies and disasters would have been averted. But the absence of armed force led to weakness, pathetic weakness, lamentable weakness, in every way.

The constitutional arguments of the leadership were useless. The legal arguments of the legal representatives were also futile and useless. They were advanced without the force needed to back them and were confronted by an overwhelming armed force which was used successfully by the enemy. An argument backed by armed force is a forceful argument. It is particularly irresistible when a whole people are determined to fight to protect their rights. Undoubtedly the Muslim people, in the main, were prepared to engage in such a fight, but their hands were tied by the invisible albeit strong cord of constitutionalism created by the leadership.

The Muslims suffered further in this grave, complex and confused situation. While the majority community was unanimous in its demand for Akhand Bharat; while they had the extremely active support of the Sikhs and the tacit agreement of other minorities who were too small or scattered to be effective as groups, the Muslims were handicapped by fragmentation. There were bodies of varying opinion which were far from being conducive to cohesion. The so-called nationalist Muslims of many hues caused the greatest disharmony. Their differences led to plebiscites being held in areas like the then North West Frontier province, with a Muslim majority of well over ninety per cent, to ascertain the wishes of the people concerning their wish to join Pakistan or remain in India. Of course the verdict was overwhelmingly in favour of Pakistan. But it did prove that the weakness of the Muslim defence positions was aggravated by some Muslim political leaders (in some majority areas) following a policy diametrically opposed to the larger interests and programmes. Not only could support not be expected from such quarters but actual hindrance could be anticipated; indeed fierce resistance continued until the very last moment. No such methods for ascertaining peoples' wishes were found to be necessary in the Hindu majority areas. If no help could be expected by Hindus from some less communally biased areas, organisations or individuals, they were absolutely sure that no hindrance in the execution of their programmes would take place.

There were those who wavered and could not decide as to what stance they should adopt. Their attitude, therefore, varied with different situations. But one factor was clear, and that was that no help could be expected in the preparation of defence, until the fact of Pakistan had completely crystallised. Once this crystallisation took place people threw themselves into the idea of Pakistan with apparent enthusiasm which grew in scale after the establishment of Pakistan. The enthusiasm was greater than it had been during the struggle for it. One such example may be quoted here to illustrate the point. General Mohamed Zaman Kiari of the Indian National Army had been clearly associated with me since we joined the Indian Military Academy at Dehra Dun as Gentlemen Cadets in February 1933. He was several years my elder, as he had entered the Academy through the army in the capacity of what was termed 'Y' cadet. The age limit being eight years higher than in the case of those who entered the Academy, as I did, through an open competition under the Public Services Commission. I was probably the youngest in my term while Zaman Kiari was among the oldest. He was tall, slim and an excellent athlete; he was intelligent, mature, experienced, shrewd and worldly wise. I looked up to him for a lead and tagged along with him. We were commissioned from the Academy together. Were served our first years as officers together doing what was called 'attachment' with a British Unit. We selected 2nd Battalion, the Highland Light Infantry (City of Glasgow Regiment) stationed at Peshawar. We participated, separately, in the 1935 Mohman Operations, which were designed to teach us practical 'Frontier warfare' but of course, more so to teach the truculent tribesmen a lesson in how to accede to the British imperialist wishes and demands. To this day I am quite unaware of the assumed or real reason for that operation. However, the operations, under the command of Brigadier Claude Auchenlick, were successfully carried out. The units added another name to their standards, another ribbon to adorn the imperial breast; another occasion to award distinction, the highest being posthumous; another occasion for the units, British and

Indian, to engrave their crests into the rocks of Nahaki Pass. To leave their footprints on the sands of time, so to speak.; to leave them to posterity but perhaps even more for, to leave them for the tribal children to gaze at, throw stones at and spit at, the onlookers wondering whether the last act was a purely local habit to remove the dust from the throat and the mouth or whether it was a gesture of more profound significance.

Having acquired the benefits of practical training and having become conversant with the etiquette expected of an officer in the imperial army, Zaman Kiari's and my paths forked. We went to our separate Indian regiments. Later I joined the Indian Air Force and Zaman found himself with Netaji Subhash Chandra Bose, having been captured by the Japanese imperialists in the campaign in South East Asia. After the defeat of Japanese imperialism he was re-captured by his former colleagues and brought to Delhi, to stand trial for services rendered to the enemy. The enormous political pressures, after the war, brought to nil the efforts of the British to punish the members of the Indian National Army. When Zaman was released I was in Air Head Quarters in New Delhi.

It was then that we came face to face after twelve years. We were both invited to tea by Mr. Siddique, a Muslim business man dealing in items of refrigeration, who was to become a mini tycoon in the same line in Pakistan. By this time Zaman had become aware of my deep involvement in the struggle for Pakistan, without knowing the practical extent of it in my making weapons available for defence. But he knew me and how seriously I was capable of being identified with a cause of this nature. At that time the slaughter of the Muslim minority in the districts of Gurgaon, Rohtak and Karnal was in progress. Therefore, the subject was topical and under discussion. I vividly recollect his words to me; they were indelible because symbolically he had dipped his fingers in that blood and written the words across my eyes, "Well, your friends are having their scalps taken off. They are being put through the process of 'Shudhi'."

Shudhi is part of the process of conversion to Hinduism; purification. I am unable to recall the exact words of my retort. I was provoked into uttering words of rage. How well aware I was of the plight of those very people, of those very human beings, who faced death and destruction; a blood bath was their lot; surrounded on all sides by a ferocious enemy, who was engaged in the achievement of unpolluted and unpollutable Mother India, Akhand Bharat! How deeply aware I was that they were the first people whom some of us were trying to assist in order to save some blood! How profoundly conscious I was of the meagreness and inadequacy of that aid! The moment was psychologically charged and it was not possible not to be provoked and to retain those words.

Yet the same Zaman Kiari was whole-heartedly engaged in helping the people of Poonch and Mirpur to throw off the yoke of the tyrannical Dogra ruler of Kashmir and Jammu. The oppressed Muslim subjects had risen in revolt, had routed the Dogra troops and had virtually freed themselves. Zaman and I collaborated quite closely in this. He wrote me a sorrowful and anxious letter about the conditions on the front. I responded to the best of my ability, but he was located too far away for me to give him all he needed, or as much as I was capable of doing and did on the fronts within my reach. This was in the later months of 1947, when Pakistan had come into being, was reasonably secure behind the wall which had a million martyrs for its foundation stone, their blood running in the moat round it. In these conditions of security, Zaman had rendered quite valuable service in various capacities over a prolonged period.

Then there were those who gave themselves and their audience the most profound psychological reasons for adhering to the theory of Akhand Bharat, but in fact to satisfy a far greater personal psychological need. There were few of them but they were persons of strong moral fibre; most devastatingly effective in their own way. They convinced themselves of the sincerity of their belief and set about their task sincerely, steering a course divergent to the majority of their people, and, wittingly or unwittingly, but positively, acting in a manner which could and did add enormously to the difficulties of their people. This type was symbolised in the person of General Shah Nawaz of the Indian National Army. He was the most famous of the I.N.A. officers after Mohan Singh, but caught the limelight more than the latter and probably more than any other I.N.A. officer. This was quite in keeping with his character; 'glamour' might quite easily have been his middle name. I remember him so well when he was at the Academy. He was a term behind me but in same company. I am unable to think of a clumsier athlete; he had the stamina for long distance running but not the speed for sprinting. He was not outstanding at either and his style used to reduce us to tears. But after an attempt at 100 yards, which he covered in thirteen seconds flat, he would come over to us, with a grin of delight, and say in most expressive Punjabi:

"You know, Khan (referring to me), when I run I feel the wind whizzing past my ears!"

His style in boxing was no less clumsy; and being a south-paw did not add to its attractiveness. But he had a powerful looking physique and was able to overcome many of us lesser beings during sparring practice, prior to the inter-company matches. I was about three weights lighter than him, and this must have been the reason for my having been so terribly impressed. He would inch at me from a distance, his left fist drawn well back; as he brought it forward he would set his jaw and grunt words, which roughly translated would be,

"Oh, I could knock the stuffing out of you!"

I would pull myself well back, guarding my stomach, and would feel that had he completed the move, his fist would have gone crashing through my ribs, but magnanimously he would never complete the stroke. He would then throw out his chest, flap his invisible wings and crow like a victorious cock, in a manner of speaking. And well he might, because his gestures had this kind of effect on all those lighter in weight. Shah Nawaz was a Welter Weight. In those days, the first string welter weight fought last. There were odd numbers of fights and if the last but one fight led to a draw then the welter weight first string assumed tremendous importance and the excitement reached fever pitch. This was the situation on the first day of the boxing competition. Our 'B' company and the opponents 'D' company had won an equal number of fights. It now depended upon Shah Nawaz to 'knock the stuffing' out of his opponent by the name of Litchfield, an Anglo-Indian boy. As far as all 'B' company was concerned the match was in the bag. Shah Nawaz would make short shrift of the bout; such was the awe-inspiring impression created in all minds – no exceptions in 'B' company anyway; and probably most of 'D' company also felt sorry for Litchfield. 'B' company all relaxed; 'D' company all tensed. The moment came; the bell rang; the seconds went out; the two boxers shook hands. Shah Nawaz went through the now expected and universally dreaded posture; pulled back his left fist; and before he or anyone else knew it, Litchfield had crashed his fist on the completely exposed nose of Shah Nawaz; he had obviously read the signal correctly. Shah Nawaz had forgotten that some boxers read the boxing telegraphs and responded to them with alacrity and agility. After that Litchfield made circles around him. Speed was never Shah Nawaz's strong point but it was Litchfield's; style was never considered by Shah Nawaz to be of any importance, but it was by Litchfield; science did not matter to Shah Nawaz but it did to Litchfield. The end was inevitable: Shah Nawaz lost, mercifully only on points. The cock so accustomed to crowing was now crestfallen.

But that was thirteen years earlier. We had all undergone many changes. I expected Shah Nawaz to have done the same. I met him briefly during his trial, in the Red Fort in Delhi, for his part in the Indian National Army. But after his release I met him on numerous occasions and for prolonged periods, some lasting all night and the greater part of the following day. The reasons for this close association were two-fold. Firstly, that we were at the Academy together for two years; secondly we were at Rawalpindi Division, and thirdly we also belonged to the same clan; Shah Nawaz too is a Janjua.

We resumed our relationship when political activity was at its zenith; when conditions of conflict prevailed in which neutrality was really not possible. I had undergone a metamorphosis and was firmly, positively and deeply aligned with a group of humanity which faced the most crucial phase of its existence. Had Shah Nawaz undergone the same change I wondered? Had he made his decision? He certainly sounded more mature even if his exuberance appeared to be uncurbed and unrestrained. He was extremely busy; meeting delegations, attending functions and ceremonies of which he seemed to be the centre. Together with some I.N.A. officers, he had been acclaimed a national hero in India. But he outshone the others and stole the limelight. In this he revelled most; giving speeches, being garlanded, receiving the 'tilak' of a Hindu hero, (a red marked placed on the forehead, generally by a most attractive young lady) processions, shouting slogans: in fact, "roses, roses, all the way"! When I met him he had returned from Nagpur in central India having attended a function. I think it was an athletics meeting. I found the cock crowing once again; ready to knock the stuffing out of everyone; the wind whizzing past his ears! He was in his element. A good organiser; his opinion and guidance were being sought. A sincere, indefatigable worker; the demands on him and his time were non-stop. On the one hand his talents were being fully utilised and exploited; on the other hand the floodlight was fully trained on him. This was an irresistible combination. It brought out the best in him. It would also keep him in one place, performing duties regardless of their effect on others.

My heart sank when I saw the situation and type of work on which he was engaged. I made a desperate bid to change his mind and commenced a series of discussions with him. These would be either at the bungalow where he lived or in my room in the I.A.F. officer's Mess in Central Vista, not far from the Secretariat and Air Head Quarters. At some of these meetings there were other friends present, prominent among them being Lt. Col. Gulzar Ahmed, later Brigadier in the Pakistan Army. Shah Nawaz had considerable regard for Gulzar Ahmed, who was married to a third cousin of mine.

"Well Shah Nawaz, the die is cast now. We have achieved independence for two separate homelands." I would say, "How about coming home?"

"No Khan, I cannot forget the image of a United India." He would say.

I said, "But we all had that image at one time. That was a long time ago. Things have changed, you can see that."

Shah Nawaz: "That picture is so firmly fixed in my mind."

I responded, a little irritably, "That picture has been smashed and trampled underfoot by the very heroes you adore so much. It no longer exists."

However Shah Nawaz insisted that the image remained with him.

"Here you have all the glamour; you can have a belly full and more to spare. In your homeland you will be required to tie a loincloth around you and work harder than you have ever done. I know that hard work is the one thing you relish most. So do come; your type is needed." I tried to appeal to the best in him.

There was silence from Shah Nawaz.

At that moment a Gandhi cap, loin cloth clad person entered and greeted Shah Nawaz in the traditional Hindu manner; palms joined together in front, at breast level then raised rapidly to touch the forehead. Maybe that was to indicate his superiority over the other; maybe he was still unaccustomed to the form of salutation and was his

68

usual clumsy self; maybe my presence had made it slightly difficult for him.

"Concerning the training camp at X-pur Sir!" said the man.

"Yes, what about it?" Shah Nawaz asked.

Then a conversation ensued which showed that the training camps were being organised and operated for Hindu youth, boys and girls, under the unquestionably capable, serious and sincere guidance of Shah Nawaz. Their training included physical exercise to toughen them up and the use of arms, mainly swords, daggers, sticks, knives and other such close combat weapons, but the handling of small fire arms was not excluded.

The wholesale slaughter of the Muslims in Garh Mukteshwar and Bihar had taken place so recently that the bloodshed had hardly had time to congeal. Shah Nawaz had visited the effected areas on 'peace missions', sometimes accompanied by other 'national Muslim leaders', but more often by Hindu 'leaders'. Then occasionally we would see Bapuji (Mahatma Gandhi) talk about the riots; yes, just talk about them: there is nothing they could do to influence in any way the main trend of events. The Mahatma's creed of non-violence was in shambles. He ran from place to place, mainly after the event, by which time the ferocity had more or less spent itself. After all there is a limit to the amount of blood that can be shed in a given time! I do not for a moment suggest that some lives may not have been saved through the Mahatma's efforts, appeals, counsels and other interventions alone, or in conjunction with other leaders such as Mr. Hussain Shaheed Suhrawardy. But the fact that millions and millions of lives were lost by the application of the most violent and bestial means, stares us in the face, and this, at a time when not only was non-violence most necessary but when the Mahatma preached it with all his soul. Then who can say how effective his preaching and his personal, undoubtedly Himalayan efforts were in preventing loss of life? Who can say how many more lives may have been lost had he not preached or intervened?

I for one would be too happy to revise the estimate of lives and property saved. I only know the phenomenal estimates of the losses suffered. But I can say one thing with confidence and without hesitation and that is that had the Muslims armed themselves for their defence they would not have suffered such terrible losses. If, instead of clarion calls, weapons had gone out to them for their protection, they would not have suffered as they did and would have achieved their entirely legitimate aim of a full, un-truncated, Pakistan. If Mr. Suhrawardy had concentrated on defence instead of issuing, quite unnecessary out of place empty warnings of Changiz-like action, such losses could have been averted. There was no aggressive action required or planned for the achievement of their aim: purely and solely defensive action was required. The adversary was armed for aggression; his aim was to prevent the partition of the 'sacred Motherland'. He carried that plan out ruthlessly and it was not because of lack of effort on his part that he did not succeed. Under these circumstances Shah Nawaz, or the Mahatmaji himself, could not stem the tide of violence. But not only was Shah Nawaz not attempting the obviously impossible, he was actively participating in preparations for further possible aggression and atrocities. He was engaged in carrying out training of quasi-military Hindu youth.

I questioned Him on these matters.

"You have been to Bihar. What were the conditions like?"

Shah Nawaz replied "Yes, I was there. I met Bapuji also. Khan the conditions are terrible."

"And in Garhmukteshwar?"

Shah Nawaz said, "No better. Indeed they may be described as even worse."

He was quite composed when he started to describe the nature of the atrocities but as he proceeded with descriptions from place to place his emotions began to become perceptible. He literally gave up, but put up a façade of cool courage; indifference to such sufferings – sure sign of a great leader; he tried to shrug them off as being a necessary part of such a momentous event as the independence of India. He appeared to be struggling. A conflict appeared to be raging within him. He had witnessed bestial treatment meted out to the Muslims; their unspeakable plight. He was able to do practically nothing to prevent it. But worse; he was giving further training to those responsible for those dastardly acts. Is it impossible that these thoughts would create a sense of acute guilt? He had to resolve this.

He was passionately attached to the image of a united India. He would do everything within his power to retain it. They had decided to rend that image apart but he could not rid himself of it. Although all parties were responsible for the destruction of that sacred image, he implied that one was more responsible than the others! The part of the sub-continent which was to be Bharat was more sacred than the part that was to be Pakistan! By what logic, only he could know. He had been proclaimed a hero by a vast majority of Hindus and not by vast numbers of Muslims. He had had the 'tilak' on his forehead on numerous occasions, but not once had he had the crescent on his breast. The Muslims had no organisation, no youth volunteers to be trained. Even if they had something resembling the Hindu mass movements, they had never asked to help. In any event this was the real Indian youth and moulding it for the future glory of India was indeed an honour. Now he felt better. He was working for the glory and greatness of India; the India of the sacred image. No sacrifice was enough or too much and if that sacrifice was the blood of millions, so be it.

"Can you stop it?" My question startled him. His reverie came to an abrupt end.

"Eh?" he murmured.

"Can you stop this carnage? Can you prevent it? Can you even reduce its intensity?" I asked.

Silence.

"Can you stop training the potential butchers of your community? Because this is precisely what you are doing." These were more or less my last words.

Shah Nawaz embraced me warmly, as was his wont; managed an affectionate smile. This must have soothed him. I wanted to weep and cry in anguish. Inwardly I sobbed. Oh, how complex we are. I am no exception. But I was leaving behind forever an able, sincere, honest person. How much he would be missed I could not say. Nations and people have a habit of getting along without the indispensable. But individuals do make some difference to their progress, if they are capable of positive contributions. I thought Shah Nawaz was one of them. He decided to contribute elsewhere. He preferred the present certain glamour to the possible future one. He alone can know the real reasons. We can only speculate and venture intelligent guesses but we may not be entirely justified in drawing our conclusions. In the common and mundane term, 'he did well for himself'. He attained a ministerial post in his chosen Motherland. He was, indeed, well rewarded for his hard work and services rendered. I believe he came to Pakistan at a later date. He did not find the situation encouraging for himself. I sincerely hope that he was not surprised that such was the case.

Then there were men of little or no calibre, but they added to the numbers. Everyone who was unsympathetic potentially endangered some aspect of the already weak position of Pakistan. At best they would be, or were obliged to remain neutral, and at the worst they could be spokes in the wheel. They had no cogent reasons or arguments. Two examples of such persons were in the Rajputana Rifles at Palam. I visited that unit frequently because my first wife's sister lived there with her husband, Major M. Hayat (later Brigadier in the

Pakistan Army) who later became ambassador in the diplomatic corps. He was a good officer; gentle, quiet and unassuming. These traits made him amply suitable for a task where minimal use of speech was an asset. He later had such an assignment and it can be assumed that he did it adequately. A man of few words and those words at that time were favourable to the need of his community, but not so those of Major Sawal Khan, (later Brigadier in the Pakistan Army). He was in the same unit as Hayat and was married to Hayat's sister. He did not see 'why' the army should be divided. He did not see 'why' he should have to go over to Pakistan, if he did not wish to. Muslims from areas in Pakistan could not opt to stay in the Indian Army. Sawal Khan came from such an area. In fact he did not see anything! He was exasperating. I was beside myself with irritation at his unintelligent repetitive utterances.

"The army of Pakistan could do very well without you. It does not need your kind. So, if you feel so terribly emotional about what you call the indivisible Indian Army, then all you have to do is to submit your resignation and rejoin the INA. If they are as emotional as you are about them, you have nothing to fear." I said; to put an end to a futile discussion, devoid of any sense or logic.

Obviously Sawal Khan's emotions were not reciprocated. He did not resign. He remained in the army, came over to Pakistan and carried on working and getting promotions in a set up he had opposed vehemently, at least in theory. Well, things and people can change. He forgot all about his previously held views, probably he rendered good service within his limitations, of which he had a surfeit. I was told by Hayat that Major Sher Bahadur (later Major General in the Pakistan Army) was even worse in this respect. But I did not have the occasion to meet him. All I could say was that it was their good fortune that there was a country like Pakistan for them (in which they could work) and that it was Pakistan's misfortune that there were people like these working for her.

There were men in all these categories who together numbered millions. Then there were religious and politico-religious bodies who passionately wished to remain in a united sub-continent. They believed that a way could be found for settling the communal differences peaceably. They were romantically and emotionally attached to the soil of Hind. The glory of their conquering forebears and the zeal of the early Muslim missionaries lingered in their minds. But instead of it remaining a distant, hazy, albeit colourful memory, of days long past, they let it assume a concrete shape. The times had changed and would continue to change but in a relentless forward movement, not ever looking back, at least not for the purposes of those harking back to images of a united India. There were others who also wanted to restore the ancient glory of India but their aim included the complete eradication of the very picture that these Muslim politico-religious gentlemen were conjuring up in their minds. That picture was a painful reminder of the foreign yoke and subjugation of Indians under Mogul rule! Of course, they had settled the Motherland. They had made it their home. Their numbers had multiplied. But they were Arabs, Turks, Persians, Afghans, and Moguls. Yes, all foreign conquerors. Admittedly India had been conquered by others before them, but that was past history. The British had conquered India after them. But the British were being ousted by the Indians themselves. They were not being forced out by another foreign conqueror. After many centuries a situation had come about where India was to be in Indian hands. No-one must forget that it was Hindustan; that it was the land of the Hindus; that it was Bharat; indeed, that it was Maha Bharat (Mother India). Any people living within its boundaries would be well advised to remember that. This was the overwhelming desire of the majority of Hindus.

But the Muslim visionaries did not hear this clear warning; they did not see the writing on the wall. If they did, then they singularly failed to give it the interpretation that was obviously intended. They kept going in pursuit of rainbows. Overtaken by events they begged and prayed for wise counsels to prevail. In fact they were imploring the wolf to protect the lamb. This had no more effect than the Mahatma's exhortations. It added further to the confusion in the already sorely tried Muslim ranks and subtracted from their ability to organise a defence.

Such were the forces, if they can be so called, at work. Some actively engaged in helping to cause damage; some sitting on the fence; some passive and neutral in a situation where neutrality was tantamount to connivance with the opposing forces; some just myopic if not blind, looking backwards, not able to see the dangerous collision course we were on. The sum total of it all was the creation of weakness after weakness in the ranks of the people threatened in every possible manner with physical elimination.

But what about those who were determined to achieve Pakistan in order to forestall the plan for extinction or absorption? No evidence could be seen of a cohesive, organised and planned defensive action. Was the plan then to achieve Pakistan, which would have large numbers of Muslims within its boundaries, but let the others run for their lives and the devil take the hindmost? This is virtually what it appeared to be. If any organised movement existed it must have been most inefficient and ineffective; it failed miserably to defend and protect. But I would say that no really effective organisation to deal with the situation ever existed or was even seriously contemplated. The attitude of the policy makers would make this fact reasonably clear.

Shortly prior to the announcement concerning independence and the reconstitution of the sub-continent, an interview was arranged with Quaid-e-Azam M.A.Jinnah, for some Muslim officers of the armed forces. To my chagrin I was appointed spokesman. In the discussion the Quaid-e-Azam stated that he was confident we would achieve an independent Pakistan.

"And I cannot accept a Pakistan without its own defence forces. It is inconceivable that an independent sovereign state should not have its own armed services", he said.

"Could the argument of the impracticability of division of the armed forces be advanced for shelving the issue of Pakistan?" I asked.

"No, I must have Pakistan and I must have its own defence services. They must find a way to divide them" he said.

Being aware of the certainty of irritating the Quaid-e-Azam, I asked,

"But what if they do not agree to divide the armed forces?"

"You want me to consider unconstitutional means! I will not do so." He exploded, but mildly.

This to my mind at least summed up the situation. The Quaid-e-Azam was naturally right in his political, but strictly constitutional analysis; Pakistan was on the way. Logically, no country could be without its own armed forces, when at a political level separation was agreed, it was up to the specialists to devise ways and means to practically divide the departments. The armed forces could not be an exception. There could be no two opinions on that point. And that is exactly how it took place theoretically. But there was many a slip between the cup and the lip, which is another story to be told elsewhere.

We asked a few more questions about general matters, occasionally coming very close to the edges of the subject of civil strife and the critical situation of the Muslims in several parts of the country. But the line was never crossed. Not one hint of any defensive measures. Possibly that was not the place or the time. But some of us later came into intimate contact with the policy makers and were taken into their confidence on matters of importance. Not once did we step across the line, into the subject of practical defence. There, indeed, there was no such subject for discussion! There was little to do except to plunge into the 'constitutional' work, to prepare for Pakistan. But temperamentally, some of us could not remain entirely 'constitutional', another word for inactivity, as far as we were concerned, when strong action was desperately needed. We continued to throw straws into the torrent so that some may clutch at them for safety; that was how inadequate I considered our efforts to be.

Our disharmony, disunity, discord, apathy, confusion, day dreaming and lack of practical action were met by complete harmony, unity, accord, enthusiasm, clarity and practical thought and action on the part of the Hindus. While the Muslims were in disarray with no allies, the Hindus were fully organised and had the minorities actively or tacitly with them. The Sikhs did much of their work for them. There was no division of opinion. Some, very few indeed, did accede to the right of the Muslims to have their own homeland, but they would shed no tears if it were not achieved. Generally the tempo of resistance to Pakistan was increasing and continued until the last day before independence and even beyond.

When I was at the Services Selection Board in Dehra Dun, we had a visit from Brigadier Thakus Nathu Singh in the latter part of 1946. He was the Head of the Department concerned with Selection Boards; I do not recollect the exact designation. The Brigadier and I had served with the same Indian Unit, 1st Battalion, 7th Rajput Regiment. He was several years my senior but was quite friendly with me. This was in 1936-37. Now, ten years later we met again. The inevitable topic was Independence and the Pakistan Movement; it was not long before his Rajput whiskers began to bristle and he said:

"We will fight you tooth and nail. We will fight you to the last."

"That's saying a lot", I said.

"We shall wipe you out if need be." He went on, his face taking on a darker hue and I could almost hear the bristling under his nose.

In such situations I have not always succeeded in remembering differences in ranks and other such demarcations between individuals.

"You will find us ready for that. You will find wiping out of a people far more hazardous than you imagine. When you come you will find us prepared to die and this coin has the other side, which is much more important; we will be prepared to kill!"

After my outburst we lapsed into silence. Some minutes later our old regimental camaraderie came to the rescue. Just as I had forgotten our ranks in anger, Brigadier Nathu Singh chose to forget them in calm. We repaired to the Mess where he had his double Scotch and Soda and I sipped my lemonade. In how many more Messes was this taking place? Did it all end in a similar manner? Did it? Would it continue to end like this? And if so, for how long? I could not see it continuously and indefinitely following that course.

On my posting from the Selection Board to Air Head Quarters, New Delhi, later in 1946, for some time I lived with the family of one of my best friends, Lt Col. Moti Sagar (later Lt. General in the Indian Army). I had lived with his family on numerous occasions commencing in 1937, in Lahore. I was closer to them than to any other Hindu family; as close as my father was to Amin Chand, except that we were able to cross some of the barriers which they did not. Moti Sagar and I entered the Academy together, through the Public Services Commission open competition, we were commissioned together and found ourselves together again in the same Indian Army Unit, 1st Battalion the 7th Rajput regiment. We became intimate friends. Moti was a highly intelligent and efficient officer. He was literally of sober taste and of exceedingly high moral fibre. I relished his quick wit and simple but subtle humour. His family, brothers, sisters and sister in law and I had taken to one another instantly. The relationship deepened with every exchange of visit. I was with them again at a critical phase in the history of the country. I would be with them for a few weeks, perhaps a few months and then depart perhaps never to see them again. I cannot but be emotional here. I was enormously happy that the eldest of Moti's sisters, Bibi, was married, literally days before I left them forever. They were sad that I did not assist in the preparations for Bibi's wedding as much as they had wished and expected me to; they were, however, glad that I was there for the function. I had been busy elsewhere, trying desperately to prevent Bibi's community giving the waters of the Jummuna a hue to match the henna on her hands. A hopeless task, indeed, but it had to be attempted.

During my stay with them a young Hindu man was a frequent visitor to the house. We got on very well together and our relations were normal and even friendly. I do not recollect his name. One day as he came in my first name was under discussion. As he heard it he became tense and almost choked as he said,

"Are you a Muslim? Then I am ninety per cent against you."

"When you say it like that I am one hundred per cent against you. Why bother with the ten per cent?" I said.

After that whenever he came during my stay, he was so aloof that I may easily have been in Pakistan already. He represented the overwhelming majority of Hindus. We his hands already stained? He was entirely capable of using a dagger; many daggers were visible in his eyes. And I had been almost a friend, only hours before. How about those who had only ever been enemies?

At the Air H.Q. the Head of my Department was Air Commodore Aspy Engineer (later Air Marshal and Commander–in-Chief and Chief of Air Staff, Indian Air Force). He and I served together on several occasions. I was his Adjutant when he commanded No.2 Squadron I.A.F. and officiated as Commanding officer whenever he had to be absent from the Squadron. Socially he was rather snobbish. He and his wife Ruby, from a rich Parsi family were what was then called 'modern'. My background was quite different and my temperament, vastly so.

Professionally we had a healthy regard for each other. He was a very capable officer, especially in staff duties. He did, however, have a reputation for being exciteable and for flapping. Whenever he was nervous or engrossed in some serious subject, he would place his elbows on the chair and if standing, on an imaginary chair, hold his hands in front of him, finger and thumb apart and curved inward. He would then repeatedly and rapidly touch the tips and while he spoke in an agitated manner he would suck in his breath and make a hissing sound.

Aspy had a redness of face that made him look as though he had tasted and swallowed a red chilly. He would get flustered and go a deeper red which was when I knew he was flapping. This is how I often found him in the hectic days shortly prior to and after the 3rd June, 1947, when the announcement was made concerning the reconstitution of the sub-continent. Prior to this he would broach the subject of Pakistan and discuss it interminably. His primary argument in favour of keeping India united, at least militarily, was the theory of 'defence in depth'. A very laudable military principle indeed, but certainly not sufficiently laudable to be a reality at the cost of matters vital to the continued existence of people whose numbers had reached one hundred million. I would then give him all the reasons why a separate homeland had become inevitable.

"It is not only our defence in depth but yours also if you achieve Pakistan" he would say. He would then proceed to measure the supposed width of West Pakistan at its narrowest and give the distance in miles, pointing out how there was no 'depth in defence'.

"In modern warfare this is entirely inadequate." he would conclude.

"Defence against whom? Are you contemplating an attack on Pakistan when it comes into being?" I would ask.

"No. No." he would add hastily.

"Then if you do not plan to attack us there is no other power against whom we would need the 'defence in depth' about which you are so anxious. Even if you decide to attack us, believe me we have enough territory to manoeuvre in. Besides that, it is not necessarily always the decisive factor. You may find it rather difficult to cross a twelve mile width" I said. There was a brief silence after which I continued.

"If you think we might attack you then you have all the depth you need. And should we be on the same side in a larger conflict the situation for you is even better. But should we be on opposite sides then who knows who may need greater depth?"

As time passed these and similar discussions became more frequent and assumed a certain sharpness. Aspy appeared to be becoming more loyal than the king. He would take up cudgels on behalf of others. He would repeatedly ask about various Muslim officers to ascertain whether they had opted or would opt for Pakistan. Then one day the argument between us became really hot.

"It's a damn shame, this partition. Something should still be done to stop it", he said.

I said, "Forget it Aspy. The decision is taken and it's final. Let's get on with what we are required to do to implement it."

"I will see you in Pakistan in ten years. It will be a poor destitute country. You have no industry. How can you last even ten years?" Aspy said.

"I will come here after five years and see Cyrus with a 'chutia'" I retorted. 'Chutia' or ' Choti' is a tuft of hair allowed to grow by Brahmins and orthodox Hindus. It is at the dome of the head, while the rest of the head is either shaven or hair is kept short and even. Cyrus was Aspy and Rubi's only son and child; they were very proud of their Anglo-Parsi culture. By my remark I had suggested that their culture would vanish and that their son would be practicing another culture which I am reasonably confident in believing. Aspy associated with low class Hindus. The implication behind my remark cut Aspy to the quick. That was my intention and I continued to tell him that that was how some of us thought conditions would be in India in due course. The minorities and their cultures would be overwhelmed, primarily in a planned manner, but in any case by sheer weight of numbers. We did not intend to allow our culture to be crushed out of us. The conflict between the cultures was too great. Other minorities were not in a position to adopt the course that we had. History and geography had made it possible for us to have a homeland. As for industry and other aspects of progress, when one hundred million people put their mind to it, there is hardly anything they cannot achieve. We have the manpower, the talent, the energy, the vigour and the will. We could manage very well in due course.

Shortly after this incident we were at an evening party given by a senior British Officer. Sardar Baldev Singh was the Minister for Defence and a guest. As he entered I happened to be standing with Aspy Engineer. A sharp nudge in the ribs from me nearly made him jump. I pointed out a spectacle to him I thought I would never see. Ruby of the impeccable European and Parsi manners and culture stood up from her chair, faced Baldev Singh and greeted him in the traditional Hindu manner, palms joined in front of her and head slightly bowed to meet the fingertips. My elbow was still in his ribs.

"That is what I meant, Aspy" I said. There was a distant look in her eyes. He coughed a bit to clear his throat, turned slowly away from me and walked off. Of course he knew it was going to be like that. But he was welcome to it. He had to submit. I did not have to do so and would not.

Some years later Aspy Engineer, after a full term of office as the Commander-in-Chief and Chief of Air Staff of the Indian Air Force, was appointed the Ambassador of India in Persia. But when his tenure expired he did not return to India. He decided to stay in the land of his ancestors. The fire lit by Zoroaster in the temples of Persia had been extinguished more than a millennium earlier, but it seemed to kindle a spark in Aspy's heart!

We had to continue to work together as officers of the Indian Air Force and to sit at opposite sides of the table, Aspy as number two for the I.A.F. and I as the senior member of Pakistan Air Force, at the meetings of the Armed Forces Reconstitution Committee' Air Force sub-Committee, which was formed following the Reconstitution decision. Aspy pursued his 'defence in depth' argument relentlessly until a few days before the date fixed for handing over Independence to the two countries by Mountbatten. When the Radcliffe Commission sat for the boundary award Aspy would stand in front of the map and point out to me as to where the boundary line should be, of course, always keeping in view the 'defence in depth' of India. When the deadline neared, he became more positive and began to say where the boundary line would be. He told me that Ferozepur would have to be included in India; there was a large depot there! The sub-division of Ferozepur definitely and a large part of the district, was a Muslim majority area contiguous to the unquestioning Muslim majority areas to the West. But he did not stop at that. He pointed his finger, with the tip touching if not actually piercing, Lahore.

"Aspy, not only is a large part of Ferozepur district a Muslim majority area, a large part of Amritsar district also is, and Gurdarpur district as a whole is Muslim majority. So even if the minimum conditions of the terms of reference were met, Amritsar city would be in an untenable position. It would have to remain in Pakistan. But the Punjab is a Muslim majority province and in the larger meaning of the terms of reference it should be in Pakistan."

Aspy was not only confident, he was adamant that his idea of a boundary which must be drawn after giving due regard to India's defence requirements, was the right one. And that is where the boundary would be. Aspy Engineer was number two in the Indian Air Force. He was being consulted about the defence of India. He had access to the Indian members of the Cabinet. Did he know the shape of things to come? Had matters already been decided? Even if they had not, were the Indian members confident of getting the line drawn where Aspy's pencil roamed? This was many days, possibly even weeks, before the Radcliffe Award. Aspy was apt to be quite secretive, but when excited he would unwittingly let the exuberance penetrate his defence mechanism. He would give out the crux of the information in a camouflaged manner. Those who knew him intimitely could draw reasonably accurate conclusions. I had known this of him over seven years of close professional association. His demeanour now showed that some truth lurked behind his assumed personal analysis. When the boundary Award bombshell came, I was in Pakistan. Aspy's words and gestures came back to me. The line appeared almost as if it had been drawn by him. Intelligent as he most certainly was, this could not have been a guess on his part. It followed too literally what he had said. His attitude of supreme confidence and cocksure manner, then the nature of the 'Award' and the shape of the map, coincided too well for it all to be a coincidence. He did know something. One can only make an intelligent guess, from where and why was it possible for such knowledge to percolate to some on the Indian side! If it was merely a brilliant guess then why could not our even more brilliant personalities have guessed a fraction of it? If it was information than why did our side not have such information or sources which could give them, at least, an inkling of what was in store for us? I believe that just as our leadership was entirely ill-equipped for an active defence, which is the minimum requirement for a people's struggle, so was it completely at sea in assessing the situation with regard to the subject under discussion. Should it be claimed that our leaders did have even an iota of knowledge, then why did they accept such an outrageous situation? Why did they not walk away and make the strongest possible protest?

Why did they allow such injustice to take place? According to them, the Award was a grave injustice. Everything points to the fact that they did not have the vaguest notion about the treachery taking place right under their noses. While, as I have already said, Radcliffe's mind was in all probability influenced by the events in the vital sectors of the Punjab, it is not beyond the bounds of possibility that those very events were influenced by an inspired leakage of information about the shape of the intended 'Award'. Indeed, an unofficial conspiratorial compromise and even alliance is not an improbability.

The timing of the announcement regarding Radcliffe's Award was just four days before the date of the establishment of Pakistan! Had the 'Award' been according to the all important clause 'contiguous' majority areas – the boundary would have been far, far to the East of where it stands today. This would have meant firstly, that the Muslims from the areas farther East would have stopped there and not gone so far to the West; secondly, that the Muslims from the West would have come to the rescue of their harassed brethren, and thirdly, that the Sikhs would have left those areas and gone farther East. This precisely is the process which took place when boundaries were drawn. Muslims on one side and Hindus and Sikhs on the other, exchanged places and went over to their own majority areas; Muslims to Pakistan and Hindus and Sikhs to India. Of course, I maintain very strongly that that had the Muslims armed themselves for their defence and had it been known to the Sikhs and the Hindus that the Muslims were in a high state of preparation, then the carnage would not have taken place; and they would have achieved mainly if not entirely the Pakistan as envisaged in the Muslim League resolution of March 1940, which would have spanned the North of India.

It may be, and might quite conceivably at that time have been argued, that if the Muslims had armed themselves as I had suggested, there would have been a bloody civil war. But there was a bloody civil war; and it was virtually one-sided. It is absurd to suggest that one side should follow the path of peace when the other, openly and actively belligerent, pursues the attainment of its aims, by force of arms. The unarmed party would either have to surrender, or if conditions for surrender did not exist, or if they did exist but were unacceptable, they would have to accept crippling losses and suffer untold misery. Neither the question nor the thought of surrender could arise on the part of the Muslims. The masses were mentally prepared for a struggle. They did carry out the 'constitutional' campaign in an admirable manner. They would never surrender. They were never armed. They were prepared for any sacrifice. They made the supreme sacrifice in being an unarmed army, without strategy; without a plan for defence or withdrawal, which are among the most difficult actions in a war. The outcome was logical and obvious. Many tears were shed; much wrath and horror expressed at the human tragedy. What did they expect from an enemy, fully armed, with the declared aim of using force either to make us desist from our demands or to make us pay for it in blood? And how we did pay!

The contrast between the attitudes and activities of both sides could not have been greater. The Muslim leaders divided; the so called intelligentsia and other thinking persons holding divergent views thereby completely confusing and misleading large numbers of Muslims; the Muslim masses generally realising the vital necessity for a separate homeland and mentally and morally prepared for a struggle, while not being equipped for it in physical terms. The Hindu-Sikh leaders united, holding identical views which led to ambiguity in the minds of their masses, concerning their aims and actions; the Hindu-Sikh masses being mentally, morally and physically prepared for a struggle. All shades of opinion were mobilised; ninety per cent against us at the mere mention of our name! Prepared to fight us to the last and wipe us out, persistent propagandists seeking to enlist the support of larger numbers of Muslims and demanding more territory to provide greater depth for the defence of India. The results achieved by the parties could only be, in direct proportion to the attitudes adopted and actions taken by each.

The impossible task of stemming the tide of Hindu violence, and breaking its force, was continued. Due to the paucity of sources for the supply of defence weapons; due to the dangerous nature of the operation in an overwhelmingly Hindu-Sikh domain, and above all due to the virtually hostile attitude of the Muslim leaders to these 'unconstitutional' methods, the work was made immensely difficult. Its effectiveness was necessarily limited, but the leadership's constitutional struggle was, of course, open to all Muslims and others, who alas were not forthcoming in any significant numbers. There were some zealous young officers who were busy collecting material information concerning the number, percentages of Muslim officers on staff duties in various departments of the Army, Navy and Air H.Q.; of course, these were always lamentably small. The instances of injustice with regard to promotion to key appointments and such matters were always painfully present. Prominent among these workers was Lieutenant Maqbool Elahi of the Indian navy. It was he, through whom I first met Mr. Altaf Hussain; editor of the daily 'DAWN'. While these officers collected and compiled information about victimization and other injustices suffered by the Muslim officers, 'DAWN' publicised it to bring it all to the attention of the world. The officers worked extremely sincerely and passionately, believing their work to be a contribution of great value in the argument for Pakistan. I have no doubt that it played a part, unfortunately a minor part, in mobilizing public opinion. However, the leadership must have been naïve to give it more than the minimum importance. I did find them taking it very seriously; as if a great deal depended upon it. On occasion I was dismayed by it all but working on the theory of 'every little matters' I worked closely with both officers and 'DAWN'. Deep inside me was the ever present urge to tell those leaders with whom I met, that this aspect of the argument for Pakistan was long past; now it was time to fight for it! But my effort was akin to trying to penetrate a wall with an aching head as the only weapon with which to batter it. The leaders seemed to be like protesting and demanding schoolchildren banging their spoons on the table to ask for their pudding from a chef unwilling to part with it. In chorus:

"We want Pakistan; we want Pakistan. Hindus are unjust to us. We want Pakistan."

But the Hindu chorus was deafening. Not only was it harmonious and united, it was equipped with far more effective instruments than spoons. It had the backing of the kitchen knife. It could, and did, inflict injustice and made no secret of it, nor was it a secret from the other parties who were involved.

We went on with our collection of the instances of injustice. I commenced constitutional action which I thought would be of greater value, when an independent Pakistan was on the horizon, and increased my efforts when it became a reality. With the very active, sincere and enthusiastic assistance of many Muslim officers stationed at New Delhi in Air H.Q. and other I.A.F. units, I began to collect information in respect of Muslim personnel in the Indian Air Force, branch and trade wise, in order to assess the nature and size of the programme for the expansion of the Pakistan Air Force, which was to be put into effect without a moments delay. A target was to be set, based on the personnel, equipment, training and maintenance facilities at our disposal.

It was by sheer chance that I found myself in the position of the most senior Muslim officer in the Indian Air Force. When I seconded to I.A.F. in 1938, there were two Muslim officers already in the General Duties (Pilot) Branch. The more senior was Flying Officer Aizad Baksh Awan, Zaidi to his friends, who was the same seniority as F/O Shobroto Mukerjee (later Air Marshall and the first Chief of Staff and Commander in Chief, Indian Air Force). There are few more charming, gentle and kind persons than Zaidi. I always said that he should have been an infirmary missionary, taking care of those who needed tender, sympathetic handling. The additional qualification which would have made him admirably suitable for this assignment was his sense of humour, which kept those around him in fits of laughter. He had regard for most people and things but unfortunately none for the orthodox administration which applied to his profession. His unorthodox methods met neither the approval of his superiors nor the needs of the organisation in which he happened to be. The gap in the recognised methods of operation and those adopted by Zaidi, grew wider. I believe that apart from deliberate injustice, which may have been inflicted upon him, this was the basic reason for Zaidi fading into the background. Despite his long service and rank he began to be overlooked when assignments for which he would be qualified, were being considered. He was made to command an operational squadron when he should have been on relatively senior staff duties. The reason given was that Zaidi should gain operational experience at that level before assuming staff duties, so as to better qualify him for higher duties in future. It was said that it would benefit him professionally! Of course those who were so anxious to better equip him for his career overlooked the fact that Shobroto Mukerjee and indeed, about half a dozen other officers at the top of the Indian Air Force list, had not commanded operational squadrons in the real war; only one or two had been operational on the North West Frontier. If Shobroto Mukerjee did not need this experience, then why was Zaidi Awan, who was of the same seniority, required to have it? If it had been a professionally necessary rung on Zaidi'd ladder, then why not Shobroto's? This injustice continued for a long period. During this period Zaidi became involved in a forced landing. He was in the rear cockpit of an aircraft which he let one of his pilots fly. Due to a combination of circumstances a forced landing had to be made. This was the last lap in the relentless pursuit of Zaidi. He was blamed; why did he not take over and avoid the forced landing? Why this? Why that? Until Zaidi, in disgust, threw in the towel. He resigned in 1944.

The other officer was F/O Habibullah Khan, Bulbul to his friends. One would have to go a long way to find an officer more different from Zaidi.

Bulbul was extremely forceful, vigorous, abrupt and quite ruthless in the execution of his duties. Professionally there were no flies on Bulbul. He had a curt manner. No smiles as a tacit form of greeting! Smiling seen perhaps as a sign of weakness! A hearty, raucous laugh whenever approval of his own or another's wit was acknowledged. I first met Bulbul in the Air Force Officers' Mess, Ambala. I was introduced to him and F/O Henry Ranganadhan, together. The latter had a reputation for drinking round the clock; his perpetually bloodshot eyes bore witness to that. Henry offered me a cigarette.

"No, thank you. I don't smoke" I said.

"Have a whisky?" said Henry.

No thank you, I don't drink," I said.

Henry almost exploded, as if I had hurt him personally. He shrieked.

"You don't smoke! You don't drink! What the hell did you join the Air Force for?"

Bulbul burst into one of his robust laughs, although he himself did not partake of alcoholic drinks.

"Well to fly aircraft, if there is no objection." I said in an assumed meek manner. Within seconds Bulbul had put on his mask of sternness. What he was trying to conceal behind it I never did discover.

"What's your name?" Bulbul asked me gruffly.

"Janjua" I said

"Yes, yes, I know that" he said impatiently.

"But what is your name?"

The impish side of me took over. But semi-seriously I repeated.

"Janjua"

"What is your other name?" Bulbul's impatience was mounting.

I would like to have continued irritating him, despite his ferocious demeanour, but I could pretend no longer. So I replied;

"Mohamed Khan"

"Why didn't you say so? We can't pronounce these other anglicised names."

Bulbul gave his verdict.

"I am sure you have not found it difficult to pronounce Linlothgow, McIllhinney, MacFarquaharson, Higginsbotham, or bottom, to be nearer the mark. My adopted name is composed of six letters and three syllables; maybe that's why you find it difficult?"

This terminated the conversation on addictions, alcoholic beverages and anglicised names. We were all good friends during one service together. There were only fourteen of us after all, including two officers in the equipment branch. Bulbul formed No. 4 Squadron I.A.F. at Kohat on 1st February, 1942. I took it over from him in September, 1942. He took over command of an operational squadron, on the Burma Front. While flying a Hurricane, fighter bomber, near Ranchi, he had to carry out a forced landing. He selected a large and even field to touch down and to come to a halt within its boundaries. His intention seems to have been to take-off, in due course, without having to resort to repairs or having to haul the aircraft back on a trailer. He decided to make a normal landing; under carriage down and locked. He had not been able to detect clearly a channel which ran right across the field and landing run. The aircraft ran into it and came to a violent stop. Bulbul could not have been prepared for this impact. His harness broke and his head hit the aiming sight in front. He died instantly of the head injuries he sustained.

The one minor and one major tragedy conspired to leave me in the position where I found myself during the hectic days of the struggle for Pakistan, during reconstitution and during the initial expansion programmes of Pakistan Air Force. Had either or both Zaidi and Bulbul been present in those critical days, things might possibly have been dealt with in a vastly different manner. I cannot say definitely what I would have done with my eruptive nature, which could remain dormant under most circumstances. I am quite sure that they would have given their best to the national effort. I am equally positive that I would have given them all my help and loyalty. But would I have found Zaidi's approach vigorous enough? Would I have been able to bear, thoroughly and ruthlessly efficient as his approach was likely to be, the one-sided, iron-fisted methods of Bulbul? Mainly and often entirely firm, not tempered with kindness? This went contrary to my temperament, where kindness was preferential to firmness. Why indulge in futile speculation? I was where the vagaries if history had placed me.

I sought help from all other officers in preparing to bring into existence an Air Force which would be worthy of a country the size of Pakistan, and of people who had the diverse qualities of Pakistanis. Among them were officers of high calibre and professional ability. Their achievements in the air force of Pakistan amply proved this. These qualities of vigour, energy, courage, boldness, meticulous application of professional knowledge, patience and endurance, were to make possible the formation of an air force at once vital and efficient. There was a good cross section of officers who displayed the best of these qualities. We arranged meetings to be held at my house or at the residence of Sardar Abdul Rab Nishtar, the Minister for Communications. This was made possible because of my association with Sardar Nishtar's younger brother Sq. Leader Ghayyus, who had transferred to the Ministry of Defence and assumed duties in New Delhi. Altogether twenty six meetings were held. The minutes of the meetings were kept by Fl. Lt. M. M. Piracha (later Air Commodore, Pakistan Air Force). Fl. Lt. Piracha was in the personnel branch and most of the information needed was available from the branch or could be acquired by it. For us this was most invaluable information, plus of course that obtained from the contribution of all these and other officers. Without all of it, such a thoroughly worked-out plan could not have been possible. From these efforts emerged what may be termed the first five year plan of Pakistan Air Force. Taking into account the number of officers and airmen of all branches, in particular the vital General Duties (Pilots), technical, the equipment available, or which could be obtained without undue difficulty, the stations and their locations, facilities and other such factors, a target was set for 1952.

It is neither possible nor necessary to go into the detail of all the work done, over a period of six months, carried out by the officers and some airmen. Many airmen came to me offering help. Unfortunately, it was not possible to avail myself of this wonderful gesture; they were not in a position to be of positive help, which they so much desired to give. However, a few did repeatedly contact me and A. C. I. Bhuiyan, in particular, spent long hours with me taking dictation and typing. Later, in Pakistan Air Force, he qualified as G. D. (Pilot) but was killed when his fighter aircraft crashed. I was immensely grieved when I learnt about his demise, because I was not able to pay my last respects and once again express my profound gratitude to him. I was fighting for my life in a battle in which every material advantage was with the adversary, but not the moral and patriotic, which I had. I was in Hyderabad central prison, defending myself against a heinous charge, in what was the Rawalpindi Conspiracy Case.

Let it suffice to say that the men working on the programme of their nation's Air Force were specialists in their fields. They gave all they had with unparalleled zeal. They were passionately patriotic. It was manifest in their indefatigable efforts. These words are so inadequate in the description of all that took place in planning the birth of the Air Force of Pakistan to ensure correct delivery and rapid growth. Teething troubles are unavoidable and are expected and accepted. They can, however, be aggravated and they were, which I will cover in a later chapter.

In the meantime, my contact was limited to Raja Ghazanfar Ali and to Sardar Nishtar. I was trying to get closer to the policy makers to be able to assess their policies but more so to seek advice and guidance, to exchange views at least on matters concerning my service if not the defence services generally. I was also making attempts to establish contact between the politicians I knew on the one hand and senior Muslim Army Officers on the other. There seemed to be no desire or interest on the part of the former and reluctance, bordering on mild hostility as a reaction, on the part of the latter. However persistent endeavours began gradually to bear fruit. Lt. Col. Sher Khan (later Major General, Pakistan Army) who had been my close friend for several years, was in New Delhi. I asked him to come with me to Sardar Nishatr's residence.

"I have not been invited. They don't give a damn about us! Why should we bother?" said Sher Khan, with acrimony.

"Isn't it possible that they may be saying the same sort of thing? That we don't care enough to call? After all they are senior to us. We all know where to locate them. They cannot know where to find us all." I said without much conviction, but there was no other way to persuade Sher Khan and others to meet the politicians.

"Let us do the first call and then see how it goes", I suggested.

Sher Khan was a patient, charming person. He gave a mild shrug of the shoulders and agreed. We went to Sardar Nishtar's residence one evening, but since the air force officers used to gather there to meet quite regularly, we became a crowd. We sat on the lawn, sipping tea when Sardar Nishtar returned. He waved from a distance as he passed into the house.

"There you are! I told you. He didn't even bother to come over for a few seconds." Sher Khan said, disappointment and disapproval written all over his face.

I explained to him that Sardar Nishtar was quite accustomed to seeing us there at that time, in that manner. He could not know that we had anything special for him, and in any event he did not wish to disturb us and interrupt whatever we may have been doing. Later Ghayyur and I managed to introduce Sher Khan to Sardar Nishtar and they got on famously. Lt. Col. Akbar Khan (later Major General, Pakistan Army), and some other officers were brought in, in a similar manner. But even before these introductions I had conveyed the names of these officers to Sardar Nishtar directly or through Ghayyur. Muslim officers of the requisite seniority and status were required to serve on the Armed Forces Sub-committee of the Reconstruction Committee. Sher Khan and Akbar Khan were eventually made members of the Army Sub-committee. The selection of the senior member was made a few days later. The choice lay between Brigadier N.A.M. Raza and Nazir Ahmed. The former was the senior Subaltern in 1st Battalion the 7th Rajput Regiment during my three year service with that Unit. I did not know the latter professionally but he enjoyed a good reputation. He hailed from my district, from a village about eight miles from my own. So I had some knowledge of him. The honour ultimately went to Brigadier N.A.M. Raza (later Lieut. General, Pakistan Army and Ambassador twice to the Peoples Republic of China).

I had no difficulty whatsoever in selecting my number two. I had never any doubt that it was going to be Squadron Leader M. Asghar Khan. It was not necessary to consider an alternative. In my opinion, no one measured up to him at that rank. In due course he was to assume duties of the first Pakistani Commander-in-Chief of his country's Air Force in 1957; ten years after it came into existence! That a free country the size of Pakistan, waited a whole decade to entrust the affairs of its first arm of defence to one of its own sons, spoke volumes regarding the ineptitude and utter absence of self-confidence on the part of some of those who were at the helm of its affairs. But that is yet another story. Flt. Lt. H.V. Bhatty was the third member, acting as the Secretary maintaining minutes of the meetings and other records from the discussions of the Air Force Sub-committee meetings. He was fully qualified for this task and did it exceptionally well. He was acquainted with my method of working, as he was already in my department, that of Manning. Captain H.M.S. Chaudhrey (later Vice Admiral and Commander-in-Chief of Pakistan Navy) was the most senior Muslim naval officer. He had no problems of any magnitude on collecting his team for the Naval Sub-committee. We exchanged some notes in New Delhi, but it was never really necessary to keep close contact. He had no particularly strong views on any matter, except in his adherence to the Moral Rearmament (MRA). He propounded to me, on several occasions, its laudable but rarely practical, four 'absolutes', absolute honesty, absolute trust, absolute love, absolute selflessness. Many long discussions were had on this subject during 1950, our year together at the Imperial Defence College in London. When I asked him during a very long talk in a hotel in Dusseldorf where we were on tour, whether he ever found himself planning and taking action against a person whom he considered to be a threat to his position, he said that he did but that it was a normal human defensive action and precaution.

"Indeed it is. But it is not absolute selflessness". I said. Then I told him that up to the 5th January, 1949, I did not ever imagine that one human being would deliberately plan to harm another one. In answer to a question I told him that I did take disciplinary action against officers and airmen but not one of them threatened my security in any way; the law of the services was applied to deal with specific defaults. I had considered any acts of injustice on the part of others to be an error of judgement. I had had violent differences of opinion and quarrels with several superiors, but I did not carry these as grievances with me to my house or anywhere else, to nurse them for vengeance. I had an attitude of it all being like a boxing bout; shake hands at the beginning, knock hell out of each other during the bout, shake hands at the end and leave the fight behind. There was no planning for revenge for differences of opinions and quarrels; those had to be solved within the service policies, rules and regulations.

"Either you are an angel or I am the devil" said Chaudhry.

"Neither" I said. "But I am going to give you a statement of facts. I know differently now. I realise that deliberate plans are made to harm and damage people. When they are unable to better one professionally, intellectually and morally, they do plan to destroy by other means. Up to 5 January, 1949, I was too naïve to appreciate all this. I am no longer so naïve. It will not be easy for me to adapt myself to the new situation. But I can only try. Maybe it's already too late in some respects."

Commodore (as he was in 1950) and Mrs. Chaudhry took me and my wife to several MRA meetings, functions and private gatherings. At that time the slogan or the theme was 'Go to Caux' (pronounced Coh)! This is a small town in Switzerland, where MRA had obtained accommodation for their adherents to enable them to practice their four 'absolutes'. There they gathered; no servants or staff to help them run the establishment! They assigned various tasks to one another, from cooking to dishwashing, bed making to dusting, sweeping the floors and so on and so forth. We were informed that the atmosphere was ecstatic; one experienced a spiritual uplift which had not been possible before; so calm, so serene, so blissful! They all gave of themselves, no one expected to receive; each working for the others, no thought for oneself. How noble it all sounded. But any group of people who agreed to work together, without staff, even on a picnic, did precisely the same. They all really and truly showed immense enjoyment. But we were told this was spiritual and not purely mundane. At least I could not be convinced that the joy was less intensely experienced by them in this location than those on a staff picnic. But no; 'Go to Caux; Go to Caux' was the chant. Alas, I was unable to get into a trance. Maybe I was lacking in the spiritual. Those ecstasies were not for me. I was not able to bring myself to attempt something, the absolutes of MRA. So I would not 'go to Caux'.

I was introduced, at a private meeting, to a renegade Communist, Copeland by name. He showed us a film, I think about Caux. A discussion ensued.

"If we practice MRA we are practicing Christianity" Copeland said, stressing the 'absolutes' and explaining to me how MRA and Christianity could be considered to be synonymous.

"But I have been taught, and told about, these 'absolutes' since even I can remember." I said. "To the best of my ability I have been practicing them. These are the basic tenets of the creed to which I adhere. Therefore, if I practice Islam I am practicing all of these. When you practice MRA it is like practicing Christianity. When I practice Islam I am practicing what you are trying to preach to me, and a great deal more. Then I see no particular advantage in joining MRA, I suggest that we practice Islam, which would encompass all that MRA has to offer and many other social aspects in addition. At least I do not have to practice MRA to improve in any way."

"That is very interesting" said Copeland. "It's certainly worth closer scrutiny."

He was not in the least sincere about it. We parted company that evening, perhaps never to meet again.

During our tour of West Germany, we met some representatives of industrial workers and coal miners. Some or all had been enlisted into the ranks of MRA. I never discovered whether we just happened to be at the same place as the MRA function or whether we were intended to participate in it. The theme there was not one of inviting everyone to make a pilgrimage to Caux. The audience was of a quite different calibre. The specific experience of working for others or for one another as in Caux, was not the principal point of the meeting. In Caux there were conditions of equality; no staff, so each one did according to one's ability; and received according to one's need. Not so in that industrial area of West Germany. There it was 'more blessed to give than to receive'. The stress was on labour relations. 'Absolute love', of man for man demanded a friendly, nay affectionate, relationship between the management and the workers. 'Absolute selflessness', of course, must lead to everyone giving without even the remotest thought of expecting to receive in return. When applied to the situation of the workers it could mean nothing but that the workers 'love absolutely', in other words submit to the managements' policy of greater profits; 'absolute selflessness' could only mean that the workers gave their all and received a pittance from the management, while the latter received all from the workers and gave a pittance to them. Since, for both, it was more blessed to give than to receive, the workers at last could be blissfully happy, having literally adhered to the tenets of their creed. Can there be any doubt about the ecstatic happiness of the management! I can say with 'absolute honesty' that that was the 'absolute truth' as it appeared to me. But we are asked not to overlook the fact that all disputes, a harsh word in the gentle creed, are thus settled in a most amicable – perish the thought – brotherly manner.

But I run ahead too far. Let me return to the events that were taking place three years earlier. Constitutional activities were assuming a tempo seldom experienced before. An immense upheaval was in progress, the earth literally shook. Some had the temerity to refer to it as a 'bloodless revolution'! I was now legally and formally involved on the deliberations concerning the reconstitution of the sub-continent. I was appointed the senior member for Pakistan on the Air Force Sub-committee. It was of very great importance that all concerned had prepared themselves well for the task, for I.A.F. Air Commodores S. Mukerjee and Aspy Engineer with Wing Commander Arjan Singh as their Secretary. The latter succeeded Engineer as the Chief of Air Staff and

Commander-in-Chief of Indian Air Force. Sq. Ldr. M. Asghar Khan with Flt. Lt. H. V. Bhatty as our Secretary, and I, made up the team for Pakistan Air Force. It absorbed most of our working hours. There was however abundant energy left for other matters. I went in search of the policy makers, who were also exceedingly preoccupied in what is often termed as, the larger affairs of the country.

At some time during that period prior to 3rd June, 1947, a conference was held in Delhi, called the Inter-Asian Relations Conference. A function was held one evening at one of the clubs, possibly the Delhi Gymkhana, if my memory serves me well, to meet the delegates from the Asian countries. I was also invited to this; not because of any special status which I may have acquired, unbeknown to me, but because one of my friends was on the committee managing the programme. That friend was Mr. A. Quddus of All India Radio (later Wing Commander Pakistan Air Force, as Public Relations Officer). His entire family and I were intimately friendly. When Quddus told me that members of the Cabinet, Pandit Nehru downwards, were to be at the function I accepted the invitation with almost indecent haste.

Indeed, they all came. I stood talking to Quddus and to Professor I.H.Qureshi, to whom I had just been introduced, when Nawabzada Liaquat Ali Khan walked in from a door to our left rear. He came directly over to us. He knew both Dr. I.H.Qureshi, a senior Muslim Professor at the Delhi University, and Quddus. The latter introduced me to Mr. Liaquat Ali Khan. After a formal word with me, he turned to Dr. Qureshi and asked;

"Are you in contact with the delegates?" I dropped the first of a series of bricks, which were inevitably to pile up on my own toes in due course. I did not let Dr. Qureshi answer the question immediately.

"I am sure he is in close contact with the delegates" I cut right across the conversation, "But there is no contact here." And I pointed my index finger at him and then at myself. I was in uniform. He looked puzzled and there was a hint of astonishment and irritation. I had waited for this occasion. I had virtually prayed for it. I could not let go now. He recomposed himself and said with a smile, I thought to cover the embarrassment:

"Ah! You are afraid of coming to us."

"Quite the contrary, you are afraid of having us." I replied.

"I am in uniform. In a public place, talking to you with all these gentlemen not even an arm's length away" I said, pointing at Pandit Nehru and Sardar Vallabhar Patel, who stood immediately behind me and Lord Mountbatten, who had just then arrived and stood in a corner. Naturally, not one of those lofty gentlemen could have had the slightest notion as to who I was. But the implication was quite clear. At least I was not afraid.

Mr. Liaquat Ali accepted the situation and said, "You can come and see me any time you like."

"When?" I asked.

"Anytime you wish" and he did mean it at that moment.

"No Sir, I would like an appointment" I persisted.

"Alright, Soofi will arrange it" he said, and passed on an instruction to that effect to his secretary.

This incident could not have lasted more than a minute or so but to those around, it seemed like hours. Other conversations which had been pushed to the background were soon resumed and probably Dr.Qureshi was able to answer all the questions. We all soon drifted from place to place and ultimately out of the club, to tread the earth like other mortals and make our way home.

Subsequently I met Mr. Liquat Ali at his official residence, Finance

Minister of India, at the appointed hour and on the appointed date. Our talk stretched to forty minutes. The first subject to be discussed was concerning the necessity, of dividing the Air Force between the two countries. Although the Quaid-i-Azam had stated categorically that Pakistan would have her own defence services, arguments were being advanced about not only the undesirability but the impracticability of dividing the Indian armed forces. No less a person than the British Commander-in-Chief of the Indian Army, Filed Marshal Sir Claude Auchinleck was said to be advocating a joint defence, not by means of an alliance, but by keeping the defence services in their shape and form as in August 1947. No doubt 'defence in depth' stood at the head of the list of so-called cogent reasons. It is difficult to believe that the protagonists of the retention of the Indian Armed Forces as the Indo-Pakistan Armed forces did not read the signs which pointed in the opposite direction; that they did not feel the pulse which had ceased to beat in harmony; that they did not look up at the heights the emotions had reached. Surely a soldier of the eminence of Sir Claude Auchinleck could not be serious in this suggestion! Why this impracticable solution? Was it to go along with the Hindu desire for a semblance of unity, to be later converted to union in reality? This could be a reason. About a year earlier the Quaid-i-Azam had agreed to a three zone India, each zone to be autonomous, except in matters of 'defence', foreign relations, currency and communications. The zones were to be the North West and the North East, these being the Muslim Majority areas, and the rest of the sub-continent. Mahatma Gandhi having given his (tacit) agreement later retracted from it. Jinnah would have got more than even the Pakistan of 1940 Muslim League resolution, it was said. The matter of retaining unity in at least the field of defence was being discussed again.

We went over this matter in more or less the following sequence. Mr. Liquat Ali asked me to prepare a paper laying out the feasibility of division of the Air Force. I had already compiled the relevant information, with the aid of other officers, while planning the expansion of P.A.F. I asked A.C.Bhuiyan to type it out. It was handed over to Mr.Liaquat Ali within two days. We also discussed the political situation in general. But when I brought up the matter of defensive preparations for the Muslims in general and in the districts of East Punjab in particular, the response from the General Secretary of the All India Muslim League was extremely discouraging if not painful. There seemed to be reluctance, an attempt to brush the subject aside. I pursued it persistently and repeatedly. There was no coherent answer; there was obviously no plan; therefore, a great deal of fumbling took place. I gave my views and reasons as passionately as I felt them. Leaving the people without defence must inevitably lead to loss of life and property in the most vital zones. Equally inevitably, this must lead to weakness in every sense of the word. Political argument can derive strength only from the strength of the people. If the people are crippled political argument must follow suit. We had already sustained losses in some Hindu majority provinces. It may be difficult to avoid them but they could be rendered less harmful if our defence in the Punjab and Bengal could be strengthened. We had to attain the ability to hold firmly to these areas. Failure to do so would have consequences which were not possible to be measured now but which could only be detrimental to our interests. Defence was desirable; defence was necessary if not vital. I must have sounded like a gong being beaten with mounting force!

Mr. Liaquat Ali was pensive. He mused while I spoke and continued to muse for some time after I had finished.

"We will try our best. Please continue to help wherever you can." He said.

We thanked each other; I for taking his time, he for my views. I returned, if anything, more unhappy than before I went. It was far too late; even if they made efforts now, they could not make adequate arrangements to meet the needs of the people and the times. The prospects were gloomy indeed.

The constitutional activities went ahead. Meetings of the Air Force Sub-committee proceeded under the chairmanship of the British Air Officer I/C Administration (AOA) of Air H.Q, Air Vice Marshal A.L.A. Percy-Keene. They were conducted in a neat and fair manner. I found no reason to complain and Air Commodore Mukherjee seemed satisfied.

Our own meetings to discuss P.A.F. continued apace. The formation and expansion programmes were decided. I commenced work on devising the symbols of the Air Force of a free nation, the Pakistan Air Force ensign, the crest, the motto, the markings on aircraft and vehicles. We set up a committee to design them; this was soon completed and approved. I had them approved by the skeleton Ministry of Defence, taking care of the interests of Pakistan. In my enthusiasm I had five ensigns embroidered by Rankins, tailors of great repute, in New Delhi. The ensigns were flown over to the five Air Force stations in West Pakistan, which Pakistan Air Force were to take over from the R.A.F. The ensigns were hoisted on the flag staffs of the five stations on the 14th August, 1947, When Mountbatten handed over the relevant independence documents to the Qaid-i-Azam. They made bold attempts to flutter, to join in the mood of the people of Pakistan! They were too heavy to do so whole-heartedly, except in the strong wind of Drigh Road; but they were symbols, to be retained as historical pieces.

The ensign of Pakistan Air Force had to be based on the flag of Pakistan. I do not recollect whether the flag was already physically in existence. Possibly, we were slightly ahead in our preparations. But we obtained a detailed description and went ahead with the design of our ensign. The flag was to be green, with a white strip, to represent the minorities, with the crescent and the star in the top corner, nearest the flagstaff. A red edge (border) might well have been a part of the design. Enough blood was flowing along the would-be borders of Pakistan to justify it.

We moved towards the date set for independence. It is not easy to describe my own feelings at that time. They stretched from one extreme to the other. Achievement of independence brought exhilaration which can only come when liberty arrives and the chains of bondage lie at one's feet broken and scattered. One spreads ones arms to their full extent as if to test ones wings; to touch that which had remained beyond one's reach; to take long strides forwards; indeed, to fly in the fresh air, the oppressive, suffocating atmosphere having been overcome, self-expression, shaping of ones own destiny through the vigour, energy, talent of ones own people becomes possible. What glorious future lay ahead for the people of Pakistan! Then came the rather sad, but at that time, subdued thought, concerning the complexity of human societies, which had evolved over many millennia, which divided man from man. More reasons had been found to create divisions despite professions to the contrary. Amongst these were the call for conditional unity; each one setting his own rules and laws for uniting mankind, some advocating force for the purpose; even when reformers preached against and forbade violence, it was applied by their adherents in order to ultimately eliminate the necessity of violence and, of course, to spread the word. Violence was used to spread non-violence; persecutions in the name of one, oppression in the name of another; massacre, carnage, destruction in the name of the third. These various ideas came, now here, now there, subjugating, persecuting and inevitably exploiting us all. We were at the crest of that tide.

Hindu communalism, the demon of pseudo-superiority, was rampant. It would destroy all in its path that was foreign to it. But it could not be allowed to do that. It had to be contained. A safe abode had to be found for its intended victims, the Muslims, so that it would recoil back into its den and be left there to devour its own parts if so inclined. Our only option was to cross the western and eastern borders into Pakistan, leaving a resentful Hindustan behind. We would not submit to forced unity on terms that would lead only to one end – the assimilation of a people; absorption into a system where they would cease to have a defined identity. I was, and am, in favour of the removal of all barriers between men and women, people and people, but only by the people themselves and not at the behest of any exploiting class. When those classes are removed by the people, the causes of friction would have been eliminated. But that was a long way ahead. At this stage, it was necessary to part. And that is what we were preparing to do.

The final feeling was one of gloom and foreboding. Much too much blood had already been shed. It continued to be shed as we approached independence. I had been informed that large scale preparations were afoot, unchecked, unhindered and in all probability with some official connivance, for a virtual civil war. I also knew that no plans for defence were in existence. Not a glimmer of hope did I have in this respect. A mass slaughter was staring us in the face; but there is none as blind as those who refuse to see. When it came it far out-stripped all my worst fears. Later I often wondered whether the heads that wore the crowns ever really lay uneasy! I was immediately absorbed in the affairs of Pakistan Air Force and some other matters, following partition. To confront anyone with the situation as it emerged in East Punjab and as it had been predicted. It could cause discomfort to some.

Chapter Four

Rises the Stained Sun

Constitutional activities and decisions came to an end by the latter part of July or early August 1947. Piece by piece we were given the policy decisions as they applied to Pakistan. A discussion started concerning the policy and commands of the armed forces of Pakistan. I was completely aware of and fully prepared to commence implementation of programmes for Pakistan Air Force. We had not only finalised them in every possible detail, but we had obtained sanctions from the interim Ministry of Defence and Finance. Stations had been selected for various functions, personnel appointed, equipment allocated and other provisions made to enable the functions to be performed efficiently. To my mind the discussion was purely academic. But it continued none the less.

Field Marshal Sir Claude Auchinleck had invited all members of the Reconstitution Committee and all the armed forces Sub-committees to an evening function at his residence. It was only a few days to independence. All parties had, to a greater or lesser extent, adjusted themselves to the situation. There was 'shop talk' about transfer of equipment, personnel and other related matters. I was at one end of the lawn. I saw a crowd in a semi-circular or crescent formation in the middle of the lawn, with the floodlight playing fully on it. I walked across to join in what appeared to be a deeply attentive audience. It was around the Quad-i-Azam, who was talking about the powers of civil authority and those of military authority. This was probably in answer to some question. Quad-i-Azam was stressing the supremacy of the civil authority. As I listened I felt that that supremacy was being over-stressed and it seemed to prevail, even in matters of general detail which the Commanders would be fully competent to deal with. Policy making was a civilian domain or preserve.

"But Sir, while formulating policies the specialist opinion and advice of the defence service commanders must be taken into account."

I had barely finished the sentence when Quad-i-Azam swung round and sharply said,

"No Sir, the civil authority must remain supreme in all circumstances."

He then cited examples of Curzon in India and Churchill in the Western Desert during the Second World War.

I had not suggested that larger policy matters were not political, or that military commanders should have the last say in the formulation of those policies. I thought my meaning was quite clear, that in the matter of these policies which affected or included the defence of the country, the specialist opinion of the defence commanders should weigh heavy. This seemed natural enough and I was unable to see the objection to it. The audience were silent. As Quad-i-Azam continued to talk on the subject, no further interjection came. I considered that I had said enough for the evening. I seemed to have thrown the last straw on the camel's back. That was neither the time nor the place for a discussion, even to explain what I had in fact meant. Quad-i-Azam moved elsewhere and the audience melted away, as is the wont of all audiences. I wondered. Had I spoken off the subject? But neither the

Quad-i-Azam nor any member of the audience of whom I knew many, said that I had. Had I spoken out of place? Again the answer was in the negative. Indeed, I was later told by some acquaintances that my remark was quite in order. Then why did it bring such a sharp reaction. I thought one day I may be able to revert to it with the Quad-i-Azam.

Not long after this incident I was informed that our Cabinet had decided to have British officers as Commanders of the three defence services of Pakistan. This was announced at a meeting of all Pakistani members of the Reconstitution Committee and Sub-committee. It was indeed, the prerogative of the civil authority to lay down national policies. They must be accepted and implemented to the best of one's ability. This I had every intention of doing. But I would be less than honest if I said I would do so willingly under these circumstances. Secondly I was quite keenly disappointed. I was also surprised because as much as I tried, I could not see the necessity for British Commanders. I was disappointed because we had worked out a thorough programme for our Air Force, towards which no non-Pakistani had contributed; we had no need for any outside contribution. We had talent of our own. A person who had no part in the formulation of the programme may not go along with it, in which case conflict would become unavoidable. However, deep in my heart, I was determined to carry out that programme, regardless of who came to head our Air Force.

I did exercise my right to speak even on matters which were closed. Expression of a view could not take away from it; it may add to further thinking on the matter. I put my arguments forward. We were all small services but senior officers were sufficiently experienced to organise, train and expand them in accordance with the needs of the country. A British Commander-in-Chief could make little or no difference, especially to the Air Force and the navy. We had made all our programmes without any external assistance. They had been approved as workable. In case of a national defence emergency, when commanders are most needed, we would not have the services of the

British Officers. It had been made clear by the British that in the event of a conflict between the 'two dominions', India and Pakistan, all British personnel in the armed forces of the 'two dominions' would be withdrawn.

I was told that by stressing the need for a Pakistani Commander-in-Chief, I would give the impression that I was aiming to be one myself. This was a peculiar argument. In order to avoid giving such an impression, I was being encouraged to give up all my sincerely views, which I considered to be in the best interests of my country. It is true that I was the most senior Pakistani Air Force officer and would therefore be the first C-in-C of the Air Force, if the policy were to be altered. And what was wrong with a Pakistani taking command of the Air Force of Pakistan? What could be more natural? A non-Pakistani taking command of the Air Force of Pakistan would be unnatural and could be wrong. I had seen nothing, nor had any senior officers of our Air Force, which we could not manage ourselves. We had known no British Officers who had extraordinary experience or ability to organise our Air Force, better than we could. If we must have non-Pakistanis as senior officers, they should have the status of advisors; not policy makers. No non-national could possibly identify himself with Pakistan as much as a son of the soil. Indeed, the more senior a foreigner the more likely he was to serve the interests of his own retreating imperialism. Those were the conservative empire-building types. According to their logic the empire could not be saved, but much could be salvaged.

The implication was that we were too young and had insufficient service and experience! This argument was ridiculous and senseless; unjustified and irritating. Take my example. I had had nearly fifteen years experience including my training. Many army officers had several years greater experience. How was I or Captain H.M.S. Chaudhry, who had as much service, possibly slightly more than me, less qualified to run the administration of our services, than those who were to manage the affairs of the entire nation, after a couple of years of apprenticeship? The game of playing politics was over now. The serious problems of a nation of one hundred million people needed to be tackled. If the new members of the cabinet of the brand new country of Pakistan were qualified and could be entrusted with the task of administrating the vast country, it was strange to argue that officers of the Armed forces, who had gained experience in their respective services all their working lives, could not be entrusted with managing their own very manageable services. We were all old enough for the purpose and passionately devoted to our country and dedicated to our services. I was confident that we were wise enough too, if wisdom came with age, to be left entirely alone to perform our duties in providing the best possible defence for our country.

I could come to no other conclusion than that it was the talk of petty men who were projecting their own petty mindedness, petty motives and lack of self confidence onto others. It was an insult to one's intelligence, one's sense of history, one's patriotism, to hear them suggest that the officers had any motives other than those of giving the benefit of their experience to their country. No non-Pakistani could ever do the job with the devotion that was needed. I was sure of it then and had it proved to me repeatedly in the months after partition.

It did not need a genius to know or to realise that fact. Imagine the Russians asking for German officers to command their armed forces and lay down policies for them; the Chinese seeking similar help from the Japanese! If the Germans were to formulate policies for the Russians and the Japanese for the Chinese armed forces, it could be either as occupying powers or with the connivance of self motivated weak Russians and Chinese respectively and because of the dictates of national interests. The argument that the Indians were to have British commanders-in-chief made not the slightest difference to the basic principle of national interest. Indian politicians were not supermen whose example had to be followed as though it were a holy injunction;

despite the involvement of the author of 'Discovery of India', Jawahar Lal Nehru. How easily he forgot that period when he spent time in isolation, making that 'discovery', all wholly and solely in national interests! How readily he was denying the right to the younger generation which he exercised to the full himself, that being to strive for the interests of the nation. Could the interests of a nation be best served or striven for only in bondage? Why was it better or holier to make errors and sacrifices when in shackles rather than when free? Or did these men want to cling to the monopoly of being national heroes, suffering martyrdom for a cause and all that went with a struggle against imperialism, for the liberation of a people? Why did they think that the officers were more hasty when they showed desire to render service to their free countries, for which they were amply suited and qualified, than these gentlemen were in demanding freedom for their countries so that they could be served by their own people? Their stand was utterly illogical. The leaders had claimed for decades that we, the people of the sub-continent, were fit to manage our own affairs. That was what the whole struggle was about. We did not want foreign rulers on our soil. We must have the freedom to choose our own methods for our progress. That struggle had now culminated in victory. We had won our freedom. The imperialist power had conceded the point. But now, judging by their attitudes, the politicians were telling the world that we were not in fact ready to run our own show, whereas the leaders were; the politicians considered themselves ready. They would have no foreigners in their cabinet. They had decided that they were ready to shoulder the burdens of such large nations. They had also decided that they could assume the role of rulers and they alone would decide as to whether, and which other citizens were capable of rendering service to the nation. They were using the same arguments against their own people as the imperialists had used against them; we were not ready to manage our affairs! If we were not ready then why were we rushed to premature independence? Independence for a country and its people should normally mean freedom from external intervention in the lives of the people. That intervention is prevented and freedom defended by the armed forces of a country. I can say with certainty that the personnel of the armed forces were positively capable of performing their functions, at higher and lower levels, without any outside assistance from the policy makers. By their very nature these services led themselves to rapid organisation and re-organisation.

Why did these politicians withhold the right of some citizens to serve their nation while themselves exercising that right to the full and in the larger interests of the nation? By what logic did they come to the conclusion that the larger interests of their nation could be better served by non-nationals being placed at the head of the armed forces? Why did they think that the most oppressive instruments of imperialism would now suddenly become instruments for removing the evil effects of imperialist occupation? The struggle for freedom; freedom to define our own destiny, had to be fought for every inch of the way. Who was responsible for retarding, and attempting to snuff out, our progress? They were the very individuals whom we now expected to enhance our progress. Right up to the time of independence the British had informed us that we were not ready for progress. They had advanced every conceivable argument to prove their point. They neither had respect for nor faith in our ability to manage our own affairs. We had wrenched from them what they did not want to give. How did our leaders come to the conclusion that the disrespect and lack of faith of the British would, as if by magic, be converted into respect and faith? I can bear witness and inform those who may still be within hearing distance, that there was no regard for the British officers. But for the patriotic Pakistani officers there was a healthy regard. It is quite another matter that on account of the attitude of the leaders, many patriotic officers had had to undergo extreme hardships. This is not a new phenomenon. Every age has known it.

The whole argument was absurd. Facts were turned upside down. But the question to ask is why? It was difficult to draw any conclusion other than that the politicians suffered from complete lack of self confidence and feared those who may prove to be vastly more capable. They wanted time to consolidate their positions of power, so that they could freely indulge in their game of playing politics, in order to be able to perpetuate their power. For them politics and intrigue were synonymous. They wanted to gauge the temperaments of the officers so that their political intrigue could be most effective. They made a compromise with their erstwhile imperialist masters. This type of situation always suits the imperialists. What was agreed for their mutual benefit has had consequences which will take the effort of the entire people to eliminate. Whatever motives they may have had in coming to those policy decisions, which denied their own nationals the right to serve their nation unhindered, that of national interest could not be one heading the list. The interests of a nation are best served by its own nationals. Any notion to the contrary is false.

These views were passionately felt and passionately expressed by me. I was fully aware that the policy would not be altered. Discipline demanded that I accept and implement the policy. It was never my intention not to and I conveyed this fact to the appropriate authority. I did not at that time or later, and even now, care as to what motives were attributed to me for the stand I took. Whether or not it was believed then or is believed now, that the one and only motive I had was to serve my country through its Air Force, is quite immaterial and irrelevant to me. I am quite aware that I will be psychoanalysed; my every word will be interpreted by the analysts according to their own motives, interests and policies. I was and am conscious of only one fact; that I was and remain passionately devoted to my country and its people. I do not think that this attitude is unique in any way. Passionate devotion to one's country and people is not unknown. Those who doubt this will have to search their own hearts, if they still have the ability to do so.

On account of my close association with Sardar Abdur Rab Nishtar, I had been asked to express my opinion on several matters, often through S. Ldr. Ghayyus. I had done so in the selection of members for the Army Sub-committee. I was asked to suggest a Royal Air Force British officer of requisite seniority and experience, who should be nominated as Commander-in-Chief of Pakistan Air Force. I was told that since I had to work closely with the future C-in-C it might be better to have someone I knew. I had known few very capable officers but after the war they were all scattered. They had been repatriated, retired or transferred to other bases and commands. I had little personal knowledge of those who now remained. The Senior Air Staff Officer (SASO) at Air H.Q., Elmhurst, had a good reputation for professional ability. But I had met him only once or twice.

Over the previous few weeks I had come to know Air Vice Marshal Percy-Keene. He had conducted the proceedings of the Air Force (reconstitution) sub-committee in a tidy, calm and impartial manner. I was impressed with his staff work; reducing his deliberations to precise and concise decisions and preparing the minutes of these meetings while keeping up with other paper work. If I were to select my own C-in-C, then he was as good a choice as any known to me and still available in the sub-continent.

My opinion was conveyed to Sardar Nishtar. He was one of the big three political leaders for Pakistan; the other two being the Quad-i-Azam and Mr. Liaquat Ali Khan. He had been affectionately referred to by the Quad-i-Azam as 'my Nishtar', which also meant my lance, because it was considered that Sardar Nishtar provided the thrust in the sword play then in progress.

Percy-Keene was nominated as the first Commander-in-Chief of Pakistan Air Force. This was announced after the work of the Air Force Sub-committee had ended. We shook hands across the table in his office. That was probably the last time we looked into each other's eyes, or to be more precise, it was the last time we saw eye to eye. He appointed me Senior Officer I/C Administration (SAO) for Pakistan Air Force, and I was to be promoted to the rank of Group Captain with effect from 14th August, 1947. I forgot to thank him for it. In my case this was promotion delayed by ten weeks. Had the reconstitution not come that year, I would have taken command of the Advanced Flying Training School at Ambala from 1st June, with the rank of Group Captain.

The final steps were being taken to establish Pakistan. The families who wished to leave and the personnel who had to leave were sent to West Pakistan. I had strongly advised for the families to be sent as early as possible. I had knowledge of the circumstances at that time which gave birth to the apprehension I was feeling. I did not want to create panic by revealing my knowledge and fears, even to those closest to me. I did not know and could not predict as accurately as the situation warranted, the zero hour for the planned Sikh onslaught. Most families were able to get through. But some personnel and their families, who were obliged to depart late, did not. I knew a few personally. Their blood mingled with that of their brethren who had been indiscriminately selected to be killed. Their souls cried out for their homeland; their bodies were reabsorbed into the soil from which they had emerged and which should have given them continuing life; instead it brought sudden death.

When it was time to leave, the departure seemed too sudden. Wherever temperament and tempers still made it possible, there were handshakes and goodbyes were said. In some cases embraces were exchanged; the eyes were moist; lips trembled; voices were hoarse and choked; lumps arose in many throats. Life-long associations were coming to an end. Who knew where, if ever, the next meeting would be? There was one absolute certainty; I would never again see most of those whom I was leaving behind.

It was also goodbye to the Imperial New Delhi; good-bye Old Delhi, that collection of footprints on the sands of time, as I looked back through the rear window of the car. Was it still too early to see clearly, or was there a dewy film across my eyes? We drove to Palam Airfield on 12th August, 1947, to fly to Karachi in order to participate in the Independence Ceremony. With me was Sq. Ldr. M. Asghar Khan. We took off in a Dakota (DC3) at dawn. If I can have my choice I like to sit on a port side window seat. I was able to have such a choice that day. Our course was approximately south-west, as we headed for Jodhpur. When day broke, I turned in my seat to look to my left rear and at the sun which was about to make its multi-billionth appearance; for me it had risen twelve thousand, one hundred and thirty seven times. It arose in a leisurely manner; a huge disc which was stained and spotted red! A glowing red cloud sat across the middle of the sun. I could not shake off this red from my vision. On that day particularly the colour red was predominant. It flowed as it seldom had flowed before in the land of the five rivers. It was not generally known, nor did I know that morning that the Sikhs had started to put their plan to kill Muslims into effect on the previous day. The Radcliffe Award was to come five days later, but I thought about it with apprehension. As I say the sun was rolling on in all its majesty like a prayer which was emerging from the depths of the soul and it was accompanied by the verses of Omar Khayyam:

"And that inverted bowl we call the sky,

Where under crawling cooped we live and die,

Lift not thy hands to it for help, for it

Rolls impotently on like you or I."

These lines follow Omar Khayyam's famous and oft-repeated:

"The moving finger writes and having writ

Moves on; not all thy piety nor wit

Shall lure it back to cancel half a line

Nor all thy tears wash out a word of it."

The impotency of the skies! It was not difficult to agree with this profound philosophy of the immortal poet. Inertia, lack of effort, dependence on powers other than our own – the power of the people – was not to be accepted. But fatalism, the inevitability of 'what is to be will be', submission to forces of evil, grovelling to tyranny, abandonment of hope and struggle was not be advocated. The people would not give up the struggle. They would shape their own destiny. They would write their own history; make their own fate. They would cancel, erase, all that had caused tears, pain, misery; indescribable suffering of every kind. They would wipe it all out and rewrite that which would never again be altered. Yes, even with their own blood, as some were doing at that moment, not too many miles from where I was flying.

I looked down and saw a vast span of desert, Rajastan. It seemed to have no end. I had undergone this sensation a few years earlier, when I thought this desert must cover the whole earth, be endless.

After that I had to fly from Drigh Road in an Audax, those days my favourite aircraft. I had Corporal Atma Singh Lota as my passenger. We landed at Jodhpur to refuel. Thus far it was an uneventful flight; not that we were actually seeking adventure. Jodhpur to Ambala was probably the most difficult cross country flight in the entire sub-continent. The modern aids to flying such as homing devices were a few years away, at least from us. Compass and maps were the only aids to navigation. If one met a dust storm or other weather conditions which reduced visibility, then one was left with the compass as the sole aid. The wireless (worked by the passenger, if he was able to) provided some comfort; if we were within shouting distance and our batteries had not run down, then we could make ourselves heard and hear the control tower, not necessarily knowing the direction from which the dots and dashes of Morse code reached us.

We set course for the first leg to Ambala. Soon Jodhpur was left behind, and emptiness lay ahead. I kept my eyes glued to the compass. The weather was quite good but there were no landmarks to help me pinpoint my position on the map. I flew on until I came to a railway line which I had been briefed to follow for some minutes. It was to lead me to a point from which I was to set a new course which would take me to Ambala. I had been told that the route had several landmarks which would enable me to follow it on the map. I sat on the railway line; our term for such a method of navigation. I occasionally looked at the compass. In a very short time it began to veer away from the anticipated course. I continued to sit on the railway line. The compass was soon 45 degrees off course; the curve in the railway line, away to port side, was much sharper than my map indicated. There was no sign of the landmark I was to encounter! A very definite doubt began to arise in my mind. I decided to ride the railway line faithfully. I dived to about a hundred feet above ground level and continued in the direction of the flight. The existence of the line meant railway stations; even if they were few and far between in a desert. I had fuel for over two hours. A station soon came. I read the name and flew on. I wanted to see two stations in order to assess the direction and the course I was pursuing. The next station was a large one and almost in a town. I climbed up, circling to keep the town within my sight, and to be able to read the map comfortably. I did read it, but it brought no comfort. The town was not on the map. I looked along the edge of the map to see whether this town was indicated. Yes, it was, at a distance of 16 miles. So I was sixteen miles off the map and I had no time to work out as to how many off the course. I retraced my steps, so to speak, and went back as far as I could easily remember and identify the railway line. I reset an approximate course for Ambala. Since I was quite lost I had to make rough calculations of the course I had steered and the duration of the flight off course. I was unable to identify any landmark until I had reached a town, a long time after the ETA (estimated time of arrival) at

Ambala. There was no difficulty in reaching Ambala, but firstly I was so long overdue that they had abandoned hope of seeing me and secondly, I had made it only by the skin of my teeth. There remained two gallons of petrol in the tank.

Amid much mirth and laughter we later discovered, in the officers' mess of course, that my flight commander, during his briefing had overlooked an alteration on the ground which was not shown on our map. The railway line which he had asked me to follow had been removed. However, it still existed on our maps. I had been following a non-existent railway line. It was appropriate to quote Shakespeare; "All's Well That Ends Well!"

Almost a reverse course from the one I had steered about seven years earlier now brought us to Jodhpur. We were to take Sq. Ldr. Maqbool Rabb (later Air Commodore PAF and Ambassador) with us to Karachi. He was the Chief Flying Instructor in the Initial Flying Training School. Apart from the one landing I made at Jodhpur to refuel, en route to Ambala, my association with the airport was confined to one other visit. I had stayed in Jodhpur for a couple of days in 1944, in my capacity as Staff Officer to their Highnesses, the Nawab of Bhopal and Maharaja of Jodhpur. They had been appointed Honorary Air Commodores to the Indian Air Force. They visited nearly every Indian Air Force Station, including those on the Burma front, such as Imphal. I accompanied them on all their tours, prepared itineraries for them, and acted as liaison officer between them and the rest of the Indian Air Force.

The Nawab of Bhopal did not indulge in alcoholic beverages. The Maharaja of Jodhpur did nothing else! While the latter had his four fingers of scotch he would draw the back of his hand across his well moustached lips and smacking them, he would address the gathering at large:

"His Highness will take notes while I take in whiskey!"

If the output of the former were to match the intake of the latter, the notes would be voluminous indeed. The Maharaja was re-building his palace. It looked big enough to accommodate a brigade. We were shown around; the swimming pool, cinema, many recreation rooms and halls; the nuptial chambers all in gold, or so it seemed with beds each large enough for an indoor tennis court. At the end of the tour the Maharaja tendered his profuse apologies,

"I am extremely sorry that I cannot put you up; only His Highness. I have no room."

We giggled. We thought it was intended as a joke; or a polite way of telling us that we were not wanted. But we discovered that in that maze of rooms, chambers and halls, only two rooms were ready for occupation. I thought we could have lived in any of those rooms luxuriously. But such is the way of the Maharajas. I need not mention the contrast between the abode of the ruler and the shacks of his subjects within spitting distance of it. I wondered who would spit last!

I visited Bhopal on several occasions to help the Nawab Sahib compile his notes. We did, indeed, produce a large report in justification of Indianisation of the Indian Air Force. The Nawab Sahib signed the report. I took it over to the Maharaja. I was given it back with two words because less could not be used. "I concur." I do not think that the Maharaja even signed it. If he did, it must have been an enormous effort, not because of having to sign, but having to have to take a break from his more than favourite traditional pastime, which was drinking whiskey.

On this visit it was not possible to go as far as the palace; shortage of time accompanied by an acute lack of desire. While the aircraft was refuelled we went to the hotel at the airport. I had stayed at that hotel on previous occasions when the Maharaja could not find space for us in his thousand-room palace. Of course, I was a State guest. The hotel had the reputation of being the best, most luxurious, in the Orient. It could equal Claridges in London, I was informed. Not having lived at Claridges I was unable to make the comparison. But it was certainly the most luxurious I had ever known. Why have such a hotel in the wilderness? Who would come to that otherwise glamorous desert, to stay in such a hotel? Perhaps it was mainly State guests who occupied it; guests of the people in shacks and rags! The people who paid for all this and lived in the shadow of this glitter, glamorous pomp, where a myriad electric bulbs literally floodlit the premises and surrounding areas; those people of modest backgrounds often looked longingly at the neighbour's candle!

I could not dwell on these thoughts much longer. We were bound for Karachi; for Pakistan. Independence was only so many miles and forty eight hours away. This kind of occasion occurs only once in a lifetime. The excitement within me was mounting as we approached the place and the time for that event of momentous historical importance; the birth of a nation, a free people. They were free to shape their own destiny; freedom for the entire people to put their genius and talent to the best use for the benefit of the entire people. This is precisely what is denied a people by the occupying powers. The denial saps the morale of the people and blunts their genius; that is the most cruel aspect of foreign rule. Despite professions to the contrary, the progress of a subject people is always hindered, never enhanced, by those who subjugate and rule over them. The interests of and benefits to, the subject people have to take second place, at best. The benefits of the occupying, imperial power must always come first. It is not possible to visualise a situation in which an imperial power would undertake any project with the primary object of advancement of the people of an occupied territory or country. All projects are designed to ensure a maximum exploitation of the resources of a country and the talents of its people. Any benefits which accrue to the people are purely incidental. Improvements in the lines of communication, increases in productivity and employment, better education and higher technical skills come to the country and the people only because without them, resources cannot be exploited and maximum profits cannot be made. This is the way of all imperialists and all capitalists. The general unhindered progress of people cannot be assured without breaking the stranglehold of imperialism and capitalism and their other equally vicious allies, the exploiting classes, of all types, within a society, created for the nourishment of the exploiters at the expense of the people. It is not possible to end exploitation without a struggle. That struggle had been waged and brought to a successful conclusion against the occupying imperialist power. The people of Pakistan would now be free to harness their energies; create the wealth which their country was unquestionably capable of producing. That wealth would now remain within the nation or be used in international trading to be of further advantage for the people. That is freedom; all engaged in working for all; the benefit of all, not the few, be they foreign or indigenous exploiters.

Such were the hopes and aspirations I nurtured in my breast, as did many millions of others, as we approached Karachi, the capital of Pakistan. In this city the registration of the birth of Pakistan was to take place within hours, as that of its founder had taken place seventy one years earlier.

Chapter Five

Birth Pangs and More

Karachi was as decked and ready for the occasion as it was possible for her to be under the circumstances of extreme joy, excitement and exuberance on the one hand and turmoil, tension and anxiety on the other. It would be right to say that while Delhi enjoyed all the advantages of a well established capital, Karachi suffered from most disadvantages. The former was equipped, in every way, for the imperial administration of the entire sub-continent. The latter was the headquarters of only one of a score of provinces. It was equipped to provide administrative facilities for a few districts, of which the population numbered less than ten million. It was now required to accommodate administrative machinery for a nation of a hundred million. Undoubtedly these thoughts were exercising many minds. But this subject would be considered seriously later. Now was the time for preparations for the celebrations. We saw signs of these as we drove through one of the main streets to the house of our host. Asghar Khan and I stayed at the residence of Karim Goolam Ali. He had named it 'The Retreat' and it was located behind the Karachi Club. This address invariably provoked a titter on the part of the operator whenever we dictated a phonogram (a Telegram that one can phone in to a

Phonogram telephone number) to be sent to 'Retreat', behind Karachi Club. However, it had been a glorious retreat for me since I was first stationed at Drigh Road, in 1940, on Coastal Patrol duties. I have enjoyed the hospitality on countless occasions and for periods running into months, of this remarkable man; generous to a fault, kind, with dauntless courage and firm resolve. One could set the time by the regularity of his habits; punctual to the nearest second. Born in the Ismaili Community, his temperament led him to rebel against an establishment which he considered to be unjust to its members. Since 1922 at the age of twenty two, he had carried out a one-man crusade against injustice, his actions leading to litigation and direct clashes with the Aga Khan, grandfather of the present Ismaili incumbent. His booklets have found a place in the British Museum.

Karim Goolam Ali bears a mark on his body and a colleague carries a hatchet scar on his face, as a result of physical assault by the more fanatical members of the closed sect. He has addressed communications to several people of high status and organisations of international standing, of course, to no avail. He puts too much faith in the so-called milk of human kindness, among members of the exploiting classes. He is baffled, astonished and pained when that milk fails to flow and when, far too often, it turns sour. He has not been able to learn that a people's cause can only be served by the people themselves. They have to mobilise and take their legitimate due; it will not be bestowed on them. But he hopes, prays and hopes again for the kindness of those in authority. He was hoping even more fervently for a positive outcome to his efforts, when I met him on arrival at the Retreat on the evening of 12th August, 1947. Being an ardent nationalist he had contributed everything he could towards the freedom movement. Now that freedom was here, he considered that the foreign protection of the usurpers of the wealth of his community, would come to an end.

We were much too busy to help Karim to look closer into the crystal ball, even if we had been endowed with the ability to perform such a feat. We had to make our own preparations for Independence on the 14th August 14th 1947. Arrangements were made for ceremonial parades to be held at the five stations which Pakistan Air Force was to take over. Contingents, mere symbols of the defence services of Pakistan, were organised to participate in the main parade, at which the Quad-i-Azam was to take the salute. The entire ceremony was purely symbolic as regards the armed forces; but I shall always remember the fly-past by a few Tempests and a solitary Dakota, piloted by the only fully trained pilot of the Air Force of Pakistan, Flying Officer Abdullah Baig.

However, civilian participation was indeed, overwhelming. The shouted slogans of 'Pakistan Zindabad', (long live Pakistan) rent the air. People who have had experiences of such events or have been accustomed to celebrate or even witness celebrations of victories in wars, battles, struggles for emancipation, can well imagine the wildly enthusiastic scenes on the occasion of this celebration. The agonies leading up to the occasion were forgotten for the moment. On the morning of the 14th August, 1947, the ceremony for the handing over of Independence and for the inauguration of the Quad-i-Azam as the first Governor General of Pakistan, took place in Government House, which had been the residence of the Governor of Sind, in Imperial India. About thirty politicians, plus civil and military senior officials, myself among them, but several of them British, stood in a crescent formation to be presented to Lord Mountbatten, the last Viceroy of India, to the Quad-i-Azam and to be witnesses to the ceremony. It did not take Lord Mountbatten much effort to impress the audience. He was a fine specimen of masculine physique, adequately enhanced by the regalia, which were intended to establish his superiority. He strode in looking every inch the great grandson of Queen Victoria, Empress of India. The occasion must have weighed heavily on him. He was destined to pluck out the 'brightest jewel' from the crown of his mighty forebear; to remove a sub-continent from the Empire thus letting the sun set over it for the first time in many generations; to have been denied his most fervent desire performing the dual role of Governor General of India and Pakistan. The Quad-i-Azam had firmly declined his suggestion, to this effect. As he approached the British military officers they clicked their heels, the sound reverberating throughout the hall. They bowed their heads with violent jerks – typically Prussian style – and had they raised their right arms stiffly at an angle of 45 degrees and uttered one word 'Heil' the ritual would have been complete. The politicians and civilian officers, bowed at the waist, as trained to do so in the imperial court, some more than others giving the indication of their so-called background and upbringing, or could it be the indication of the amount of subservience could be expected of them! I detested the Prussian-Nazi form of salutation and had never been able to bow in the prescribed manner. So I was the odd man out. If I had the headgear I would have saluted. But without it I had been trained to stand to attention, shake the hand of the superior officer, if offered for this purpose, and look him straight in the eye. This is precisely what I did. This obvious departure from what was, on that occasion, the norm, led to the ever so slight widening of the regal eyelids for a mere fraction of a second. There was an almost imperceptible disapproval, on the part of at least a few of the observers. It was written across their faces. Since militarily what I had done was correct I was given to understand, in the mildest of manners, that my attitude could be construed or misconstrued as one of arrogance. But this had never consciously crossed my mind.

I was obliged to admit to myself, however, that I have never approved of one man's superiority over another man; the more glaring the display of superiority, the more adverse my reaction. I was unable to understand why it was that even at the young age of five years or less, I was infuriated by the assumption of superiority by any man for any reason. I vividly remembered an incident when I was that age. My father took me to a village about a mile and a half from ours, to visit some relations. When we reached their house I noticed extra activity and a sense of excitement and we were taken straight into the main room. As we entered through the door I saw directly in front of us, a man sitting against the wall, cross legged on the floor, on a rug. He looked well fed and robust; his shoulder length raven black hair, square beard and dark tanned face, all well greased, glowed with reflected light. He was, of course, bareheaded. He wore a bright white shirt and loin cloth, a white scarf across his shoulders and a ~~'tasbih'~~ ('tasbih' (rosary) around his neck. He sat solemnly and upright. This was in marked contrast to the surroundings and the people around him. It was this sharp difference, in almost every respect, which was being made the basis for superiority. As I was to discover later, the gentleman was a local 'pir' (teacher). He never had to do a stroke of work for his livelihood. His follower – 'murid' – gave him gifts in cash or kind, the latter being in the shape of goats, sheep and chicken, on special occasions, but never less frequently than once a year. Since the followers numbered a few hundred thousand, at least, his income was sizeable. He was not required and, indeed, not 'permitted' by his followers, to indulge in any physical labour. However, he provided 'spiritual guidance' and often talismans to his followers, to ward off or cure disease and evil spirits. This entire process needed no more effort than to write a few words or signs on a piece of paper, tie a few knots in a string, or on an object to be worn or consumed by a follower. The relatively enormous income provided the best of food and clothes and all manner of luxuries; utter freedom from manual labour kept him neat and tidy. In this manner he assumed superiority over those who not only knew the dignity of labour, but without whom he could not enjoy the luxuries of paradise on earth.

That 'superior' person now sat as we entered. My father walked up to him, bowed, touched his knees, the symbolic admission of superiority of the other over himself. I boiled with rage, stopped where I was and refused to go up and pay compliments in a similar manner. I was no less angry when other men came in and performed the same ritual. I knew some of those men, to be honest and industrious. Intellectually my father was head and shoulders above all of them, and even more so in the case of the 'superior man'. Apart from being the best in his profession, my father had mastered a dozen foreign languages, was a poet, musician, composer, dramatist, actor and a prolific writer on subjects concerning the social welfare of the people in our area and the upbringing of children. He was very religious and believed firmly in the equality of men as advocated in Islam. He had laid the strongest possible emphasis on this tenet in my presence. The discussion took second place only to the religious songs, na'at, maulud, quwwali, which were a regular feature of evenings spent at our house. Due to my father's beliefs I was all the more bewildered by my father's gesture. However, on my insistence he explained later that it was only a formality he observed at another person's residence, admitting that he had been wrong and hypocritical. In the following twenty seven years, before he died, I never again saw him exchange anything more than normal courtesies.

The only possible explanation I could find for my attitude towards people was my strict religious background according to which I must not bow to any but my Creator. I could not bow to a person because he had earthly authority or power. I would salute in the prescribed manner because I was a professional soldier. But this did not include either bowing or prostration; indeed, the rules stated that I would look the senior officer straight in the eye and he would return my compliment in precisely the same manner that I paid it. Even now, it is not possible for me to say whether I would have adopted or adhered to a soldierly profession had it included gestures which acknowledged someone's superiority, rather than seniority, other than standing upright. But I do know that my strict adherence to, what I believed to be an important feature of Islam (bow to no one except your Creator), and my passionate devotion to my country, led to extreme hardship for me and all those near and around me, in my own country.

The solemn ceremony of handing over a part of the empire took place in an atmosphere which befits such an occasion. As the saying goes, one could have cut it with a knife. I wonder how many in the hall were aware of the bloodbath which was taking place on the yet undefined eastern borders of West Pakistan; of the tattered nature of the boundary line; of the deep inroads being made into the contiguous Muslim majority areas of the Punjab, Bengal and Assam. The ceremony proceeded as if it were the only thing that mattered. The ceremonial parade and the processions went off in organised chaos and ended in a tumult. I learnt later that the Quad-i-Azam and Lord Mountbatten indulged in some mutual congratulations, each having brought the other safely through a day charged with emotion, when anything could have happened. Of course, one cannot deny the extremely delicate and emotional nature of the occasion, but in Karachi, on that day, an overwhelming majority of the people displayed positive emotions. It has since been said that a plot existed for an attempt on the life of the Quad-i-Azam on that memorable day. As I have said, almost anything was possible in those days. Those were the days of mass murder in accordance with designed plots. Those were the days of bitterness, of grievances, of hatred. When Quad-i-Azam was congratulated on having survived the celebrations of the independence of his own country, the inevitable implication was that at least one person had some knowledge of the danger to his life. Surely the preparations for the unprecedented massacre taking place in East Punjab could not have been unknown to those whose duty it was to remain well informed concerning matters of law and order. A massive arming of hundreds of thousands of people cannot be concealed, it can only be overlooked. I have since read in more than one book that the highest authorities at the centre and in the Punjab completely ignored the belated protestations of Muslim leaders, about the preparation, on a colossal scale, for riots in the province. Of course, I maintain that those preparations for aggression should have been countered by preparations for active defence. This would have forced the authorities to either stop both sides from obtaining weapons, or to shut their eyes to the Muslim preparations also. In any event I maintain that had the Muslims been as well prepared for their defence as the others were for aggression, we would not have lost millions of lives and vast territories which were our contiguous majority areas and hence legitimately ours.

The plight of those in East Punjab and other parts of India, that is Bharat, seem to have been temporarily pushed into the background as the celebrations ran concurrently with the carnage. I received my first severe shock in Pakistan during that period. I am unable to recollect now whether it was on 14th August, the day before or the day after, that an evening party was held in the gardens of Government House. Large quantities of cold beverages were being consumed to the accompaniment of martial music in the background. I have always felt guilty and miserable on the recollection of such occasions. There was gaiety and laughter, music and mirth and cold drinks of various colours. The wailing and cries of agony and anguish, from the land of the five rivers, did not seem to filter through, even if the crimson of the blood lent it's hue to the 'sherbets' on those lofty lawns. Almost insatiable thirsts were being quenched. Whereas over there the warm blood seeped into the soil, here we sipped and gulped the cool beverages.

I roamed among the throng of dignitaries, civil and military, attired in their best, much decorated in commemoration of imperial wars, where capitalist imperialism had clashed with fascist imperialism. I also carried a few multi-coloured ribbons on my breast, having participated, even if in a limited manner, in an anti-fascist war. I must admit that at that time I felt quite proud of having done so, despite the fact that some of us were torn between the desire to obtain freedom from our immediate masters by abstaining from fighting, or to fight against the onslaught of the fascist forces. On that evening as I went from group to group exchanging greetings, I came to stop near a very senior British army officer. As we talked about the events of the day, a message was handed over to him. He opened and read it and spoke to another British officer next to him. The message was from the Boundary Force Commander and the former read it aloud. It was worded to this effect:

"Estimated one thousand Muslims killed in and around Amritsar."

I choked with emotion, but managed to repeat with some vehemence.

"One thousand killed?" I cried.

The senior British officer swung round and said sharply,

"Yes! Are you surprised? After all you have killed five thousand of them in Pindi."

I looked at him aghast. But he continued,

"In any case you have a senior officer attached to the Boundary Force. He should be able to give you a better account of the situation."

The reference was to Brigadier M. Ayub Khan, later Filed Marshal and President of Pakistan.

I stood petrified. Of course, despite some attempts at retaliation in West Punjab, I did not believe that at that time the Hindu and Sikh casualties were so high in Rawalpindi alone. But my amazement was due to the British officer's utter lack of concern and sympathy. I was in a way happy about the killings in West Punjab. But I was most certainly aggrieved about the situation in East Punjab. The nature of the preparations was known to me but 'one thousand' deaths in virtually a few hours seemed a very large number to me. I felt a dull stab in the pit of my stomach. Little did I realise then that the slaughter in progress was to take the toll to well nigh a thousand thousands. The least I expected was a word of sympathy, even if qualified by the mention of losses on the other side as well. The remarks left me in anger and despair and extremely gloomy. The officer was none other than the first Commander-in-Chief of Pakistan Army, General Sir Frank Messervy. He did not remain in command of our army for very long. I am not aware of the reasons for his departure after such a brief tenure. I also did not know how he reported matters to the Qaid-i-Azam. I was far too upset then and far too busy later to try to find out. I did however mention this brief episode to the Qaid-i-Azam that evening, during one of those rare occasions when individuals could have his attention for a few moments. He looked dismayed; his face clouded and became tense; his eyes welled up and seemed to reach the point of overflowing: there was the barest perceptible trembling of his lips. But he tightened his jaw and gulped as if to drink the fluid which would otherwise stream down his cheeks, recomposed himself, shook my hand, I thought rather warmly, and was soon surrounded by other guests.

Two days after the ceremonies and celebrations, I flew to Peshawar which, due to the availability of appropriate accommodation and other facilities, had been selected for the Air Headquarters of Pakistan Air Force. I had been appointed senior officer in charge Administration (SOA) with the rank of Group Captain. The next three officers after me in seniority were Haider Raza, Maqbool Rabb and M. Asghar Khan. They were all promoted to the rank of Wing Commander and appointed in Air Staff, Administrative Staff, at Air H.Q. and Commandant of P.A.F. Flying Training School Risalpur respectively. Asghar Khan became the first substantive Commander-in-Chief of Pakistan Air Force *ten years* after the country had achieved independence.

Ayub Khan succeeded him in 1965, a few weeks before India invaded Pakistan. Haider Raza became Air Vice Marshal and Maqbool Rabb an Air Commodore and later transferred to the Diplomatic Corps, attaining the status of Ambassador. They were the nearest to me in seniority, and yet the gap stretched from the date of my commission in September 1934 to theirs in early 1940 and 1941. This distance was so great and unusual that it left me terribly lonely. It is not easy to describe that feeling. Although one is close to the others emotionally and physically, yet the system creates a barrier which is never easy to cross. However, we all tried to be as intimate as possible, but the nature of our work was such that we hardly had time to let personal relationships develop. We literally plunged ourselves into our work.

The slogan was that "We would work for fifty years and then take a day off."

A new country had to be built with all the disadvantages one could possibly imagine. Its Air Force was an important part of it. It provided the first line of defence and a counter offensive power. Superiority in the Air is of paramount importance in modern warfare. A small Air Force may not be able to attain complete superiority, but then it must deny it to the enemy; in other words, it must neutralise a larger enemy Air Force. We were extremely conscious of our small size. We, therefore, had to establish the base for a compact, but efficient Air Force which could be expanded. It would remain relatively small for the foreseeable future. Plans had to be made, firstly to make it secure on the ground against surprise enemy attack, secondly to enable it to assemble in the air as rapidly as possible because that is where its real strength lies; thirdly to train the personnel to be able to achieve the foregoing aims and finally to train personnel, the pilots in particular, to strike at the enemy air bases in surprise raids by evading his warning system. There are other roles to be considered, like transportation of supplies and men, reconnaissance and air observation for the artillery. But this is all a vast subject and would need volumes to discuss it. Indeed, the senior officers who had the good fortune to serve our country's Air Force in later years have no doubt written on the subject. Also periodically information is fed to the public concerning the development and progress of the Air Force. A reasonably accurate picture can be had from such writings and reports. But an excellent picture of the professional ability of Pakistan Air Force can be gained from its superb performance during the Indian war of aggression in September 1965. Like other arms of the defence services and indeed, any other project, the quality of the organisation necessarily depends on the men who are engaged in it at all levels. I place the men of the armed forces of Pakistan among the best in the world. I have personal experience of those who comprised the foundation of Pakistan Air Force. I hold them in the highest esteem. They were men of sterling qualities, men of all ranks. Given the tools and adequate training, man for man, they are a match for any Air Force. Apart from the obvious professional high calibre of the Commanders-in-Chief and other officers, whose performances have come to public notice in later years, I shall quote here a few examples the reason for my claim and confidence.

AT the time of partition a young Flying Officer attended an Air Gunnery course in the United Kingdom at an R.A.F. station. He scored the highest points in air to air flying ever achieved at that school up to that time. Air to Air flying requires superb skill and handling of aircraft. He let his many countrymen witness that skill in scores of displays throughout the country. His demise was, indeed, a loss to Pakistan Air Force. He died in 1969, after having attended the Imperial Defence College in London. He was then an Air Commodore.

We have always availed of the facilities at the R.A.F. training institutions in the U.K. to which we sent young officers for flying training of various types. Among these was the training for flying instructors at R.A.F. Little Rissington. Pilots from all the Commonwealth nations, and from other countries, came to be trained at this school. One of the competitions for winning a trophy was in aerobatics. This again calls for superb skill and control of an aircraft. In these courses, in three out of four of which our boys attended soon after the establishment of Pakistan, they won this trophy. Unhappily, without records, I am unable to recall the names of all those young men but I believe one of them was Masroor Hussain. He attained the rank of Air Commodore, but was killed in a most tragic flying accident when his aircraft struck a bird near Karachi in 1967. There are many other boys who, then and later, established enviable records of professional ability.

Among the airmen one boy stands out in my memory for his performance in America. He was in the technical branch of signals. He stood at the top of every class and course he attended. I vividly remember the report I received from America concerning the excellent results achieved by this airman, Tariq by name. Of course, there were and are scores of other airmen who did and continue to perform similar feats.

In late 1948, I sent twenty two pilots for training to America and the same number of technical engineering branch officers to Hamble in the U.K. The latter had to undergo a lengthy course and were still at Hamble when I went to attend the Imperial Defence College in London in 1950. One of them, Durrani, came too see me at my residence. He had three projects with him. A table cigarette lighter, which he placed on the table in front of me, and asked me to lift it. As I did so, it snapped open and a tongue of flame sprang forth. It was self-lighting. I have never smoked in my life and I, therefore, declined the offer of this wonderful gift. It was the only one he had made and I asked him to keep it. Then he explained, with the aid of a diagram, the working of an automatic kettle. It was designed to set itself off by means of a clock and the owner would be woken up by the alarm at the desired time with tea prepared and ready to be poured out. He produced yet another diagram showing the working of a wireless or radio controlled model aircraft. He later completed both these items. I was delighted to see all this. I asked him to continue to experiment with such items. I had every intention of getting him into the designing side of the aircraft industry. I had similar plans for Tariq of the signals branch. But I was not able to follow these up. Not long after my return to Pakistan in the last week of January 1951, I was put under house arrest, on the 9th March, to be precise, under suspicion of being an accomplice in what came to be known as the Rawalpindi Conspiracy Case. Neither was Durrani able to specialise in any technical field or to have financial backing for any of his inventions. He came to be regarded as a crank. After a rough time in the Air Force he was sent to the training section in Pakistan International Airlines. Yet more rough times led him to leave that too and I am unaware of his whereabouts thereafter. It is possible that the items which he had produced had been made by some others as well, although I had not, up to that time at least, seen or heard of a self-lighting cigarette lighter, or an automatic electric kettle of the type shown to me.

Such was the human resources; such were the men available to the air force of Pakistan. I had every reason to be proud and confident. We really got to grips with the problems confronting us. The plan for establishing and expanding the air force had already been prepared, as mentioned earlier. A target had been set to achieve it by 1952. However, unforeseen matters arose immediately and simultaneously, in which I became involved, due firstly to my temperament and secondly to the peculiar position I occupied, which affected the plan. As I have already mentioned, I was temperamentally opposed to all types of injustice. I was not directly in command of Pakistan Air Force, but being the senior most national I was, to all intents and purposes, in command. This brought me into very close contact with the political leadership, the senior layers of bureaucracy and other armed forces. This combination of people led to co-operation and conflicts in several matters, in a manner which I shall explain in the succeeding chapters. The most important events taking place within a few weeks of the birth of Pakistan were:

(a) Organising Pakistan Air Force
(b) Evacuation, resettlement and rehabilitation of the personnel of the Air Force and their families, who had escaped from the massacre in East Punjab and other parts of India.
(c) The uprising in Poonch against the autocratic Dogra ruler of Jammu and Kashmir.

The people in this area not only had blood ties with the people in adjoining districts of Pakistan, but their struggles against perhaps the most oppressive ruler in the sub-continent, aroused universal sympathy in the country.

It would be best to deal with the subject of evacuation and resettlement first. It had its terrible agonies and tales, indescribable and harrowing.

The bestiality displayed during those days could have parallels only in the dark and medieval eras. Every conceivable type of crime against humanity was committed. I would not wish to go into the details of the innumerable incidents which were brought to our notice. Suffice it to say that everything that is bad in human beings seems to have erupted and was rampant. On the one hand groups of humanity may suffer from collective guilt but on the other hand they also are prone to mass amnesia. Let us hope that the victims of atrocities undergo the latter condition and the perpetrators of bestialities experience the former condition. The masses awakened to overthrow the yokes which lead them to such clashes and the mutual spilling of blood ceases by the removal of the exploiters, who cause those conditions.

However, I have understood this with hindsight. At that time trends and tempers were different. We had to react swiftly to every situation. I organised rescue and evacuation parties. I put all available and necessary transport at their disposal to go into East Punjab and retrieve all they could. There were several successful sorties. It pains me to say that even under those conditions there was some misuse of the facilities given and that I had to resort to disciplinary action in one case. The Air Force conducted its own evacuation and resettlement operations for some time because, being a small organisation, it was able to act with greater speed. The urgency was such that I dealt with the matter personally. Those personnel had undergone the most shattering experiences. It was vitally important to have their families, or the remnants of them, settled in their new localities in the shortest time possible. Later all this was handed over to the larger set up of the Pakistan Army.

It will be over two decades after those events that these words will see the light of day, but even then I feel that at least two incidents, which occurred in the same period, be mentioned. Recounting them may bring tears of blood to the eyes of our people as they, and other similar incidents, brought to the eyes of those of us who were involved in the problems of those days. Of course, the impact cannot be as great now as it was then, but if those of my countrymen who happen to read these few sentences were to exercise their imagination they would, in all probability, be able to assess the intensity of the feelings which must have prevailed then. This is in no way intended to reopen any wounds. It is the recording of some historical events relating to my country. It is a brief analysis of those events. It is merely to ask to be judged for my actions in those days by providing some glimpses of the extremely trying conditions with which I and my colleagues in the Air Force were confronted; the ugly, mean and heinous actions.

It is not difficult to understand the acts of inhumanity and cruelty by those who have declared one another to be enemies. But, if committed by those who are not enemies but are, indeed, entrusted with the duty of providing protection for their own people, such acts should not be allowed to go unpunished. During the days immediately succeeding partition there was lodged, intermittently, in Lahore, a Brigadier at the residence of perhaps the most senior police official in Pakistan. They were both directly responsible for, not only the welfare of the refugees, but also for their protection in every possible manner. They were required to use every means at their disposal to ensure the evacuation and safety of the refugees. A great deal was put at their disposal for this purpose. They were visited by army officials and members of the public with the acute problems of the refugees and their unspeakable plight. Among the visitors were a journalist and a major of the Pakistan Army. The journalist, who hailed from East Punjab, took to the aforementioned two senior officers, problems concerning some refugee families and the condition of those in a camp across the other side of the border. I am unable to recollect the exact words exchanged between them. The two visitors reported that the officers were surrounded by bottles of alcoholic drinks and indulged in that past-time in the presence of the journalist. According to the latter those officers displayed callousness beyond description. Their contempt for and indifference to the plight of the refugees was such that the journalist burst into a furious rage. He threatened to kill them if they persisted in their attitude and did not take action towards a solution of the problems placed before them. This outburst literally sobered them up; their eyes boggled with amazement at the ferocity of the onslaught; they cooled down and tried to pacify the journalist. The latter however, left in anger and disgust to seek voluntary and perhaps more effective help.

On a different occasion a major went to see the Brigadier at the same place. The latter was found to be indulging in the same alcoholic drinks as in the previous incident. The major paid his compliments and spoke about different subjects for a while and then asked permission to leave. The Brigadier not only invited him to join him in a drink but far, far worse, and unforgiveable, in rape and indecent assault on young refugee girls from East Punjab. The major was advised to enjoy himself and forget about more serious matters. He declined to accept the offer and the advice, saluted and left saying:

"Thank you very much Sir, but I must get to Kasur very soon."

These are the types of incident which illustrate the almost unbearable tensions and agonies so many had to undergo. It should also help those who judge us, these many, many years later, towards the understanding of the reasons why some of us reacted so sharply to the events of those days. It would, indeed, be a hard-hearted or callous person who would fail to react to such incidents without anger, without a stabbing ache in the heart, without human sympathy and without the desire to go to any length to help the victims of a carnage, which may have been equalled but hardly ever surpassed. I would beseech my countrymen to keep these in mind when I proceed further to describe events. It is not easy, nor indeed is it possible, to recapture precisely those situations. But I hope it will not be difficult to appreciate the causes and the reasons for actions which, in retrospect, may appear to have been drastic. In retrospect, even today, I have not been able to come to the conclusion that I should have acted differently. Events led inexorably to resolute action. Had actions not matched the demands of the day, the shape of many things would have been different. I can say with certainty that the size and structure of Pakistan Air Force and the map of Kashmir would have been quite unlike what they are today. The map of Kashmir might have been completely different had some of our requests been met, initiative used or allowed and tough moral fibre displayed, as demanded by the situation. My meaning will become clear as I describe the events relating to the period immediately succeeding partition and for a few months thereafter.

In addition to the aforementioned relief work, to help the refugees, the airmen and their families, I went yet further to render aid to those in East Punjab who might still be able to use it to good effect. While the indiscriminate slaughter continued and refugee camps sprang up, there were lamentably few pockets of resistance. The most prominent among them were at Batala and Qadrian. I made available whatever weapons and other material could easily be transported to these two towns and some smaller ones, at the request of volunteers. It was never possible to obtain accurate information regarding the effectiveness of such assistance. Flying officer Latif who was retired, having been a Japanese prisoner of war, flew in some equipment in a small aircraft. I do believe that large numbers of people were safely evacuated from these towns. Of course, these were unparalleled individual acts of heroism. It was one of these that the brother of Group Captain Fayyaz Mahmud, Senior Education Officer of P.A.F. was martyred in Batala. Also the Muslim personnel of the 10th Baluch Regiment gave perhaps the most valuable protection to the completely routed and demoralised Muslims in parts of East Punjab, where they were deployed for this very purpose. Many acts of heroism and personal initiative to oppose and lessen the ferocity of that onslaught have not been related. Many of those who participated did not survive to tell the story. We seem to have the most obnoxious tradition of omitting that part of our history which does not relate directly to those who are at the helm of affairs. If ever attempts are made to portray those events, there are mainly by oblique methods such as story telling; camouflaging the facts and personalities; efforts which are utterly inadequate. They do give the trends, the mood of the people at a particular time and generally the types of events which took place, but they deny people access to actual facts and the right of the subjects of those facts, to be placed in the annals of the history of their country, community or class. This type of attitude or such tradition robs the people of one of their greatest treasures. I, for one, would like to see an end to this tradition. I would like to see the names and exploits of those who became involved in those situations, and faced them with dauntless courage, written in bold letters across the pages of the history of their country. There may be nothing unique about some omissions from history, but we have far more than our share of them and of utterly erroneous emphasis in favour of those who happen to be in power. This trend is not unknown in other countries but in our case firstly, it is extremely exaggerated and secondly there is no reason why an effort should not be made to stop it. So let the exploits of those who displayed such matchless valour in the face of impossible odds, in East Punjab and elsewhere, find a prominent place in our history books. Let those who are aware of the facts bring them to the notice of the people by writing or causing books etc. to be written about them. Many volumes have been written about the less deserving and even the undeserving. Some have usurped the place in history of the rightful owners of it, indeed, they usurped the power which rightfully belonged to the people. While I ask of my countrymen to come forth with whatever is within their knowledge, let me continue with the narrative of whatever I am able to recollect.

Air Commodore MK Janjua

Chapter Six

The Steep Climb

I have already given an account of the manner in which the programme for the establishment, consolidation, training and expansion of Pakistan Air Force was prepared. Normally it should have been a relatively easy matter to put that programme into effect. There should be no reason for the Air Force of an independent country not to develop along the lines outlined by its own nationals. They would have taken all factors into account, their limitations first, and then all the sources available to them, indigenous and foreign. The nationals of a country are the best judges of the requirements of their country and the most appropriate and effective ways to meet them. This assumes adequate and sound basic knowledge of their profession. I maintain that the personnel of Pakistan Air Force had such knowledge. They had all the qualities which go towards the making of a highly efficient air force. They had ample sense to appreciate the need for foreign equipment and technical personnel. Their programme had accepted the necessity of foreign assistance in the technical branches.

Since virtually all our equipment was British, not only had we decided to retain it, but also to re-equip with British aircraft for the foreseeable future. We also welcomed and sought all help in respect of training our personnel in Britain, and having British personnel on loan to our air force in branches where the need was greatest. However, we had not visualised, when all plans were being set, that we would have a non-national as the policy-making Commander of our air force. We were, therefore, placed in an exceptionally unusual position. This applied more to me than to the others. I found myself working with a British officer who had no part whatever in the making of the expansion programme of our air force. His initial contribution, several weeks after we had completed the programme for our air force, was that after his own appointment as Commander-in-Chief of P.A.F., he appointed me the Senior Officer I/C Administration. He later, while still in New Delhi, selected a few British personnel whom he knew, for service with P.A.F. As soon as I began to discuss the problems of our air force with Air Vice Marshal Percy-Keene our first Air Commander – as the C-in-C was then called – I became aware of a vast divergence in our views and approach. I realised that it would, indeed, be a steep climb to get to the target we had set ourselves. I could foresee serious opposition from the very quarter that should in normal circumstances be doing everything to improve on our target; pushing us all along; inspiring us to greater achievement. Instead we found ourselves at loggerheads. Instead of being pushed, I found myself being pulled and even dragged back. I can best describe the situation, which I shall discuss in detail, by quoting a small incident. I had to discuss a matter with the Military Finance department in Rawalpindi in the early days of Pakistan. Mumtaz Mirza was the officer concerned. A blunt, outspoken man, he had already acquired the nickname of "Molotov". He was reputed to have "No" as the answer to all financial demands. Of course, this was not my experience of him. I found him to be of very high calibre professionally. In that system there were not many better. However on that day I was having some difficulty in putting my point across. Ultimately I said:

"Mumtaz, can you imagine a truck going up a steep slope?"

"Yes" he said, looking at me quizzically over the rim of his glasses.

"You will agree that it is hard going" I said.

"Yes!" again from him, the monosyllable.

"Then please don't jam on the brakes!" I said.

We settled down to a relaxed discussion and managed to see each other's point more clearly. Mumtaz did all he possibly could to help in the progressive build up of P.A.F. in its initial stages.

But I felt the application of brakes from my own commander. At times, I felt it very acutely indeed. Since I was determined to push the original programme through, it made for a very unhappy relationship between us. Not only was there an immense gulf between our thinking or policy concerning the size of Pakistan Air Force and the speed of its development, but our temperaments were as different as dynamite is from a lump of coal. I was very energetic and even aggressive in my approach and was in my early thirties. He was phlegmatic, terribly slow and was near the age of retirement. Before Independence my experience of Air Vice Marshal Percy-Keene was confined to the meetings of the Air Force sub-committee of the Armed Forces Reconstitution Committee. He was its chairman. My experience of him was limited to a few weeks; at a few official and social functions. He conducted all these in a tidy manner. He was the Air Officer I/C Administration at Air Headquarters, New Delhi, one of the most senior Principal Staff Officers. This implied that he had the requisite seniority and ability to manage the affaires of a small air force, which P.A.F. was going to be on partition. These were among the factors which had led me to submit his name to our policy making body in New Delhi. Undoubtedly he had experience of administration. But in the vigour necessary to build and organise P.A.F. from its inception, he fell lamentably short of our requirements. Above all, the inclination to expand P.A.F. with all the speed, which the situation demanded and we were capable of generating, was lacking. We soon began to clash on many points.

I belonged to a generation which witnessed the culmination of the struggle for independence. Many of us had, in our own way, taken part in the nation-wide movement to remove the yoke of colonialism. I had had my share of it. While on the one hand our personal relationships with a large number of British personnel were very good, on the other hand there were many incidents of what might be called fight for privilege, between the British and our officers and airmen. I was involved in several myself. An incident which could be multiplied infinitely, as others far better than myself, waged similar struggles, will indicate the trends and experiences we had undergone during and after the world war.

It was late in 1942 that I was stationed in Kohat as Commander of No.4 Squadron I.A.F., the I.A.F. Squadron was No.3, commanded by Squadron Leader D.A.R. Nanda, later Air Vice Marshal I.A.F., who was one of my closest friends for many years. I was the most senior Indian Air Force Officer on the station. The station H.Q. had R.A.F. officers and Wing Commander Thripp was the station commander. The station adjutant was an R.A.F. Pilot Officer. A vacancy occurred for the appointment of President Mess, Committee (P.M.C.). The station commander, who had the authority to appoint the P.M.C., let it be known that he would appoint the Adjutant, a pilot officer in rank. I raised an objection to this. Wing Commander Thripp called me to his office to talk it over.

"You are being rather unreasonable in this matter" he said.

"I beg to differ" I said, "There is a preponderance of I.A.F. officers with the requisite length of service and rank. I think it is quite reasonable to have one of them perform the function of P.M.C. There are two other members on the mess committee. You could have any two you like there."

This generated some heated discussion for a few minutes until Wing Commander Thripp growing increasingly angry said,

"Who do you think should be appointed?"

"Squadron Leader Prem Nath" I said.

"But he is a medical officer; a non-combatant! He has no disciplinary powers." He literally screamed at me.

"The P.M.C. need not have disciplinary powers because he himself cannot take any disciplinary action against the mess staff" I replied.

Wing Commander Thripp was now furious. He said:

"I am station Commander. I will appoint anyone I like."

"No, you cannot appoint a pilot officer as P.M.C. According to the King's Regulations, he must not be less in rank than Flight Lieutenant" I said.

He was beside himself with fury and shouted:

"But he is going to be promoted to Flight Lieutenant soon."

"Maybe" I said, "But today he is still a pilot officer."

"From your arguments you are implying that I am anti-Indian," he said.

"I did not have any implication in my mind" I said. "I only had in mind the fact that there are two I.A.F. Squadrons here and many I.A.F. officers qualify for P.M.C. If you insist on appointing a pilot officer the implication would be clear to all."

He made a final gesture of anger and said:

"I am sorry but you are wasting my time."

"I am sorry you think so" I said and left his office.

That evening I phoned him from my house. When he answered I said:

"I still do not agree with your decision to appoint a pilot officer as P.M.C."

"But I am at home now!" he said.

"I thought it was important enough to let you know" I said.

The following afternoon, it appeared in the Routine Orders that Squadron Leader Prem Nath was appointed President of the Mess Committee.

While the political struggle raged, political leaders were imprisoned; many who fought for independence lost their lives and many thousands, like me, served and fought for the colonial interests. Yet within our own spheres there were such incidents. Many officers who had suffered heavily; were court marshalled, cashiered and victimised in many other ways. Undoubtedly, these were but a minute part of a vast struggle. But our experience had been one of progressive successes against retreating colonialism; of wrenching freedom from unwilling hands; of wresting and using initiatives, which is the prerogative of free people; then ultimately attaining independence and removing external domination.

This was the frame of mind with which many of us commenced work in the free country of Pakistan. I certainly started with the belief, assumption would be too weak a word, that we were independent and would pursue the affairs of our country in the manner we, the nationals, believed to be to the greatest benefit of our country. For many weeks I believed that our leadership and officialdom consisted of patriotic people. I was too busy to attribute motives or analyse them when I came across incidents which were not strictly patriotic and were anti-people. My awakening came abruptly.

I acted as a free person of an independent country. I was not capable of acting in any other manner. Many of us were sensitive on this point. On the other hand some British officers were unable to adjust themselves as rapidly as the new situation demanded and some not at all. They could not readily adopt the role of serving. It was too distant from that of command and rule, which they considered to be synonymous with their right. So there were clashes at several levels. Of course, little did I realise at that time that our policy-makers would yield to every pressure and whim of some British officers, even those of lower ranks. The leaders displayed such utter weakness in this matter that they were not held in any great regard by the foreign personnel. In later months they were referred to in contemptuous terms. Our first Prime Minister was referred to as 'Liquid Ali' and our second Governor General as an 'Olive on Toothpicks'. We had to fight against this type of contempt.

In the air force the first instances of contempt came from an officer whom Air Vice Marshal Percy-Keene had appointed the senior air staff officer (SASO).

He was Group Captain Davy. His attitude in every way resembled that which we had experienced in the I.A.F. during the war, at the hands of some R.A.F. officers. Every possible opportunity was taken to condemn I.A.F. personnel units; to accuse them of inefficiency. At some stations where I.A.F. squadrons were located but the flying control was manned by R.A.F. officers, the latter would respond to the radio calls by I.A.F. pilots with:

"Crash, you bastard! Crash!"

They carried a similar attitude to P.A.F. officers like Group Captain Davy. His references to our personnel became so obnoxious that I asked AVM Percy-Keene to terminate his services and send him to the U.K., where he would feel happier not having to contend with our inefficiency. On this occasion AVM Percy-Keene complied. Haider Raza was promoted to the rank of Group Captain and appointed S.A.S.O. Maqbool Rabb was also similarly promoted and took charge of the organisation department. I was elevated to the rank of Air Commodore on 1 January, 1943, and designated Air Officer I/C Administration. I must admit that I did not feel elated by this and therefore failed to thank those who may have expected such an expression from me. I did thank AVM Percy-Keene for the peak cap he gave me. Up to that time we had no such caps for officers of Air rank. It was my country's air force. I would serve it to the best of my ability. The rank was quite immaterial. Accidents of history had put me in a place from where I was required to spear-head the development of Pakistan Air Force. This was all that mattered. I tried to abide by the policy of the Government with regard to having a non-national as the commander of the air force of my nation. I found it extremely difficult. It was made even more difficult for me by the temperament and attitude of our Air Commander.

We soon settled down in Peshawar. The regular conferences commenced between the Air Commander and the Principal Staff Officers. It was not long before I became aware of the programme the Air Commander had in mind for the development of the Air Force, and of the painfully slow methods adopted by him. On some points I found it desirable to maintain silence, on others it was impossible to do so. A pattern of moves emerged, designed to promote British commercial interests at our expense. Yet further acts appeared to be utterly opposed to the security interests of Pakistan. I will give details as I proceed.

The Air Commander told me that taking into account our lack of equipment, trained personnel and flying instructors, we should make a programme for recruiting ten pilot trainees and one hundred airmen trainees a year. I nearly jumped out of my skin, but managed to keep control over myself. I said nothing to him then. We had already made out a programme for five years. Indeed, the recruiting campaign came into action immediately on partition. There was no similarity between his programme and ours. He prepared a paper and gave me a copy. Of course, it was circulated to senior officers in other departments. They consulted me in time. I told them to disregard the circular and to continue with the original plan. I vividly recollect Group Captain Abdul Hai, technical branch, coming to me with that circular. He looked dismayed. He was one of the officers who had helped me with the preparation of our expansion plan. I told him to throw the circular into the wastepaper basket. As he crumpled it in his hand, made a fist and then threw it in the receptacle, he looked very relieved.

On or about 1 January, 1948, I reported to AVM Percy-Keene that thirty pilot trainees had reported at the Flying Training School at Risalpur, commanded by then Wing Commander M. Asghar Khan. AVM Percy-Keene nearly threw a fit.

"But I thought I told you that we would have ten pilot trainees a year!" He said.

"I think we can manage more than that." I said.

"We have insufficient equipment, we are short of technical maintenance personnel and we have hardly any flying training instructors" he went on.

"Do you agree that the trainees will be engaged in ground training for six or even nine months and we have enough instructors to give them that training?" I asked.

"Yes" he replied.

He also agreed that flying instructors were not needed for that period. He further agreed that the initial flying instruction begin six to nine months later, would be on Tiger Moths, which needed very few technical personnel. There was yet more agreement between us on the fact that advance flying training on more sophisticated aircraft was a year away.

"Then if we are unable to obtain a few training aircraft, afford a few technical airmen and train a few flying training instructors in this time, we are not worth the name of an air force." I said.

While he fumbled for words, I continued,

"The Lahore Flying Club could train more than ten pilots. A nation of one hundred million people expects more from its air force. It must have an air force befitting its size and status and above all its foreseeable defence requirements."

It can be imagined that we did not part on the best of terms.

It was an extremely unhappy situation, but I and senior P.A.F. officers were determined to continue with our original programme. Despite the tragedies attending partition, due to the heavy fatal casualties in East Punjab and elsewhere and due to the uprooting of hundreds of thousands of families, the officers and airmen were in excellent spirits. They were equal to the task of building an air force necessary for the defence of their country. They performed their duties with dauntless courage and enviable vigour. I vividly recollect that we used to leave for work while our children were still asleep and when we returned they had gone to sleep again. This was the routine for some considerable time. In this way they laid the foundation of an air force which more than neutralised an air force with enormous numerical superiority over them eighteen years later. It needs no genius to imagine the consequences to the security of the country if we had adhered to the so-called expansion programme advocated and, indeed, prepared by the first Chief of Pakistan Air Force.

On the 1st April, 1948, a further thirty trainees reported at Risalpur. I had yet another unpleasant encounter with the Air Commander. For two quarters thereafter I commanded the air force and the programme continued unhindered, while the pilot trainees were reporting to the Recruits Training Centre at the rate of one hundred per month instead of per year, as envisaged by the AVM Percy-Keene. In each case the intake was twelve times greater. In addition, recruitment went on for all other branches and officers and airmen were trained mainly at home but some went abroad. In order to convey an idea of the enthusiasm, capacity and ability of those fine men of Pakistan's Air Force, I would like to mention that not only did they carry out the original plan superbly, but they met all emergencies with a zeal which had to be witnessed to be believed. They helped in supply lifts of food, clothing and medicines into Gilgit and some other parts of the so-called territory of the Dogra ruler. In this respect the great help rendered by the embryonic civil aviation authority must be acknowledged. Later, during the so-called crisis over Nizam's Hyderabad, the intake into Risalpur was increased and the period of training shortened. The intake to the Recruits Training Centre was increased to 125 a month. Operational training also stepped up. The operational wing was placed under the command of Wing Commander M. Asghar Khan. It carried out an extremely intensive training programme, under his exceptionally able direction. I will say more about these two incidents later; incidents which added enormous pressures to the work of all concerned.

I have mentioned these factors here merely to indicate that the first Air Commander's plan was entirely inadequate, did not meet the needs of the situation and was hopelessly below the capability of the young service. He had either grossly underrated the quality of the personnel or was quite unaware of what was at his disposal, in men and material. At that time I could not think of any other reason. But could his motive have been to keep our air force small, so that he, a retired officer, might continue to be employed? This is not impossible. Could he have been given a policy directive from elsewhere? This, also, is not unlikely. However, his underestimation or lack of knowledge, were amply proved by the facts I have already mentioned. Obviously we had prepared the programme correctly in New Delhi. Not only were we able to carry out the programme but we were able to meet emergencies and unforeseen situations. We did all of this despite the problem of having to collect some of our training aircraft from India. Every effort was made by the I.A.F. personnel to delay the delivery. The I.A.F. station at Jodhpur, from where Tiger Moths had to be collected, actually resorted to sabotage. They put sugar in the carburettors and some aircraft had to carry out forced landings en route to Risalpur. The R.A.F. personnel, officers in particular, stripped most of our stations bare of equipment, especially the messes, before they left. One officer's mess had all carpets, and curtains, taken and shipped to the U.K. We managed to get payment for them after a struggle. We were too small to have been able to watch over what was happening in all the stations. However, despite these and many similar problems the recruiting and training programmes went ahead and a basis for expansion was laid.

At the beginning while the Air H.Q. was located in Peshawar, the Ministry of Defence was in Karachi. Although for day to day matters we could refer to the skeleton Ministry of Defence and Ministry Finance Departments, with the General H.Q. being in Rawalpindi, for matters of policy we had to visit Karachi quite frequently. During one of his visits, AVM Percy-Keene spoke to me on the telephone from Karachi.

"You know, Jan, there are fifty Spitfires at Drigh Road. I think we should take them." He said.

"What for?" I asked.

"Well they are lying here at the Depot" he replied.

"That is no reason for us to take over something we don't need" I said.

"Well we can use them for training" he went on.

"But we are not going to use them for operations" I retorted. "We are going to continue with the Tempest and re-equip with the Fury. Therefore, Spitfires are no use to us."

"These are photographic Spitfires." He said. "We can use them for that purpose."

Now I was becoming irritated.

"In which case there is even less reason" I said. "They are no earthly use for operations. We have ample maps and photographs of Pakistan. We do not want to photograph Pakistan. We want to defend it."

He seemed to have run out of argument and our conversation came to an abrupt end. Those aircraft were not bought by me.

It does not need much effort or genius to work out Percy-Keene's motive. Here was our Air Commander who had suggested, very seriously, that we should have an expansion programme which would produce five or even four pilots in a whole year, leaving us with as many trained pilots. The same Air Commander was now seeking purchase of fifty aircraft, enough for three whole squadrons or for two squadrons with eighteen aircraft in reserve. If his suggestion of photographic survey were to be taken seriously, then these aircraft would last us forever – and, of course, he knew and we knew, that we did not want them for an eternity. There could be only one conclusion. The attempt was to sell on war surplus amounting to a vast sum of money and that too at the expense of the country whose air defence policy he was being paid to run and whose other interests he was expected to safeguard. Had we agreed to purchase those fifty aircraft we would have consumed the largest portion of our budget and been saddled with a very large number of aircraft we did not need.

This would not serve the interests of my country. Indeed, its interests would be injured beyond calculation. But the interests of the other officer's country would be served most admirably, by the sale of such magnitude, on site. I cannot but admire his loyalty to his country. While separate nations continue to exist, patriotism must remain among the topmost of positive human attitudes. It was in the interests of his country, that he made that attempt. The same sentiment on my part made me foil it. The interests of my country came above all else. I was able to resolve this matter in our favour.

We had British aircraft and equipment. We were familiar with it. We had decided not only to retain it, but to re-equip with British aircraft. Even if we had any option at that time, we did not look for it. On one point we were firm. We would acquire progressively more modern aircraft and never take a step back. We would not take over war surplus and obsolescent aircraft, except as reserves. In so far as the operational aircraft were concerned, the next logical choice as a successor to the Tempest was the Fury. We decided to re-equip with this type of aircraft before taking on the jets. The transport aircraft we selected was the British Freighter. Oddly enough, this again was contrary to the wishes of our Air Commander. He had some other type in mind. I do not recollect the name. His main argument against our selection was that it had fixed, as opposed to the retracting, undercarriage and that it looked clumsy. For us it had many advantages. It had the same type of engine as our operational aircraft. Therefore it did not interfere with our training and maintenance problems. It could carry small ground transport and had a greater payload than the alternative. It could land on small, even unprepared airstrips at high altitudes, which we had an abundance of in the Frontier Province and in East Pakistan. The Bristol Freighter did not have a very high cruising speed but for the purposes of transport aircraft that is no great disadvantage.

These were the factors which led us to the decisions to re-equip with Fury and Bristol Freighters. From the Fury we went on to acquire the first jet aircraft. I was still in the Air Force when the latter decision was made. But I understood, about sixteen years later, that the Bristol Freighter, despite its ugliness, stayed with the P.A.F. all those years. However, the typical attitude of imperialism was amply displayed when an attempt was made to persuade me to purchase fifty Spitfires: dispose of the war surplus, regardless of the enormous financial and even national security injury to our country.

Up to 1964, there were still some Fury and Bristol Freighter aircraft with the Pakistan Air Force. I was told about this and asked if I may be able to help with their disposal. I was in London. I wrote to both the companies, seeking some information on this matter and assistance towards the disposal of the aircraft, which they had been able to sell to our country. Of course, they must have made huge profits from those sales. One of them replied to the effect that my letter had been forwarded to their Head of Department. The other company perhaps found that a three-penny stamp would shatter their budgetary calculations and did not acknowledge my letter. I heard no more from the former also. I am sure that the P.A.F. was able to dispose of its surplus equipment. I am also sure that these firms of British industry have been able to find further markets for their undoubtedly superb equipment. However, while capitalism and imperialism remain there will be a continuing process of betrayals of nations, the only motive being profit. And this will continue to be made at the cost of the people. It is only the people who can put an end to it. This will come when the real patriots that is the working masses, decide as to what is in their best interests and that of their country. While a system which enables a few to claim, establish, impose and retain the monopoly on 'patriotism', there will remain the certainty – not merely the possibility – of the interests of the people being betrayed. When this 'patriotism', in actual fact power, is in the hand of a few, it is so easy for it to be used in a manner prejudicial to the people's causes and interests. The patriotism of most, if not all, of those who wield power, coincides with their own and their class interests. In any event, the interests are those of the exploiting classes, with which most of those in power identify themselves and take measures to protect. While all projects are prepared with the aim of promoting capitalism and profit-making, it is proclaimed that they are for the benefit of the country – that is the people. And while enormous profits are made by the few capitalists and monopolists, some benefit accrues to the people, purely incidentally.

Indigenous capitalism and external imperialism work hand in hand against the people. Some of those who identify themselves with the people wage a struggle against the enemies of the people's interests. If they work in isolation without a mass movement, and active support of the people, they normally come to a disastrous end. I believe that I was acting in the best interests of my country and its people, which to me are synonymous. I have never since been able to come to a different conclusion.

Not long after partition AVM Percy-Keene took up the subject of transfer of equipment to India with me. Just as some of our aircraft and some of our other equipment were in India, some of the Indian Air Force aircraft and equipment were in Pakistan. We exchanged some of it. I have already given the example of the Tiger Moths from Jodhpur. We sent them some of their share from our depots and stations. However, in some instances the Indians had adopted the attitude that they would not send our share in kind but would adjust it against cash. This applied particularly to large quantities of important and even vital equipment in respect of the Pakistan Army. I decided to adopt a similar attitude concerning some I.A.F. share. Not only did we need it for ourselves, but it would be used against our people, if we were to let it be transferred. The struggle in Kashmir had already become armed and fierce. The so-called legal accession by the Dogra ruler had taken place. Above all, the Indian Air Force was sustaining sizeable losses due to lack of spares and reserves and poor maintenance.

We had in our depots thirty seven Tempests which were the share of I.A.F. They needed these desperately to replace their losses and the high rate of un-serviceability. While we were not to use our air force in support of those who were waging a courageous struggle against the Indian Army, after its invasion of Jammu and the valley of Kashmir, the Indian Air Force came in support of their ground troops. While the Indians were 'legally' and openly in Kashmir, we were not at war with them. It can be seen that they had every conceivable advantage over the freedom fighters, the volunteers, and later the Pakistan Army. Air cover is of the most vital importance. The Indians had it. Those who rose against a most oppressive ruler and those who went to their aid had no such support.

It was under such circumstances that AVM Percy-Keene asked me to agree to the release of those thirty seven Tempests to India. I firmly refused.

"But we are morally bound to hand these over." He said. "It is their share."

"They are as much morally bound to hand over our share." I said. "But they do not". They offer us money instead. We cannot be wrong if we were to offer them the same."

Our discussion on this subject was spread over several meetings. He argued in favour of handing them over. I resisted this obviously damaging move. In my exasperation I had to tell him plainly:

"This is akin to making a gift to the enemy of the most deadly weapon to use against oneself." I said. "Within hours of delivery, these aircraft will be used against our own people."

Of course he could not be concerned about the people of Poonch, Mirpur and Gilgit and about the volunteers who had gone to their help. But I was extremely concerned. However, after a few attempts, he decided to maintain silence.

Then one morning when I went to his office for the conference, I found AVM Percy-Keene in an exceptionally happy, relaxed mood. Two or three other officers came in to attend the conference. Percy-Keene lit his pipe with deliberate care and soon began to emit puffs of smoke from the side of his mouth. His enjoyment seemed quite intense. He was still standing behind his desk when he addressed me.

"Well, Jan! I attended the Inter Dominion Conference yesterday." He said. I was not aware of his presence at the meeting between the highest dignitaries from Pakistan and India. I became suspicious immediately. I looked at him intensely and waited for him to proceed.

"I have obtained the Prime Minister's permission to release the I.A.F. Tempests." He said triumphantly.

Those were tense, anxious and angry days. I had experienced these emotions more than once. But I am unable to recollect any occasion when I have been more angry, tense and anxious than when I heard those words. I literally exploded.

"These Tempests are not going!" I said fiercely. "I will not allow them to be taken."

"Are you going to disobey the Prime Minister's order?" he said, with a mixture of irritation and astonishment. Perhaps he thought I would accept the lofty decision meekly. But I was angry beyond description. I was furious.

"I do not mean to disobey anyone. But the Tempests are not going, and to hell with your conference!"

I stormed out of the room. This was incredible. I could not believe that those Tempests would be released to the I.A.F. by anyone in our government, under conditions of an undeclared war. I had already said that money should be offered in lieu. I went to my room and asked the telephone operator to get Squadron Leader Ghayyur, Deputy Secretary, at the Ministry of Defence in Karachi. He soon came on the phone.

"What is happening Ghayyur?" I asked.

When I told him about the incident he said that he had no knowledge of it. I asked him to find out and revert to me as soon as possible.

In fact Percy-Keene had gone to Lahore the previous day. The Inter-

Dominion Conference he had referred to had been attended by the Quad-i-Azam, the Prime Minister Nawabzada Liaquat Ali Khan, Secretary General in the Cabinet, Chaudhry Mohammed Ali and some other Senior British and Pakistani officers representing Pakistan: and for India, among others, it was attended by Lord Mountbatten and Pandit Nehru. At that conference Percy-Keene had managed to manoeuvre the transfer of the Tempests. Squadron Leader Ghayyur phoned me later and said that he had spoken to Chowder Mohammed Ali. The latter informed him that the government now stood committed and unfortunately nothing could be done about it. I was still furious and recounted all the reasons why the Tempests should not be released. Squadron Leader Ghayyur was aware of my views and agreed with them. He found himself helpless but promised to do all he could.

"Ghayyur, these aircraft must not go." I said to him.

His voice choked with emotion when he said that he would continue to exert every effort to have the decision reversed. He pursued the matter with all the vigour at his command. We needed the aircraft. Let us pay the Indians as they were doing for some our equipment lying in their territory. These aircraft would be used against our people. If they are desperate for aircraft, let them go elsewhere for them. All these arguments and pleas fell on deaf ears. Chaudhry Mohammed Ali, the Secretary of the Secretariat, remained rigid on his stand of the Government's commitment. Our Government's commitments seemed to have become more sacred than those of the Indian Government, which made and unmade commitments to suit the needs of their country.

Ultimately when Ghayyur was unable to break through this stonewall of un-reason he gave up in despair and disgust and informed me accordingly. I sent a personal note on the matter to the Prime Minister. He took the opportunity at an evening party, where we happened to be together to inform me that nothing could be done now. The

Government could not dishonour a commitment. I argued fiercely, repeating all the points I had previously made, in particular the one about handing over a deadly weapon to an enemy, all to no avail. However, at my request that – short of sabotage – we must not permit the Tempests to leave our shores, Ghayyur contacted the Chief Minister of Sind, Mohammad Ayub Kure. The latter promised not to let the Tempests sail from the port of Karachi. He raised the question of customs duty and held them back for three months. The Central Government finally intervened to say that customs duty was their subject and Sind as a province could not levy such taxes. It was under the aegis, if not the bayonets, of the central Government, that the most deadly weapon against our own people was handed over to the enemy. Who can say as to how many people of Azad Kashmir, how many of the volunteers and how many of our own regular troops; how many of these fell martyr to these Tempests? There can be no certainty about the number of those who became victims but there can be no doubt that many became martyrs.

Why did Percy-Keene not keep these Tempests for his own Air Force? Why did he not agree to the offer of money to the Indians in lieu of the aircraft? Why did he insist on handing over the aircraft to the Indians, against every possible interest of the country by which he was employed? Why did he go to the lengths of presenting the case at the Inter-Dominion Conference and obtaining a sanction which could not be reversed? This action does not conform to the normal definition of representation let alone loyalty.

Then again why did those at the helm of affairs, at those lofty heights, permit this obviously injurious action to be completed? This does not match up to the standards of patriotism. Patriotism demands strong, firm and resolute decisions; it demands moral fibre which enables one to stand up against the enemy and his machinations: it demands personal sacrifice. The leaders yielded to a so-called moral aspect of the affair while the Indian Government firmly and successfully resisted it. In the system which still prevails there is nothing more moral than the security of one's country and its people. The Indians assured it by withholding our equipment and taking their share. On the other hand our people were exposed to the onslaught of weapons released by their own Government.

The expansion of Pakistan Air Force continued in these agonising conditions. I completely disregarded our first Air Commander's directive concerning the number of pilots and airmen to be recruited and trained. I refused to purchase the fifty Spitfires. He succeeded in having the thirty seven Tempests released to India. It is possible that by doing so he thought we might find ourselves short of aircraft and perhaps reconsider our attitude to the purchase of the Spitfires. I went right ahead with the programme of re-equipping with the Fury and the Bristol Freighter, after the initial discussion with AVM Percy-Keene. As regards the Fury, however, I did have some anxious moments. When we made enquiries as to the availability of aircraft, we were informed that although the firm had some on the line, they were already allocated to two other countries. I conveyed our firm resolve to equip with the Fury to the representative. I said it might be well to consider that our future requirements were likely to exceed the combined needs of the other two countries. We wanted British aircraft, but it must be one of our choosing. And our choice was the Fury. We would not be satisfied with less. The firm finally agreed and gave us a date to confirm the order, failing which they would be obliged to release the aircraft, to their original clients. I was told that although the firm would experience considerable difficulty with their other clients, they would somehow manage.

I prepared a formal case for the purchase of the Fury aircraft, and handed it over to the Ministry of Defence. At an appropriate time I was informed that the file had been agreed and sent to the Ministry of Finance for financial sanction. Time went past quickly, as it does under certain conditions, especially those of great activity. Soon it seemed, but actually many weeks later, I was reminded by the manufacturers of the Fury that the order had not yet been confirmed. I contacted the Ministry of Defence, who informed me that the case was still with the Ministry of Finance. Further reminders failed to produce results. Now there were only two days left to the deadline agreed with the manufacturers. It was 29 May, 1948. The deadline was 31 May. I went to the Ministry of Defence in Karachi, from Maunipur, where the Air H.Q. had moved that month. I met A.T. Naqui who was the Joint Secretary of Defence. He told me that the file had been with the Finance Minister, Malik Ghulam Mohammad, for the past weeks.

"But why not give me his formal sanction?" I asked. "We already have provision for it in the budget."

"I honestly don't know." He said. "I personally see no reason for delay."

At my request he made contact with the Secretary of Finance. The file was still with the Finance Minister. He was told there was no possibility of having it expedited.

"You have agreed with the case and know how important it is to get these aircraft!" I said.

Naqui nodded in the affirmative.

"The Government of Pakistan has to confirm the order. I am not the Government, but you are." I said. "This order must be confirmed if we do not wish to join the ranks of the outmoded and inadequate air forces of some countries of the Middle East."

My voice rose as I proceeded. We had known each other well. Naqui realised that this was a serious matter and that I was very serious about it. I concluded by making out a message confirming the order. I placed it before him.

"Please sign this." I said.

He became serious and tense, as he watched my face, set firm and angry.

"Of course, you are quite right." He said, as he set his signature to that message. We had it transmitted to the U.K. immediately. The Government had now formally and officially confirmed the order. It could either purchase the aircraft or pay cancellation charges. The aircraft were purchased. Naqui told me later that the Finance Minister was beside himself with rage when he was informed that the order had been confirmed – without financial sanction! That was not the only occasion upon which I was made aware of Malik Ghulam Mohhamad's rage.

During this period Nawabzada Liquat Ali Khan was on a tour of the Punjab in his capacity as leader of his political party. Mr. Ghulam Mohammad wanted to visit him and asked the Air Force to make an aircraft available. When, in answer to my enquiry I was told that it was a political tour and the visit was in connection with the political party's affairs, I declined to put an air force aircraft at his disposal. I sent a message that if an aircraft were required for non-government and unofficial purposes it could be hired for Rs 1000 an hour, and that too if it were available. I do not remember whether Mr. Ghulam Mohammad took a civil aeroplane or the train, but I do know that he went in a rage. I was unwilling to depart from the procedure laid down for use of aircraft by individuals.

Some time during the period when Percy-Keene was in Pakistan, I was called to a conference of the Cabinet Secretariat. The Prime Minister was in the Chair. Mr. Ghulam Mohhamad, Sardar Abdur Rab Nishtar, Minister for Communications, Chaudhry Mohammad Ali, Secretary general, and Iskander Mirza, Defence Secretary, were present. The Prime Minister explained why I had been asked to come alone and not with Percy-Keene, and why the latter had not been consulted. The subject for discussion was the R.A.F. staging post at Maunipur. The R.A.F. was of course still staging its aircraft through Maunipur. R.A.F. personnel and equipment were located there. We had, however, started training our personnel to take over flying control and other duties from the R.A.F. We had prepared a programme for phasing them out, while we took over the entire functions of the post. This was very good training for P.A.F. personnel and kept them in touch with several types of aircraft and equipment, at that time more modern than our own. In addition it would help P.A.F. obtain some foreign exchange for its budget. The R.A.F. would be charged appropriately for maintenance.

"The proposal is that the R.A.F. be asked to withdraw from Maunipur and their aircraft should stage through Karachi airport." The Prime Minister said.

"It is proposed that maintenance should be carried out by a civilian firm. Would you please give us your opinion on the matter?"

"I would not recommend that this method be adopted. Of course, the R.A.F. staging post should be wound up, as soon as possible." I said.

"We have already started training P.A.F. personnel who are gradually taking over duties from the R.A.F. We should be able to man the whole station in due course." I explained the programme in some detail.

"Also as an air force officer I would not trust civilian personnel with my aircraft, unless they were technically fully trained. I do not believe we have such personnel in Pakistan outside the air force." I continued.

"There is some operational equipment which is peculiar to the air force and only air force personnel could effectively maintain it. I would, therefore, suggest that P.A.F. should continue to phase out the R.A.F."

"Air Commodore, this is not advice! It is prejudice!" Mr. Ghulam exploded

"I beg you pardon, Sir!" I replied. "I have been asked for my professional opinion. I have given it. It is for you to agree with it or not. But there is no prejudice in it."

"You want the whole world to be regimented." He retorted in his customary emotional exaggeration.

"No, I don't want the whole world to be regimented, just the air force." I replied, as calmly as I could manage.

"Don't you know the British have a history of getting a foothold and then expanding from there?" He continued vehemently.

"Don't you remember Surat?"

"Political analysis is not really my province." I said. "But in my view, the process has been reversed. The British are on the way out. This is the last outpost and not the first foothold. This should be wound up in due course. It is implied that the British would spread into Pakistan and re-occupy it because of their staging post. Should we allow this to happen then we do not deserve independence."

This had gone far enough. The Prime Minister and Sirdar Nishtar intervened. They managed to get the discussion back to the subject. Malik Ghulam Mohhamad was still red in the face. I elaborated the point as much as I could. The Prime Minister and others thanked me and I departed.

I have often thought about the attitude displayed at that meeting. I could not at that time attribute any motives to Ghulam Mohhamad. I took it at face value. Later I wondered whether some firm would have gained from a contract with the R.A.F., of course, assuming that the latter would agree to the proposal. There were some domestic airlines springing up in Pakistan. Maybe they would have wished to expand their activities to cover the technical handling of the R.A.F. It could be quite lucrative. But our programme was to the best advantage of the country. The money would come straight into the Ministry of Defence. Our personnel would gain valuable experience. At least one person must have regretted having sought my advice. The worst aspect was the assertion of foreign interests at our expense. The domination by the former colonial power was assured and not so slow to show itself. In the armed forces, it was greatest in the army, the relatively large size of which dictated the intensity of domination. The Commander-in-Chief, the Chief of Staff and the Deputy Chief of Staff were all non-nationals; and many more officers beside them. In the earlier days, I managed to overcome that domination in the air force. Of course, it was not possible to counter every manoeuvre. I failed in my attempt to retain the thirty seven Tempests. I resisted domination by the army. It was suggested by the British officers that the three services should have one Commander-in-Chief. The air force would then have become what was termed as, the army air force. This would have led to no particular benefit as regards men and materials. But it would have brought almost unbearable pressure on the smaller services. Had that suggestion been accepted, I believe my difficulties would have increased tenfold. However, we succeeded in keeping the air force separate in all matters which were particular to it. We were, therefore, able to continue our development in our own way. We built up a momentum which it was not possible for anyone to lessen for some considerable time. Indeed after Percy-Keene's departure it was improved.

Chapter Seven

Various and Varied Encounters

There was a spirit of sacrifice, which showed itself in many small practical ways. The officers and airmen volunteered to forego many of their privileges. One example being that whenever I went to tour the stations or to visit units of other services, I was always entertained and accommodated as a guest. Since I did not incur any expenses on my travels, I claimed no daily allowance (DA). Many officers also voluntarily gave up their D.A. claims for a considerable period. However, although it was necessary to economise wherever possible, it was vital to maintain and improve the standard of men and material. The airmen had been accustomed, for over five years, to standards, to rations and accommodation, higher than the men in the army. It was considered more than desirable to retain those standards. After a sharp, short encounter, I managed to prevent the Ministry of Finance from lowering the standards to the level of an Indian princely state.

I tried some extremely unorthodox methods to affect economy and to improve welfare facilities. An electrical appliance was required in a building at Maurpur. The Military Engineering Service (MES) gave an estimate, which to me, appeared to be very high. I asked a local electrician to submit an estimate for the same. His was only one eleventh of the M.E.S. estimate. I asked him to install the appliance. When the invoice was presented for payment, the Ministry of Finance declined to pay. It took me some strong arguments to have the invoice settled. But that was the end of an economising drive on my part as regards maintenance. I was told that all work had to be done by M.E.S. regardless of the cost, so long as the budget was not exceeded. This was a system which permitted one thousand per cent profit. Hence the budget had to be many times higher than it need have been. It was difficult, at least for me, to see it in any other light.

I officiated as Air Commander of Pakistan Air Force from May to October, 1948. Some time during this period, a gentleman, Sydney Cotton by name, operated in our part of the world, as what might be called an armaments dealer. He came to me with an unusual request. He wanted me to help him in transporting an aircraft engine to Habbaniya in Iraq, for an overhaul. Habbaniya was then an R.A.F. station and their aircraft used to stage through there, to and from the Far East. We also used their facilities for our aircraft to fly to and from the U.K. Sydney Cotton wanted me to allow him space for his engine on one of our transport planes going to Britain.

"How much would it cost you to have it flown by civil aircraft?" I asked him.

"Sixty eight thousand rupees" He replied.

"Alright, make out a cheque for this amount for P.A.F. Benevolent Fund." I said.

He noticed the firmness and finality in my tone. He made out a cheque as required. I let his engine be taken. From this money the first Maternity Ward, it would be too much to call it a hospital, was provided for P.A.F. personnel at Drigh Road. The Ministries of Finance and Defence were informed about the transaction. The former protested very strongly. They said that any such transaction must have their approval. There were again some heated exchanges between the Minister and myself. However, since there were not likely to be such windfalls again, I agreed that approval would be sought should such a contingency arise in future.

This may be an appropriate time to mention that on some matters I used to submit papers directly to the Prime Minister for his personal attention and consideration. I will refer to some of them later, but will mention one such paper as it relates to the subject I am discussing here; building up the country speedily and affecting economy in the process. I submitted a comprehensive case for the employment of the armed forces in general, and the army in particular, in the nations building projects. My argument was that the armed forces had technical personnel who were fully and best qualified in the country at the time; for laying telegraph and telephone lines, for constructing railways, roads and bridges; even for building canals; perhaps many more similar projects, could be worked or at least supervised by the armed forces personnel. Of course, the people's labour would be abundantly available to work, with the armed forces as the nucleus. This would provide excellent training for the forces personnel while assuring a rapid build-up while reducing the cost of development. Indeed, the only cost would be the unavoidable payment for the imported material and machinery. This could be a combined civil and military operation on a nationwide basis, a gigantic exercise, planned and executed by the most qualified men in the country.

This paper stayed with the Prime Minister for a very long time without response. After repeated reference to it by me, I was informed that the paper was deeply appreciated but there was no way to implement it. The paper was a futile attempt to provide some ideas for development on my part. Had my suggestion been accepted it would have turned the forces into the people's army. In such an event the so-called free enterprise, in the extremely important field of contracts, would have been stifled to a large extent. It was naïve of me to make a proposal which would hurt the profiteer, the contractor, the tenderer, the monopolist.

I was still officiating as Commander-in-Chief of P.A.F., when preparations were to be made for the first independence anniversary of Pakistan. A conference was called at the Ministry of Defence at which Major General Cawthorne, Deputy Chief of Staff, represented the army, Admiral Jefford the navy and I represented the air force. Iskander Mirza, Defence Secretary, was in the chair. It was decided that Major General Majid, General Officer Commanding the local division, would command the parade. Major General Cawthorne suggested that as the Prime Minister drove past, the troops posted along the route should shout the slogans "Pakistan Zindabad" and "Liaquat Ali Zindabad". I would like to state here that the Quaid-i-Azam was already seriously ill and was in Ziarat, therefore, the Prime Minister was to take the salute. I raised an objection to Maj. Gen. Cawthorne's proposal.

"But don't you want your services men to be patriotic?" He said irritably.

"They are great patriots. They do not have to be made patriotic." I said.

"In any event we do not want them to be more patriotic than the British troops."

Admiral Jefford and Iskander Mirza, both of whom knew me well, supported Major General Cawthorne, but not very vigorously. They asked me to elaborate on my reference to the British troops.

"The British troops, I believe, are extremely patriotic. But on parade, or duty, they do not shout 'Britain Zindabad', or 'Churchill Zindabad'" I said. "They do give three cheers to their Monarch on what is known as the Proclamation day. For occasions such as this a regulation is contained in the manuals; a detailed drill is outlined there. This is uniform practice throughout the British armed forces. If you wish you can make it a part of the manual that a particular slogan would be shouted by the troops according to a special drill. We must not have the local commander devise his own slogan or procedure. In the armed forces uniformity in such matters is of great importance. Otherwise there would be chaos."

Despite my argument they wanted to carry it through. When Major General Majid was consulted he also agreed with Cawthorne's suggestion.

"I am sorry, but the air force personnel will not shout slogans unless you incorporate them in the manual with the complete drill." I said as we rose for the day.

Of course, I was serious about it because in that system, in that type of army or air force it was necessary to conform to the regulations. We were being asked to conduct ourselves in a manner not laid down in any of our drill manuals. I wrote a short note to the Prime Minister on the matter. I emphasised the importance of adhering to a drill. I explained to him that in the armed forces the personnel, even when 'standing easy' could not do two things, they could not move their feet and they could not talk. The reasons were obvious; moving of feet would break the formation and create disorder and talking would divert attention from the task and the word of command could be misheard. I illustrated my point by relating the scene when Quaid-i-Azam went to P.A.F. School, Risalpur, on 13 April, 1948, where he inspected the P.A.F. parade and declared it to be a P.A.F. College. He then inspected an army march past on the air field. Although Wing Commander Asghar Khan, the P.A.F. Commandant, was a rigid disciplinarian himself, I had issued orders that during the parade there was to be no shouting of slogans, not even for the Quaid-i-Azam. The guests and spectators from Nowspera and other places were asked to refrain from expressing their emotions while the parade was in progress. This was strictly adhered to, except that once a few spectators in the rear tried to raise slogans. They were quickly silenced. The P.A.F. parade went off beautifully. The Quaid-i-Azam looked thoroughly satisfied and pleased at the superb turn out, the flawless and precise presentation for inspection and march past. Any parade commanded by Asghar Khan could only be superb. After the parade we proceeded to the Mess for breakfast. The people en route shouted slogans to their hearts content. The Quaid acknowledged them, and relaxed. He smiled almost all the way.

After breakfast Quaid-i-Azam drove to the nearby airstrip to inspect the army contingent and to take the salute at the march past. As we went over a low bridge we saw the troops lined up on the opposite side of the saluting base. Behind them were the spectators and the families. Major General Nazir Ahmed Commander of the troops rode with the Quaid. He took the Quaid to the far end and drove in front of the row of troops. As the car passed, the troops threw flowers at the Quaid-e-Azam and their slogans rent the sky. When I saw and heard this I felt apprehensive. This was ominous. Soldiers don't throw flowers, nor do they shout slogans, they are required to stand to attention on parade when the Head of State is present. I would rather see them show their loyalty, affection and respect by standing to attention for hours if need be and to fall from exhaustion. This was no way for the soldiers to display their emotions. The Quaid-i-Azam and Major General Nazir Ahmed returned to the saluting base. I was placed very near the dais. As Nazir Ahmed passed he winked at me and grinned from ear to ear, thoroughly pleased with the performance. Flowers had been thrown and slogans shouted, coming from the lungs and, indeed, the hearts of thousands of young soldiers in Pakistan.

The columns of mechanised and armoured units drove past and the Quaid took the salute. Soon the last vehicle went past and suddenly the parade had ended. But just as suddenly a thunder of thousands of feet – fully shod in tough army boots – burst from the far side. The roar increased as those boots made contact with the tarmac at full speed. A wall of uniformed men, followed by civilians and families, advanced towards the saluting base, in full battle cry. It was a stampede. Before the Quaid could step into his car he was mobbed by those same men who had thrown flowers at him earlier. It was impossible for him to move. Nazir Ahmed, tall as he was, six feet three inches, was completely overwhelmed. He swung his baton at those nearest him. He hurled unprintable, most expressive Punjabi abuse at his own troops. It was no use. The Quaid turned dark purple with rage.

"I thought these were the officers and men who are supposed to maintain order and control mobs! This is intolerable. They are a mob." He burst out. I stood near him as helpless as a child. I could do no more than try to put my rather small body between him and his uniformed admirers. There was some other officer who also tried to shield him. We could only wait till the ferocity of the onslaught had subsided. The car moved away and I stood back in the corner of the tent, dazed and gazing in amazement at the scene. Soon the dust raised by thousands of feet, and by the Quaid's car settled and all was quiet. The contrast between the two functions that morning was immense. One was conducted and carried out in a solemn military manner which befitted the occasion. The other, as parades go, left little to be desired but ended in chaos and disaster. In one case the manuals had been strictly adhered to. In the other they had been disregarded.

I described all this to the Prime Minister. The difference between adhering to the regulations and disregarding them was the difference between perfection and chaos. The Prime Minister agreed with me. Orders were soon issued for a universal, uniform procedure to be adopted on the parades for Independence Day and the Quaid-i-Azam's birthday. I believe it stands to this day.

Left:
Air Commodore MK Janjua

Below:
Air Commodore MK Janjua (left) greeting
Quaid-I-Azam Mohamed Ali Jinnah and his sister
Fatima Jinnah. Also present is Air Vice Marshall
Richard Atcherley (second from left)
of the British Air Force.

Above Left to Right: Air Commodore MK Janjua, Arjant Singh (later to be the Commander in Chief of the Indian Air Force, and the Nawab of Bhobal, Hafiz Muhammad Hamidullah Khan.

Below: Air Commodore MK Janjua with his wife and children in Lahore, Mrs Tahirah Janjua, daughter Shahidah (centre), son Ali (front left) and daughter Rukhsana (front right).

But here was an interesting point. Some were trying to be more loyal than the king. Pakistanis were being told how to be patriotic by non-nationals. I am also reminded of another peculiar trick being played on some of my countrymen. General Gracey had trained his dog to make no attempt to snatch a biscuit from his master's hand until he uttered the magic word – 'Pakistan'. This type of attitude made me feel disgusted and angry. It was being considered that we would react to these in the same manner as the African Chiefs of the nineteenth and early twentieth centuries reacted to the white man's alarm clock or colourful beads.

It was probably in the third quarter of 1948, when I was asked to a select gathering at A.T.Nagir's residence. Also present were Iskander Mirza, Major General N.A.M. Raza, the Adjutant general of the Army, and Commodore H.M.S. Chaudhry, later C-in-C Pakistan navy. The occasion was to meet and listen to the poetic work of Hafeez Jullundari, one of the most celebrated poets of the Indo-Pakistan sub-continent. He was the author of Shahnama-e-Islam, which I had read with profound emotion a few years earlier. He had put the words to the music of our National Anthem. The words were glorious, celebrating the glory of Pakistan. But like the words of most of our poets, they are beyond the comprehension of the vast majority of our people. Traditionally our poets use language which is beautiful, profound and mostly rich in its use of a mix of Urdu, Pharsee and Arabic words. This had enormous appeal to the minority of intellectuals. The masses find it beyond them. Iqbal, the poet for the masses, is not of the masses. The most revolutionary of all his words do not penetrate the understanding of the rural millions.

Hafeez Jullundari had been attached to the Adjutant General's secretariat in the Public Relations branch. As we sat sipping light beverages, we discussed poetry in general and its application to the occasion in particular. Hafeez had recently addressed the Cadets at the Pakistan Military Academy. He told us that for a long time he had been at a loss to find an Urdu word for Cadet.

"Then I had a revelation. The word came to me suddenly." He said with obvious delight at the discovery of the century. He was ecstatic. "It was Qayadat" – leadership!

He was duly applauded. He acknowledged it in the manner befitting a great poet! He then proceeded to recite a poem which he had addressed to the cadets. It was, indeed, a superb poem. Charged with emotion it held our attention and greatly moved the more emotional among us. This was his address to the 'Qayadat'. It was, indeed, most moving and we expressed our admiration. I had to admit to myself that it was a masterpiece. But I was not at all happy that the young men should be subjected to such high emotion on a parade ground. This type of verse should be recited to the troops at the battlefront. It built up such immensely acute emotion that it should be followed by an immediate order to fix bayonets and charge the enemy. In the parade ground there is no enemy to be attacked. But the tension has to find release.

"You know" said Hafeez, "Some of the 'Qayadat' broke down and cried."

I was not surprised to hear it. Although it is not a pretty sight to see young men in uniform crying, yet that was perhaps the most harmless way of tension being released. It could lead to indiscipline. Young men cannot be subjected to emotion of this nature without having a release for the unbearable tension. Hafeez continued to relate the effect.

"The Commandant told me," he said, "that I had achieved in a few minutes what the Academy had not done in two years."

"That is precisely what is wrong with it." I remarked.

I had become accustomed to the stares and gasps which I witnessed around me. I elaborated.

"There is a process of training and preparing men for battle. It can be shortened. But years cannot be contracted into minutes; into months, maybe weeks, but not minutes or days."

Due to the regard and esteem in which Hafeez was held further discussion on the subject was avoided. However, I asked Naqvi and Iskander Mirza as to what the object of the whole exercise was. They told me that the Adjutant General had asked for Hafeez to be employed as a Public Relations advisor. He was now on a 'morale' raising tour of the army units. Of course, there was no doubt about the high calibre of Hafeez's poetry, specialised as it was. But was there really need for morale boosting in the early days of Pakistan? I told them that I had some views on the matter and if they had no objection I would write to the Prime Minister. They did not disagree. I wrote a comprehensive note to the Prime Minister, discussing in greater detail some of the points I have already mentioned. In my view the morale of our troops was already very high. It needed no boosting. It was especially undesirable to repeatedly work up very tender emotions in the manner described. We did not wish our fighting men to weep through emotion, it could even be dangerous. How about those who were tormented by unbearable emotional stress but did not shed tears? How would they react to repeated recitals of highly charged poems? No one could say exactly, but they would suffer from frustration. They could become unnecessarily and unduly aggressive.

I suggested that normal training and preparation methods should be employed. They were volumes upon volumes of military books intended for this purpose. While the system remained what it was, there should be no departure from them. The types of poems recited were no doubt extremely valuable, but only as the last bit of preparation, prior to hand-to-hand fighting. That is the time when emotions should be at the highest pitch. Hafeez's poetry produced precisely such emotions but the young men and the soldiers addressed by him had no enemy in sight to attack and destroy. The actual and possible consequences have already been mentioned. After a few days, when I was at the Ministry of Defence, Iskander Mirza and Naqui told me that the Prime Minister had asked them to inform me that he agreed completely with my views. However, it would not be advisable to either show my paper to the army as it would upset them, or to immediately abolish the post held by Hafeez. At some opportune moment the latter would be done. I conveyed to the Prime Minister that I did not mean for Hafeez's post to be abolished, but only that the temperature of his type of Public Relations should be drastically lowered. I believe this was done in due course.

Some time in the latter part of 1948 I was on my way to Karachi from Peshawar. I landed at Chaklala to pick up General Sir Douglas Gracey. We had to attend a conference together at the Ministry of Defence. As I alighted from the aircraft, I saw General Gracey pacing up and down the tarmac. He was unusually agitated. Major General Nazir Ali Khan had come to see him off. I went up to General Gracey, as courtesy demanded, saluted and asked him to board the aircraft as soon as he was ready.

"It's a retrograde step!" He said, as if addressing no one in particular; just the world at large. "It's a retrograde step." He repeated.

"What is this retrograde step, Sir Douglas?" I asked.

"The Prime Minister asks to tighten our security." He went on vehemently.

"And yet he is going to invite spies into the country. How can we maintain security that way?"

I had no idea about the subject under reference, so I asked him to enlighten me on it.

"The Prime Minister has decided to exchange diplomatic relations with Russia." He said. "They will have a network of military espionage. Our security will be in jeopardy."

I was surprised by this observation, and attitude. I could not conceal my surprise and agitation. It was being suggested by a very influential non-national that Pakistan, an independent nation of over one hundred million people, the largest Islamic nation in the world, should not be free to pursue her own foreign policy.

"Have you an embassy in Moscow?" I asked abruptly.

He looked at me sharply, with an exclamation mark written right across his face.

"Yes." He said

"Do the Russians have an embassy in London?" I asked

"Yes." He said, a little thoughtfully.

"Similarly, I believe there are American, Canadian, French and other Western embassies in Moscow and Russian embassies in Western Capitals." I said, and he listened seriously. "If Russia is secure with all these hostile embassies located in Moscow; if the security of all these countries is not jeopardised by the presence of Russian embassies, then surely the security of our country cannot be in peril. Exchange of Ambassadors between two countries merely means that they recognise each other and would like to maintain friendly or diplomatic relations."

General Gracey remained silent but glum as I spoke.

"Pakistan and Russia are not more hostile, as countries, than Britain, and above all America and Russia." I continued, "I think, Sir Douglas that this is a matter for the Government of Pakistan to decide. Should they believe that their relations are cordial and the future relationship would be to the benefit of the country, then they must naturally exchange ambassadors."

General Gracey had already started walking towards the aircraft. There was silence for some time then we talked about other matters. I remember quite clearly, that on the same aircraft there was a gentleman by the name of Teddy Miles. I had been requested by Military Finance to take him on board. He had gone direct to a high official in that department with an almost fantastic proposal concerning the purchase of a number of Howard, advanced training aircraft. In my view the price was ridiculously low. There was the virtually impossible task of flying them out of India, or, indeed, to have them brought out in any other way. However, Miles seems to have impressed the officials concerned with the low price and his ability to deliver the aircraft. For this enterprise he needed some money in advance to grease several palms! My opinion was sought very briefly; their minds were already made up. We did need the aircraft. When I learnt that the deal had been accepted, I shrugged my shoulders and told an official of the Ministry of Finance;

"I suggest you do not give any advance. Payment on delivery only."

I do not know whether any or how much money was given to Miles. I do know that no Howard aircraft were delivered to us from that source. Some days, maybe weeks later, we read in a local English daily a notice concerning the death by violence, in a café near New Delhi, of Edward Miles. That chapter was closed.

Teddy Miles had been known to me about seventeen years earlier. We were in the Grammar School in Quetta together for one or two years. I recollect that he had extravagant habits. I had not seen him since he left Quetta in 1931 or 32. Now in the aircraft he sat near me on the floor in the aisle. He talked almost the whole way to Karachi. It was a continuous drone. After we alighted at Manipur, Teddy Miles said goodbye to me. I never saw him again. But General Gracey came to me.

"My God! That fellow can talk!" He said. "What a monotonous voice."

General Gracey and I talked on several matters but never again on our foreign policy. The fact, however, is that there was no immediate exchange of ambassadors between Pakistan and Russia. The Prime Minister was invited to visit Russia. One day, in 1949, as I drove with Air Vice Marshal Atcherley from Mauripur to Karachi he spoke to me about the projected visit of the Prime Minister to Moscow.

"The Prime Minister would like to take some senior armed forces officers. I have told him that you should accompany him." Said AVM Atcherley.

I asked him about the date of the visit.

"We don't know that yet." He said.

"I would like you to go with the Prime Minister because you are the sort of person who can see through and behind things."

I found it difficult to acknowledge that compliment. I thanked him with a nod and a smile.

The Prime Minister, however, did not visit Russia. Instead he went to America in 1950. By that time several walls had been erected between us. I was unable to discuss the subject with the Prime Minister and know the reasons or influences which led him to completely ignore an invitation from one country, while accepting with alacrity another issued months later. The brief encounter with General Gracey gave a clear indication that the British were unhappy about the prospect of Russian-Pakistan diplomatic relations. It is fair to assume that our policy was being influenced by external forces.

In 1968, Professor Golam Wahed Chaudhry, Professor of Political Science at the University of Dacca, wrote his book 'Pakistan's relations with India 1947/1966'. There is a wealth of information in this book on most if not all the matters of which I had personal experience and about which I am now writing. He has quoted scores of statements made by our political leaders on the exceptionally delicate and emotional subjects such as Junagadh and Kashmir; the Indian intransigence; the futility of placing cases before the Security Council and the United Nations. Syed Nur Ahmed's book 'From Martial Law to Martial Law', also contains detailed information on these matters. He refers to some of the incidents I have touched upon and has quoted similar statements.

Yes, it was all statements and no action! The helplessness, the utter lack of courage, the humiliating subservience, nay cowardice, of our policy makers, is summed up by Professor Chaudhury in the following words:

"Moreover, Pakistan's Western allies had, by 1960 become sensitive to India's objections. The growing rift between China and India led them to support a policy of boosting India in Asia, even if it meant disregarding her continued defiance of international commitments, and even if it was vigorously opposed by their 'ally' Pakistan. The object of the wrath of the Soviet Union, Pakistan now had to suffer coolness from her allies. Such is the plight of a smaller country in power politics."

It is difficult to think of a more humiliating commentary on the leadership of a country. Pakistan, with a population of over one hundred million stalwart people, a small country!

Our leadership never tired of proclaiming Pakistan as the fifth largest State and, indeed, the largest Islamic State, in the world. Many countries with no such claims and populations of only a few million, or even hundreds of thousands, have successfully maintained their independence. They have cocked a snook at the so-called big powers and run their affairs to the best advantage of their people.

Professor Choudhury is quite right in placing the word 'ally' in parenthesis. We have to be exceedingly naïve to believe that any imperial power would be our ally and protector because of affection or some overflowing of the milk of human kindness. Imperialism is only there to exploit. If it finds it can exploit larger numbers it will literally ditch the lesser numbers. The most faithful allies, for instance the Nizam, have been abandoned in times of the greatest need and crisis. We may be their ally. They were not, and cannot be, our allies. We were expected to fight their battles, not they ours. The British had always said that in the event of a conflict between India and Pakistan, the British personnel would be withdrawn. They knew and we knew, that the only possible clash in which we would be at a disadvantage in men and materials, could with India. And yet that was the only country against which we could not expect British personnel to be with us. Of course, we did not need them. We, the people, were capable of fighting our own battles. But our leadership always succumbed to their threats of withdrawal. Had we the courage to call their bluff we would have had them eating out of our hands. They were as much in need of our market to sell their goods as we were of their goods for our development. They would never have taken a risk to lose a market of a hundred million people. The leadership, which had caused the loss of millions of lives and hundreds and thousands of square miles of territory, could not be expected to resist those imperialist pressures. The leadership which left the country and the people so weak and demoralised that 'Beggars can't be choosers,' became our national phrase. This was the depth of degradation to which the utterly dependent foreign policy led us. The seeds of this subservient posture were inherent in the weak-kneed policies devised during the final phases of the struggle for Pakistan. When we accepted a truncated Pakistan, we invited foreign domination. The latter got a grip on us the day we came into being and has never loosened since. It was not possible to agree with it then. It is not possible to agree with it today. It is not ever possible to agree with it. No self-respecting people can ever submit to domination. It is the self-seeking leadership which accepts domination from abroad. In turn it imposes domination on the people by implied and actual force through the police and the army. The only way this kind of domination can come to an end is by the people and the army, when the leaders cease to protect vested interests and instead protect the interests of the people against domestic and foreign domination and exploitation. Until that day comes the people of Pakistan will continue to suffer the terrible consequences of the weak and subservient policies of their successive Governments.

Air Commodore MK Janjua

Chapter Eight

Kashmir

I have been unable to find words more suitable for a caption concerning the subject of Kashmir. There are no superlatives which would make for a short heading for this chapter. There are too many factors involved; all equally important, equally tragic, equally emotional.

Apart from its earlier history, during which the people of Kashmir had known domination, the British sold the State to Raja Gulab Singh in 1846, under the treaty of Amritsar. It was not the land alone, beautiful as it is, which the British exchanged for about seven million rupees. In fact the people of Kashmir and other hill states were sold. Land alone is of no value whatsoever unless people inhabit it and work on it to extract the wealth contained therein. The people of Kashmir were thus sold into bondage. The tyranny and oppression of the previous ages pales into insignificance when compared with that which the Muslim people of Kashmir suffered at the hands of the autocratic Dogra ruler.

The rule of Gulab Singh commenced with the most barbaric form of punishment for resistance on the part of the Muslims of Poonch. When the British sold Kashmir to him, in the larger and higher interests of imperialism, the proud Sudhans of Poonch rose against the mass slave transaction. Even in those early days his troops were routed by the people of Poonch. However, the latter were ultimately overwhelmed. Gulab Singh then ordered four Sudhan elders to be flayed alive, had their skins stuffed with straw and displayed the gruesome figures on public thoroughfares. This was intended to be a lesson to his subjects as well as to his offspring. The former were given a taste of the fruits of liberation struggle, and told to submit, and the latter were shown the method of obtaining and retaining submission of their subjects. How well that lesson was learnt and practiced by the succeeding generations of Gulab Singh! No other princely rulers in the sub-continent perpetrated greater tyranny on their subjects than the rulers of Kashmir. This continued unabated for a hundred years.

Such is the way of imperialism. It extracts the last drop of blood from the people. This it does for as long as it is able. It does not only exploit them directly, but if it finds indirect exploitation more convenient, though no less profitable, then it literally sells millions of people into further bondage; the chains and shackles are even tighter. Imperialism cuts the people to the bone. The exploiters live on their flesh. The sale of the people of Kashmir to a ruler, who had every possible reason to inflict untold misery and oppression on them, was one such act on the part of British imperialism in the mid-nineteenth century. The tyranny, treachery and bestiality of the first purchaser of the State of Kashmir and his offspring, remain unequalled. The expansionist rulers of India knew this in 1947; they must know it today. Yet they were and remain party to the perpetration of oppression.

Much has been written, especially by the Indians on the problem of Kashmir, its causes and effects. Some Pakistani writers and historians have also written on this most vexed problem. It makes a long tale of betrayal, treachery, defiance of international law and opinion, abandonment of commitments and forcible occupation on the one hand and weakness, cowardice, deception of the people and absence of resolute action on the other. The former applies to the expansionist Indian Governments and the latter to the successive Pakistani Governments. The third and main party, the oppressed people of Kashmir, continue to suffer from a combination of the foregoing attitudes. They suffer even more due to the utterly erroneous analysis of the situation by their leadership in the early days, their futile faith in the United Nations and the so-called Security Council and their inability so far to wage an armed struggle to achieve the independence which they have been promised yet denied by all parties.

Regardless of the Indian Government's proclamations of Kashmir being an integral part of Bharat and its argument against the two nation theory, India remains an alien occupying power in Kashmir. The Government of Bharat knows this and the world should know it. All Hindu majority states and territories, whether they acceded to Pakistan or were Portuguese or French, or independent, were forcibly annexed and occupied by India. Junagadh, Manarvada, Mongarol, Nizam's Hyderabad and Portuguese Goa, to name the more prominent, were captured by armed force for no reason other than that the populations comprised an overwhelming Hindu majority, while the rulers were non-Hindu. However the same argument was not applied in respect of the people and territory of Kashmir, apart from the fact that the Kashmiri Muslim leadership and Pakistan Government bungled, betrayed and deceived the people. The Bharati rulers deliberately set out to occupy Kashmir in order to colonise it and in due course to reduce the Muslim majority to a minority. They have broken every promise and pledge they made to the people of Kashmir and the United Nations. Today, in violation of all those pledges, in defiance of the international organisation and world opinion, the Bharati Government continues the process of colonisation. It has moved step by step away from the position of plebiscite, until it now refuses to even discuss the matter of Kashmir. The so-called world powers and the United Nations maintain complete silence on the subject. They want the world to forget it. They are, therefore, complicit in the conspiracy which is slowly but surely converting the Muslims of Kashmir into a minority. What is happening in Kashmir is in fact a form of genocide; forcible armed occupation; unlimited and unhindered immigration which is designed to, and must ultimately, overwhelm the indigenous population until the latter loses its identity. The pressures became too strong to be resisted. This process is not unknown in the history of mankind. Another process in comparatively recent times overthrew such attempts, be they subtle, surreptitious or positively oppressive. This is the process of the people's revolution; the struggle for their own freedom. This is what the people of Kashmir will have to resort to for their emancipation. They cannot and must not allow themselves to be overwhelmed and dominated. They waged a limited armed struggle against their oppressive ruler in the third quarter of 1947. It was successful. I and a large number of persons in the armed forces, and the entire people of Pakistan considered the Kashmir people's armed uprising to be a revolutionary struggle. Everyone helped to the best of his ability. But the Pakistan Government fumbled and dithered. It was indecisive. It lacked courage. It submitted to foreign pressures including those of its own foreign employees. Later they allowed the Indian design of occupying Kashmir to succeed. The people of Pakistan looked on helplessly and the efforts of people like me, met with limited success. Now a generation later, the participants in that struggle will not find it possible to participate physically in the forthcoming revolution. There are however, far larger numbers now, with similar views. The people of Pakistan are more organised, more settled and better informed. They will undoubtedly fully support a people's revolution in Kashmir. The revolutionary people all over the world will likewise support the people of Kashmir. The Government of Pakistan, whichever it may be, will have to yield to pressure of its own people to recognise the Kashmiri people's revolution. Only in this way will the occupation, completely contrary to all the undertakings and without any moral basis, come to an end. The struggle which began twenty three years earlier, which was interrupted in the manner I have described, will be resumed. The story of treachery, betrayal and cowardice, will be uncovered and related. In the meantime, let me relate that part of the struggle which is known to me.

The Indian Government begins the sordid story of its reason for the immoral occupation of Kashmir with the so-called tribal invasion towards the end of October 1947. It cannot advance any reason in its favour prior to that period. Indeed, everything before then exposes the Indian Government's deliberate and well planned programme of annexation of as much territory as possible, in the wake of British withdrawal from the sub-continent. It succeeded in acquiring a major part of the Punjab, Assam and Bengal. It followed this up by occupying the states that had acceded to Pakistan. The most brutal massacre in East Punjab, together with one of the most perverse awards in history, cleared the decks for aggression in Jammu and Kashmir. The successes and experiences of the organised killings in East Punjab and the methods employed were extended to Jammu. In a matter of days Jammu was cleared of Muslims. About a quarter of a million Muslims just vanished without trace; massacred, abducted, converted. Others were driven across the Border into West Pakistan. These appalling acts were committed by a combination of Dogra troops, Sikhs of the type of General Mohan Singh and above all the Rashtrya Swayam Sevak Sangh (RSSS). The last of these, which would put the worst kind of fascism in the shade, had played a most active role in the killings in northern India from the second half of 1947.

Passionately dedicated to the conception of Akhand Bharat (pre-partition undivided India) and Maha Bharat (mother India), greater India, R.S.S.S. believes in reviving the glory of Bharat and advocates the extension of her borders far beyond those established for India by the British. This, of course, is ludicrous as a conception. According to a map contained in a booklet entitled "Aggressive Hinduism", which was published in 1947, the greater Bharat envelops Afghanistan in the West and the whole of South East Asia in the east. It does not stop there as it also bites into some parts of China. Apart from myth, which may prevail among the adherents of the R.S.S.S. cult, there is no historical evidence to support such a fantastic claim. Indeed, the sub-continent of India found unity, if it can be thus referred to, under the British. In ancient history the borders of India altered with successive dynasties, in most periods there were well within the boundaries as established by the British; at other times they extended beyond these boundaries but not in all directions. Never was greater territory held by any dynasty, Hindu or Muslim, than the British. Never did the ancient empire of India go beyond Afghanistan in the West. When this occurred the extension to the East did not reach the British Indian borders. Never did they approach or penetrate the borders of China and several South East Asian countries. But the advocates of Maha Bharat have these fantastic notions of their past glories. Their most passionate advocates are those who are prepared to use force and brutality of every type, these being the R.S.S.S. However, if this absurd idea of turning the clock back were to be considered seriously then these Herrenvolk, the Aryans, would have to turn about, file through the narrow mountain passes in the North West and vanish into the steppes in Central Asia, leaving the land to the Dravidians, from whom they had taken it and whom they had driven South. Need this ridiculous notion of theirs be taken further? The world; the people, are moving forward. The people of the world are now on the verge of pulling down all barriers erected between them by the savage exploiting classes. They are on the threshold of their final victory. The R.S.S.S. cannot reverse this process any more than Hitler's S.S. could. But they are capable of inflicting indescribable cruelties and brutalities as were the Swastika bearing, goose-stepping Nazi Storm Troopers.

Such were the forces aligned and arrayed against the Muslim people of Jammu and Kashmir. After the extermination of Muslims in Jammu the marauding parties moved further to help the Dogra troops in their brutal suppression of the people of Poonch. Here they met a different calibre of people. The people of Poonch were better prepared. They had a large number of serving and former soldiers of the British Indian Army. They had already commenced a rebellion against the Dogra ruler whose state troops had been ordered to exterminate Muslims in areas now comprising Azad Kashmir (Free Kashmir). The Dogra troops made a start by burning Muslim villages; forcing people to leave the territory, looting and murdering; committing atrocities similar to those practiced in other parts of northern India. By creating terror they planned for the total expulsion of the Muslim population into the adjoining areas of West Pakistan.

Another ruse used by the Dogra troops was that they discarded their uniforms, donned civilian clothes and used public transport and camouflaged their own, and mixed with the trained mass murderers. This was considered necessary because as Dogra troops they would have been expected to maintain law and order, and not destroy it.

The Muslim people of Poonch and Mirpur had blood ties with the people of Jhelum, Rawalpindi and other adjacent districts of Pakistan. While the women, children and old men could always find refuge with their kinsmen in these districts, the men from the Punjab voluntarily went to the aid of their brethren in Poonch and Mirpur. They went to the rescue of the revolutionary Muslim people, who had taken up arms against a ruler whose oppressive methods had reached a climax in those crucial and cruel months of 1947. The phase of mere show of force to exact unbearable levies had passed. The Dogra ruler resorted to the use of armed force to compel his subjects to leave their homeland, or to completely submit. The people resisted this with all the means at their command. This was a genuine struggle by the people of Poonch and Mirpur to liberate themselves from the yoke that had hung around their necks for a hundred years. Their kinsmen joined them. While the former were by able to resist the onslaught of the Dogra troops, their brothers from across the border helped to rout them. This was the beginning of a struggle that has not yet ended; which has been betrayed by every successive government of Pakistan, by the successive governments of Bharat, by the so-called big powers and above all by the highest international organisation – the United Nations. The shamefully weak and subservient Pakistani regimes, the greedy expansionist, neo-colonial and Bharati regimes; the great powers playing power politics, entirely interested in their sphere of influence and winning a market of five hundred million people; the United Nations – the handmaid of the great powers, all combined to limit the freedom struggle of the Muslims of Kashmir and deny them the right to decide their own future.

When the fight for freedom was waged by the people of Kashmir in 1947, it was considered to be a people's revolution against their oppressor by most of us. Despite the pressure of merciless events, I responded to their call in the earliest days of their revolution. In the beginning I played a very small part in it; this was confined to helping as many young men as possible to go to the front. My younger brother Aslam, eighteen years old, went to an area east of Mirpur. He had even younger boys with him. They witnessed some harrowing events, which kept them awake many a night for some considerable time thereafter. They used to wake up in a cold sweat from their uneasy slumber. Thousands of older volunteers helped to push back the Dogra troops.

It soon became evident that a far greater effort was needed if the people of Kashmir were to succeed in ridding themselves of the century old tyranny. Partly due to my extreme pre-occupation in matters which I have already mentioned, I had not been able to locate the central organisation which I believed existed, to render all possible aid to the Kashmiri Muslims. There was no shortage of men and material. There must be some co-ordinating body somewhere, I used to ponder occasionally. I thought about this during breaks in my normal work, at the Air Headquarters in Peshawar. During one of these brief interludes, in September 1947, a visitor was announced to me. I leapt to my feet when I saw him. He was Major Khurshid Anwar, with whom I had had the pleasure of working in New Delhi. What we were able to do there was too little too late. Now we embraced each other with great warmth, which is experienced by any two people whose hearts beat in unison, on whatever matter it may be.

As we sipped tea, we reminisced; going over the events and experiences of what had been happening only three months earlier. Those were anxious, harrowing, frustrating days. Current events were no less excruciating. The wounds from East Punjab and Jammu were still bleeding profusely. The fury had abated somewhat in the Punjab, but only because the ferocity had spent itself, the lust for blood had been satiated; the Muslim masses who escaped the carnage had left the nightmare land to move westward to safer areas of West Pakistan. Similarly Muslims from West Bengal and Bihar had moved into East Pakistan, after having suffered grievously in every respect. We discussed these matters. Then Major Khurshid Anwar came to the subject for which he had made his way to Peshawar to see me. Normally a bold, frank man, I found him fumbling for words. He looked apprehensive. I had to ask him to speak freely as we had known each other very well, even though not very long.

"Things seem to have changed somewhat." He said. "I have had a terrible experience and I could not bear a repetition of it."

"Things may have changed," I said, "but unless you tell me I cannot say how right or wrong you may be. Unless you tell me about it, I cannot tell you whether your experience may be repeated. So I think you should take the risk and tell me." I concluded in a lighter manner.

"I visited Nowshera the other day, and called on Brigadier Iftikhar Khan." He said. "I asked him to render whatever help he could, in material, for the volunteers in Kashmir."

"So there is, after all, some co-ordinating body." I interrupted. I apologised and asked him to proceed.

"Brigadier Iftikhar Khan responded in a manner so ferocious that it took me aback and made me sad and angry." He continued. "He told me that unless I cleared out of the Cantonment within an hour he would have me locked up in the guard room." He was red in the face with his knuckles showing white as he clasped his fingers round the arm of the chair.

I was no less astonished.

"But did he not even ask you to explain?" I asked.

"No." He replied. "He said that he had his instructions from the Commander-in-Chief and that he would report the matter to General Gracey."

"Now you can tell me who deputed you to undertake the mission?" I asked. "Have you reported this matter to anyone? After all it must have been assumed that help from the army would be forthcoming."

"Yes, it had been assumed that out army officers, who had material at their disposal, would render help." He said. "The chain of our command we can discuss later, but I am in close contact with the Chief Minister, Khan Qayyum Khan."

On my insistence he briefly outlined the so-called organisation which was in the process of being put together. I knew some of those who had volunteered to organise the resistance movement against the Dogra ruler; to train, equip and lead the volunteers. I knew I.N.A. General Zaman Kiani best of all and then Habibur Rahman of I.N.A. While their erstwhile colleagues General Mahan Singh, Colonel Dhillon and others had organised atrocities on a monumental scale, Zaman and his other colleagues on our side of the border, organised men to minimise the effect and scope of those atrocities. Later they hoped to help the people of Kashmir to liberate themselves from their century old serfdom.

I told Major Khurshid Anwar that I felt very strongly about the oppression and brutality perpetrated by the Dogra troops on the Muslim people of Jammu and Kashmir. The feeling was strong because of what both he and I had witnessed a few weeks earlier. I further told him that I would help with all within my power and capability. I asked him to arrange a meeting with the Chief Minister and others, who may be concerned, so that we could discuss matters in detail. The meeting was soon arranged. Khan Qayyum Khan himself attended. He was accompanied by his Personal Secretary, Ghulam Ishaq and Khushdil Khan, an Inspector of the Frontier Province police and, of course, Major Khurshid Anwar. We lost no time in getting down to details

I understood that volunteers were available in hundreds of thousands. The territory stretched from Kathira in the East to Kohola in the West. But the volunteers were scattered throughout the Punjab and the Frontier Province, and there were volunteers from the tribal areas in the North West. There was no problem in training them; most of them were fighters by tradition. Small arms were also available, but larger amounts of supplies would produce greater numbers. The main difficulty was transport and the means of maintaining the supplies of all types of stores and equipment. Even if public transport were commandeered, the problem of petrol, oil and maintenance would remain. Indeed, Qayyum Khan announced that he would commandeer all public transport if the other prerequisites could be assured.

I quickly assessed the situation. The army had refused to lend support in the provision of stores, equipment, petrol, oil and maintenance. Therefore, it could be definitely concluded that weapons and ammunition would not be forthcoming from that quarter. Of course, some officers would undoubtedly use their initiative and render whatever help they could from their local resources. But with obvious and definite opposition from the top there would be vigilance. An operation of this nature carried out in a clandestine manner would be inadequate, regardless of the vast supplies available to the army as a whole. The main items required were petrol and oil. The air force had an abundance of these. I had no problem in respect of my British Commander-in-Chief. I hardly ever consulted him in matters of national importance. He was a figurehead and could remain so. If I did not inform him, hardly anyone would. Even if he were to be informed he could not plug the holes, which were available to me. Above all, I had complete confidence in the officers, and airmen who would be required to handle these delicate matters. In any event, having been apprised of the attitude of the British Commander-in-Chief of Pakistan Army, I could not have placed any faith in my own British Superior. I had had more than an inkling of his trend of mind. The last thing I could expect from him was enthusiasm for a revolution by our people. I therefore decided, to place at the disposal of the volunteers, whatever was possible without impairing the expansion programme and efficiency of the air force.

Everyone at the meeting was delighted with this offer. I found it necessary to explain that I was doing no favour to them and that I would be glad if they did not consider it as such. I deemed it my duty, and it was my greatest desire, to help the people of Kashmir in their revolution against the tyrannical oppressor. Indeed, it was a sacred duty. There is nothing more precious than the liberty of a people; nothing would gladden my heart more than to be of some service to such a cause. I then told them that I would arrange for petrol and oil to be made available to them in the quantities they required. Major Khurshid Anwar and Khushdil Khan were to maintain contact with the officers, whom I was to depute for the task. Khushdil Khan proved to be perhaps the most energetic and resourceful of all, in the matter of securing and organising supplies; for arranging transportation of the volunteers from all corners of the Frontier Province and the North West tribal areas. I deputed Wing Commander Rashid Malik and Mushtaq Ahmad to maintain close liaison with various bodies of volunteers, in order to provide supplies of petrol and oil. I immediately took Wing Commander M. Asghar Khan and M. Nur Khan into my confidence.

As an immediate step I instructed that one petrol wagon, standing on the railway siding in Peshawar Cantonment, be detached and handed over to the Chief Minister's nominee and that adequate amounts of oil be supplied also. However, when I began to study the situation more closely, I made adjustments in and additions to the original requests made to me. In order to ensure that all public transport was used entirely to transport personnel, I ordered a petrol bowser (fuel dispenser) to accompany the envoy when it was ready to move. This would provide a mobile petrol station and also save space on other transport for men and equipment. I also ordered wireless vehicles to be placed with the convoys in order to maintain regular communications between the latter and their headquarters. In addition to reporting progress it would also ensure speedy relief in the event of accidents or breakdowns.

While we proceeded with these arrangements in Peshawar, a more centralised administration appeared in Rawalpindi. I was asked to visit Rawalpindi where I met the Commissioner Khwaja Abdur Rahim. We had worked together in New Delhi, where he pondered over the large-scale maps of the areas of the Punjab and Bengal and Assam, marking out, with the help of a host of young men, those areas which according to his information and findings, were definitely Muslim majority areas. Those were, alas, Loves labours Lost! I had met Major Khurshid Ahmad through Khwaja Abdur Rahim. We were no strangers to each other. We rapidly got down to brass tacks. He explained that the entire administration of the volunteers was to be carried out at his house which was the headquarters for this particular operation. He gave me as much information as was available about the several 'fronts'. The most prominent among these were Gujrat and Rawalpindi. Zaman Kiani was in charge of the former; the latter, for operational purposes, was under Major Khurshid Anwar, while the administration rested with Khwaja Rahim. In support were Sardar Shaukat Hayat and Khan Abdul Qayyum Khan respectively. This was roughly the picture given to me about our own side at our first meeting. But a soldier must have information about the enemy before all else. I, therefore, sought out such information, which was given to me by Khwaja Rahim in as much detail as he could muster.

I found that although the people of Poonch had managed to wage an armed struggle against their oppressive ruler, the volunteers from the Punjab had come to their aid and together they had carried out a limited yet successful resistance even though the enemy had superiority in weapons. The arsenal comprised long range automatic weapons which gave support to the forward troops and pinned our men down. The enemy was able to take punitive action against many villages. I went back and ordered the collection of all Browning guns on crashed or otherwise unserviceable aircraft. These guns were designed to operate in the air by remote control. On the ground they would have to be handled directly. They would be intolerably hot and were therefore modified by having wooden grips put on them. They outranged the enemy machine guns by about 500 yards. In due course they were successfully used. I hasten to mention that although I took most of the decisions, I was constantly in contact with and consultation with Asghar Khan, Nur Khan and other officers and airmen, who were specialists in their own spheres. The modification of the machine guns, for instance, was a joint effort involving Asghar Khan, Allahdad, then a Squadron Leader and our Chief armament officer and later Air Commodore and squadron Leader Abdul Hai, and me.

Soon the meetings at Peshawar and Rawalpindi became more frequent and a large number of people began to attend them. In the Frontier Province among others, we were joined by Pir Sahib of Manki Sharif. I recollect his sincerity and his innocent almost childlike enthusiasm. During one discussion at Attock he forcefully advocated that Major Khurshid Anwar should be made the Commander-in-Chief of Pakistan Army. No doubt the latter was a colourful character and could attract a legendary status, being as resourceful and able as he was. In proper surroundings and in a genuine revolutionary situation he would have made an excellent guerrilla leader. The attributes of a Commander-in-Chief of an imperialist type of army were explained to Pir Sahib but he did not budge from his stand. Did he unconsciously and vaguely have a nebulous form of a people's army in his mind? This matter was never discussed again hence the answer to the question cannot be known.

Progressively I placed more equipment at the disposal of the newly emerging 'high command'. The Commissioner's residence in Rawalpindi began to acquire the shape of a depot, transit camp, operations room, and medical centre; indeed, it seemed to meet every conceivable need of the volunteers, assembling and moving to whichever area suited them and wherever the need was most urgent.

The news of the continuing brutal oppression brought demands for greater assistance. Pressure was being brought to bear on the government from all quarters, to allow free and unrestricted movement to and from the areas of conflict. At one of the special meetings at the Commissioner's residence I asked as to what the policy of the government was concerning the struggle of the people of Kashmir. I was told that the government could not and would not stop volunteers from going to the aid of their kith and kin; individuals could participate in the conflict in any manner they wished, but under no circumstances was the government to be implicated. Iskander Mirza confirmed to me at a later date that such indeed were the instructions of the Prime Minister. I was not at all happy about this. This showed lamentable lack of resolve. Local initiative, and that too by only those – an intermediate number – who were prepared to use it, was an utterly inadequate response to the organised campaign of suppression and above all to the call by the oppressed. It was not enough for the government to shut its eyes, so to speak, and to let volunteers organise themselves willy nilly. Already I had been informed of definite opposition, if not hostility to any involvement on the part of the government, by the British Commander-in-Chief of the Pakistan Army. Under such conditions the officers and men of the army, who wished to join the conflict would be severely handicapped. They would be constantly looking over their shoulders. And they would find three top layers in the chain of command and administration of the army peering over their shoulders; the C-in-C, the Chief of Staff and the Deputy Chief of Staff – all British officers. Then, of course, there were senior army officers who would be too eager to obey the so-called orders of their superior officers as had happened in the case of Brigadier Iftikhar Khan.

I could not agree with such an approach on a matter of vital importance to the people of Kashmir, and subsequently to Pakistan. The well prepared heavily armed, ruthless action by the Dogra Maharaja against the people of Poonch and Mirpur, was abundantly clear evidence of his intentions. A ruler who had exterminated Muslims from Jammu in a matter of days and who was now engaged in suppressing, with armed force, the Muslims of Poonch, could have no friendly feelings for Pakistan. Quite the contrary, his action was an affront to the people of Pakistan. He was slaughtering their kith and kin before their eyes and was fully occupied in trying to subjugate them or push them over the border into Pakistan. While the Hindus and Sikhs had exterminated the Muslims from East Punjab, which they deemed to be Bharati territory, the Maharaja of Kashmir obviously had plans to dominate or subjugate a vast majority of the people of Kashmir. The people of Poonch and Mirpur had risen to resist this plan. The odds against them were extremely heavy. The people of Pakistan were important to them not only because of the blood ties between them, but also because no other help was possible from any other quarter. Should they be forced to surrender or leave their land, Pakistan would have a patently hostile ruler breathing down its neck. That ruler would most certainly be allied to Bharat, otherwise the slaughter, extermination and pushing out of his Muslim subjects made no sense. This scheme had to be stopped. It could not be said with any certainty that the people of Poonch, along with the volunteers, without direct government involvement, would be able to overcome the Dogra troops. The people's revolution had commenced. But it was spontaneous and disorganised. It was a response to the Dogra atrocities. In order to sustain it the people of Kashmir first and foremost needed help in arms and other equipment. Then they needed direct support from their brethren. Without preparations for a prolonged resistance and revolutionary armed struggle, a people's movement has more chance of failure than success. In a people's struggle there are no short cuts to victory over an enemy vastly superior in weapons. It is a fight to the bitter end. For instance the revolutionary peoples cannot have aircraft, armoured vehicles or heavy artillery, during the earlier stages. The enemy has all these in large numbers. The success of a people's revolution depends on the revolutionary fervour of the participants; surprise, mobility, support of the working people in general and the rural population in particular; freedom from cumbersome organisational problems peculiar to a regular imperialist type of army. The above traits render most of the enemy compromised and ineffective. The application of correct revolutionary tactics causes these heavy weapons to become so many millstones around the enemy's neck.

The people of Kashmir had every reason to fight against their oppressors. They had every right to break the yoke of serfdom. They had the revolutionary fervour. They had the moral support of all the people of Pakistan, even though active support of a painfully minute minority. But they had, alas, half-hearted weak and inadequate support from the government of Pakistan. This inconsistency, lack of resolute action, could not allow a firm base to be established. Without a firm base a revolution was doomed to failure.

Much has been written by foreign, especially Indian, authors accusing the government of Pakistan for complicity in the rebellion against the Maharaja of Kashmir by his Muslim subjects. Much has also been written by Pakistani writers and high ranking politicians, denying the accusations. The Indian and other foreign authors made the Pakistan government feel embarrassed and guilty about its non-participation in the revolutionary struggle of an oppressed people. I say that our government had no need to feel guilty, even if it had fully participated. But it certainly had every cause to feel guilty for not rendering sufficient help to an oppressed people, when it was in a position to do so.

It would have been right and just to give all our support to a people who had taken up arms to free themselves from unbearable subjugation. Instead our government displayed weakness unequalled in modern history. The leaders, who had accepted a truncated Pakistan, were at the helm of its affairs. Having submitted to gross injustice once, they could not and did not stand up against further injustices. They had obtained seats of power for themselves. They had acquired power which they used against their own people but did not dare to use against the enemies of their people. They once again submitted to every type of pressure and blackmail. There was no resolute, definite and concrete plan to help the people of Kashmir. It was left to individual politicians like Abdul Qayyum Khan and Shaukat Hayat to organise help. They in turn were at the mercy of officers of the armed forces for supplies and arms and ammunition. It is not surprising that, despite an excellent performance by many volunteers, the revolution was only partly successful. It is not surprising that having been humiliated, the leaders of Pakistan found it necessary to deny even the meagre contribution the volunteers had made.

On the other hand, the Bharati government provided moral and physical support to the people of those territories, where Hindus were in the majority or where the Muslim leaders had acceded to Pakistan. Junagadh, Manarvada, Mongrol soon fell. Later Hyderabad and Goa were occupied by force. Although there were no popular uprisings against the rulers of these territories, the Bharati government took resolute 'police action' and annexed these areas. The rulers of Pakistan clung to their seats, indulged in mutual recriminations, internecine squabbles and deception of the people. These were the hallmarks of the early rulers of Pakistan; they have remained with the successive rulers, ever since.

Had the first government of Pakistan taken the bold step to help a people's revolution, I have no doubt that it would have been successful. The Maharaja of Kashmir would have found refuge in Delhi as the rulers of Junagadh and other states had done in Karachi. I believe that the Indian government would have done no more about Kashmir than as the Pakistani government did concerning Junagadh. The latter had acceded to Pakistan. The Maharaja of Kashmir had not acceded to India.

There are some apologists for the Pakistan government who argue that Pakistan could not have intervened militarily because the army was going through a process of re-organisation, our stores and some troops were still in India and being used in other causes. The suggestion was not that large formations should be committed. No more than two companies would have been adequate. Alternatively, full scale, whole-hearted support in arms, ammunition and other supplies to the people of Poonch, Mirpur and other districts, would have achieved the aim. Neither was done.

Secondly, what applied to us concerning re-organisation and the stores and troops being in Bharat applied equally to Bharat. But, as I have already stated, those who advanced these excuses actually committed the Pakistan army to action less than ten weeks later. The vital difference was that in this case, the Pakistan army was sent in to stem the advance of the Bharati army. The problem of Kashmir as we have known it, since October 1947, had been deliberately created. Had the Pakistan army annexed Kashmir, the people of Kashmir would have suffered the same fate as the people of Pakistan, but there would not have been this most bitter dispute between the two countries, which has since plagued their relations more than any other single factor. The problem was, therefore, deliberately created.

The Bharati government has advanced several arguments in justification of its continuing occupation of Kashmir. One such argument is that it never accepted the creation of two countries on the basis of religion. In this the most progressive elements in India supported the expansionist Bharati government. They betrayed a people's revolution. They also displayed a myopic appreciation of a situation and played into the hands of expansionists on the one side and arch schemers on the other who wanted to leave the proverbial bone of contention. They failed to see that even if Pakistan had occupied Kashmir it would have been better than the blood feud which followed Bharati occupation. They seemed to forget that all states and territories annexed by Bharat since partition, with the sole exception of Kashmir, were Hindu majority areas contiguous to or surrounded by Bharat (as was Hyderabad). There was no other reason for their annexation. The Bharati government did not permit the same rights to the people of a Muslim majority state. Of course, it was made easier for her by the Pakistan government which had failed miserably to take Kashmir under its aegis, as Bharat took Junagadh, and to hold a referendum. That was the era of contiguous majority areas going to the respective countries. While Bharat government took all such areas, the Pakistan government failed to do so and allowed five million people to be taken over.

Perhaps the most outstanding Kashmiri Muslim leader, Sheikh Abdullah, was brought out of prison to head the government of the Maharaja against whom he had waged a continuous, prolonged struggle. He forgot that he had struggled for the emancipation of the Muslim people of Kashmir. He also forgot the principle of the contiguous majority areas. It may not seem so today, but in August-September 1947, this fact was too conspicuous to be missed and should not have been missed by him. Although the weak Muslim League leadership allowed a mockery to be made of this principle, it was strictly and ruthlessly adhered to and applied by the Bharati government. Sheikh Abdullah should have had the vision to appreciate this. It was absurd on his part to assume that under Bharati rule the Muslims of Kashmir would attain freedom which he had always sought and for which he had struggled. How could he have ever believed or even imagined that there would be more freedom for Kashmiri Muslims under Bharat than under Pakistan. Of course, I believe that he should have joined his erstwhile colleagues when they rose against the Maharaja.

I sincerely believe that had he thrown his lot on the side of those who had risen, the people of Kashmir would have possibly obtained their freedom. Probably Kashmir would have been occupied by Pakistan. Once again, Sheikh Abdullah, like so many political leaders in Pakistan would, in all probability, have suffered imprisonment. He did not fare any better in Bharat. Having served his purpose, he was repeatedly imprisoned for inhumanly prolonged periods. He would probably have suffered personally in Pakistan, but I say again, that that would not have been too great a sacrifice as it would have prevented the acute bitterness between Bharat and Pakistan, consequential to the problem created by the Bharati occupation of Kashmir.

As matters were then, some of us in the Air Force and in the Army considered the possibility of a swift thrust against the fascist forces of the Maharaja, but I had a prolonged struggle in mind; I therefore arranged for all surplus equipment and stores to be given to the volunteers. About 500 pilot jackets, known as teddy bears, were given to those who may be required to go high into the mountains in the approaching winter months. These were the warmest jackets to be found anywhere. We had a large surplus stock of them in Lahore and Harbanspura. There was a large surplus of parachutes for conversion into clothes, which were handed over to the welfare bodies looking after the women and children. Several cooking ranges designed for offices and airmen's messes in the field were made available. They were exceptionally light, compact and could be taken to the front to provide hot meals. A large stock of vaccines against cholera, typhoid and smallpox were also put at the disposal of the volunteers Headquarters. Also refrigerators were given to them to store the vaccine. At least one refrigerator could be worked with kerosene oil; vaccine therefore, could be taken to the forward areas for the people who had been subjected to appalling living conditions. Villages had been ransacked by the Dogra troops. Much burning, looting and slaughter had taken place. Epidemics were not an impossibility. Most, if not all of these items, and several others, were sent to the Commissioner's house in Rawalpindi. I personally checked them. They were stored and distributed from there.

Since these items were from diverse stations, and depots, apart from me, no other single individual except perhaps Wing Commander Mushtaq Ahmed or Rashid Malik, knew the overall position. These were preparations for a prolonged struggle. There were, perhaps, even greater contributions from individual army officers, or a collection of officers and men. I can only speak for the air force and its personnel. Despite the exceedingly heavy and exacting demands of their own service; despite their personal hardships and tragedies, the personnel of Pakistan air force gave support to the people of Kashmir, which I consider to be second to none. Let others speak about what they know. I wish I knew more about them. It would give me great pleasure to record their contribution.

Akbar Khan wrote about 30 pages in a small notebook in Lahore Central Prison, on his experiences in Kashmir. I do not know whether they were published. In his 'book' one single sentence appeared about the air force. The words were to the effect that "Janjua provided equipment enough for a brigade." But men of Pakistan Ai Force did more than that. Several members of Wing Commander Asghar Khan's family had been slaughtered in Jammu. His aged father, Brigadier Rahmatullah, had been imprisoned by the Maharaja, in Srinagar. At all times he performed his duties as Commandant of P.A.F. College in a superb manner; cheerfully and with dedication. Only on one subject did I see a shadow cross his face; his father's imprisonment. He told me about this in the early days. Asghar Khan can look serious but not sad. This is the only occasion I can ever recollect that I saw him looking sad. A few weeks after we moved into Air Headquarters in Peshawar he asked me if I would find some way of having his father released. I had always been exceedingly fond of Asghar Khan and my heart went out to him. I promised to do all I could. I considered it futile to approach the Ministry of Defence or Foreign Affairs. In the earlier days we had radio-telephone communication with Air H.Q. in New Delhi. I was in contact with Air Vice Marshal Sobroto Mukerjee. Many problems of personnel had to be discussed. I decided to wait for an opportunity to speak to him. It was a delicate political matter for him to handle. Asghar Khan reminded me after several days. I had not been able to speak to anyone. I was very sad indeed. Then the regular Indian invasion of Kashmir took place. We became less friendly but the radio-telephone was kept open.

The Indian Air Force became heavily engaged in the last week of October 1947, and in November. They lost aircraft to ground fire and also because of maintenance problems. I was informed one day that an Indian Tempest had made a forced landing in our area and that the pilot had been captured. I instructed that the pilot be brought to an air force officers' mess. I believe he was brought to Chaklala. I went and saw him and as etiquette demanded, I gave instructions for his treatment as an officer. He was confined to a room with an escort. He was treated as any officer under formal arrest would be except that he had greater liberty in some ways. When I returned to Air H.Q. I established radio-telephone communication with Air H.Q. India. Soon A.V.M. Mukerjee came on.

"Would you care to exchange an old man for a young one?" I asked, after the initial courtesies.

"Can you elaborate on this?" He asked, not quite believing me.

"We have your Flying Officer Sharma with us. He seemed to have lost his way." I was being impish and perhaps sarcastic.

Sobroto had a slight impediment in his speech. He mumbled

incoherently for a while, his stammer becoming aggravated by the topic. I continued when he seemed to pause.

"We have a young pilot of yours. I am sure you would like to have him back. And, comfortable as Sharma is, he would wish to go to his own mess." I said and he responded with an affirmative grunt.

"You can have him back providing we can have a retired old Brigadier whose active days were over many years ago." I went on.

I then explained Brigadier Rahmatullah's situation and said that it was on humanitarian, compassionate grounds, that I was suggesting this exchange. All remaining members of the Brigadiers family were in Pakistan and it would be an unbearable tragedy if he were to spend his last days in prison where no one from his large family could visit him. Sobroto said that he sympathised; that he would like to have his pilot but that it was a matter for his Foreign Ministry. He would take it up with the Ministry and revert to me in a few days. Obviously, for them, it was a good bargain. After a lapse of two or three days Sobroto informed me that his government agreed to the exchange. I conveyed the news to Asghar Khan. A few days later an Indian aircraft brought Brigadier Rahmatullah to our station at Chaklala. He was met by his son. Sharma flew back to join his people. Possibly he flew sorties over Kashmir again. Who can tell? And what went through his mind, if he did!

I met Brigadier Rahmatullah a few times. I had great regard and respect for him. He was a man of simple, austere habits. On the last occasion his speech had become impaired to a great extent. However, we were able to exchange some thoughts. Having been in prison himself he had sympathy for me when I met him in the early '60's. But time marched on and situations changed. When he died I was in London. I was exceedingly sad to hear about it. I would have liked to been near him. But his family forgot to inform me about his death.

Asghar Khan's contribution to the struggle of the people of Kashmir was considerable, greater than any one single person in the air force. While we assembled men and material, the fighting in Kashmir grew in intensity. The reinforcements for the Maharaja's troops were countered by larger numbers of volunteers going into southern districts of his domain. The uprising had also spread to Gilgit and other remote areas. The Maharaja's garrison at Gilgit fell quickly. It has been stated that Brown, the Political Agent, caused this sudden collapse. It is possible that he played a part. But the Muslim personnel had risen spontaneously. They took the garrison commander, Brigadier Ghansara Singh, into custody. He, along with others, was removed to a place in the North West Frontier Province. One Muslim officer who played a prominent part in this revolt was Major Hassan. I met him over three years later in prison. He was one of the accused in the Rawalpindi Conspiracy Case. At that time he and other officers and men of Gilgit Scouts moved out from Gilgit to take over the outposts further in the interior. The last of the outposts was Skardu. I understood there seemed to be stubborn resistance from its garrison as it was well fortified. It was causing casualties and tied up troops who could be better employed on other duties. Asghar Khan and I discussed the situation and decided that if the garrison held out for longer than two days we would carry out an air attack with rockets. This would be in direct violation of the government's policy, but we were not prepared to let it stand in the way of inflicting a quick blow wherever it was possible. We believed that it was not only possible but necessary to remove that vestige of tyranny from the area. Perhaps happily, Skardu fell within the time limit set by us. We could not use operational aircraft over the southern districts. But we began to fly supplies to Gilgit as soon as the Maharaja's forces had been overcome. The civil aeroplanes and pilots participated in these sorties.

All this time the fighting around Poonch and other districts in the South was becoming more intense. The preparations for a large operation by the volunteers, was going apace. The Dogra troops had been contained in the South, therefore, the organisers of the volunteers decided to launch an offensive along the Rawalpindi-Srinagar Road. It was a large operation. I was not able to take part in the detailed preparations, but I assumed that some specialist advice was available and was being used. It seemed too large an undertaking to be considered a guerrilla operation.

In the meantime I began to receive communications directly from some volunteer area commanders, Zaman Kiani and Habib-ur-Rahman and others among them. The former wrote a desperate note asking for my help in creating a better force than he had at that time. He said he was short of supplies of all kinds. Since he was a great distance from my centre of activities, I was unable to render direct assistance. We did, however, keep in contact and exchanged views on the whole matter. The two of us and some others, were of the opinion that the Maharaja may seek secret or open help from the Bharati government. There were three possible methods which could be adopted by the latter; to intervene openly by marching on Pakistan. We ruled this out. The Indians were not much better consolidated than we were. They had their refugee problem as we had, even if it was less acute. Their army was as little or as much prepared as ours. We did not expect them to undertake an open war against Pakistan on behalf of the Maharaja. The second option was to send their troops into Jammu via Kathua. There was just a pontoon bridge there, over the Ravi River. Thirdly, troops could be landed at the airstrip near Srinagar by air. Bharati troops, even in small numbers, would be effective materially and would raise the sagging morale of the Dogra troops. If the Bharati government were to agree to reinforce the Maharaja's forces and were to establish bridgeheads at Kathua and Srinagar, then firstly, it would become virtually impossible to dislodge them and secondly the people's revolution would be prolonged by years.

Therefore, these two possibilities should be denied to the enemy. One small unit of the regular army placed at each point would successfully prevent their troops crossing or landing. Placing our troops on our side of the Ravi could well be within enemy territory, but with the morale of the Dogra troops being at a low ebb, one company could take it without much difficulty, especially if it were accompanied by guerrillas with detailed knowledge of local conditions.

I took up this matter of vital importance at one of the meetings in Rawalpindi, at the Commissioner's residence. I think Brigadier Sher Khan was present. He was later Major General, but was killed in an air crash near Karachi. A detailed discussion took place; the proposition thought to be sound, was agreed. I was informed, a few days later, that the government still maintained that it must not be implicated. It was also stated that General Gracey had flatly rejected this proposal. He had declined to carry out any such operation even when ordered to do so by the Quad-i-Azam. I maintain to this day that had the suggestion been accepted and acted upon, the two best and most effective routes open to the Bharati government would have been closed. This would have meant them having to use other less effective and more arduous entry points. I still believe that they would not have attempted to use them. The alternative of attacking Pakistan was too remote. It was quite possible that, finding himself isolated, the Maharaja would have submitted to his people. It was perhaps too late to restore the situation in Jammu, but the people of the Valley and other overwhelmingly Muslim Majority districts, would have been rid of the Dogra troops and oppression.

I understood later that a request was made by Major Khurshid Anwar and others to Shaukat Hayat, to deploy the volunteers in order to deny Kathua to the enemy. This never materialised, despite the fact that Zaman Kiari strongly favoured the proposal. We have to thank some mutual bickering, typical of the ruling classes, for the failure. But the irony and indeed the tragedy, lies in the fact that not many weeks later, very large units of the Pakistan army were thrown in to stem the advance of Bharati troops into Pakistan. By that stage it was futile for

Kashmir. The people of the Valley had lost the opportunity to take the Dogra yolk off their necks. Later, it was puerile to try to conceal from the world, the presence of our troops in the Western and Southern parts of Kashmir.

These events were reminiscent of the battle in the Western Desert during the Second World War. Rommel had defeated the British forces. The Valley of the Nile lay virtually open before him. He asked for an army division and adequate air force to pursue the retreating enemy. He would have occupied the Nile delta and possibly have swung Eastwardeastward to deny the entire Eastern Mediterranean to the allies. Later, but far too late, the Germans poured dozens of divisions, with air force to match, into the Western Desert. The enemy had more resources by that time and the German troops were unable to advance initially, even a fraction of the distance that their predecessors, who had been a fraction of their strength, had done, and later they lost heavily in a confined area. Ultimately the remnants had to withdraw to the European mainland. All this for want of a proverbial nail. Had Rommel been given the reinforcements he sought the history of that war may have been different. Had Kathua and Srinagar been held, the history of Kashmir may well have been entirely different.

Jammu had been lost. The northern regions up to Skardu had been taken from the Maharaja. The Southern districts were partially liberated and the Dogra troops were on the retreat. The main struggle to be waged was for and by the people of the Valley. This exercised the minds of all those who were engaged in helping the people of Kashmir to remove the accursed yolk of the Maharaja.

Shortly before 22 October, 1947, I came to Rawalpindi and met the Commissioner and some other officers. I believe Akbar Khan was one among the officers who were present. One or two officials from the Frontier Province were present but I am unable to recollect their names. Also present were Mumtaz Shah Nawaz and her sister Mrs. Nasim Akbar

Khan. While we talked inside, the compound of the house was a bedlam. Volunteers and stores were being brought in and then despatched to their respective sectors. Everything appeared to be in a state of organised chaos. Apart from perhaps one room, where the Commissioner's family lived, the entire house seemed to have been occupied by the 'administrative' staff and many others who were straining at the leash to be involved. There were some from areas of Azad Kashmir. I recollect one young man, armed to the teeth, who had been operating in Poonch and had come to seek out more volunteers, arms and ammunition. I am unable to say with certainty, but I think he was introduced to me as Sakhi Daler.

The noisy preparations of all sorts went on in and around the house. In our room a timetable was being announced about sending a large contingent to Garhi Habibullah, Muzaffarabad and onwards. The two ladies spoke in an agitated manner and intervened on every possible occasion. I did not like the way the meeting was being conducted and the manner of discussion. It was neither cool, nor calm, nor calculated. However, I was not particularly concerned at that time. The date had been made known to us for the volunteers to enter Maharaja's Kashmir in the North. It was to be October 22, 1947.

Asghar Khan and I arranged for all arms and ammunition, which would have gone to the Indian Air Force and were surplus to our requirements, to be collected and made available to the volunteer H.Q., or to individual volunteer formations if we knew them. Asghar Khan was completely aware of the policy I had adopted; I had consulted him on several occasions. He, therefore, used his own initiative to provide whatever material he could to whichever formation he deemed necessary. Nur Khan was also aware of the policy but his activities were directed towards transport aircraft and dropping of supplies in Gilgit and other liberated areas along the Upper Indus Valley. He also participated in some of our other activities.

I do know that from among the senior army officers Brigadier Sher Khan and Akbar Khan participated in the planning and organisation of the volunteers. As they did not question me concerning the methods I had adopted to make equipment available, I also did not inquire as to the source of their supplies. Sher Khan especially, was my close friend and we enjoyed mutual confidence. I had known Akbar Khan since 1940, when he was army liaison officer attached to the Indian Air Force unit in which I was a pilot. Sher Khan was quiet, pleasant and enjoyed a good reputation for sound efficiency. He was a good operations officer and had won a military cross. Akbar Khan was verbose, possessed a keen intelligence and was an officer with great courage and initiative. He had won the Distinguished Service Order, second only to the Victoria Cross. The only other officer in Pakistan, to have won the D.S.O., twice over, was Brigadier Taj Mohammed Khanzada. The latter was unable to serve in Pakistan Army as he had been a prisoner of war of the Japanese. Most of the men who had been Japanese prisoners of war had become suspect. The British had marked them black, grey and white. Only the white and possibly the grey were admitted to the Indian Army. Taj must have been considered at least grey. In this matter, as many others, the Pakistan government followed the dictates of the British officers. Our army was therefore deprived of the services of many gallant men.

I do not recollect participation by any other senior Pakistani army officer. I have already mentioned the hostility displayed by Brigadier Iftikhar Khan against the volunteers and hence against the cause of the Kashmiri people. Brigadier Iftikhar Khan was said to be very close to General Gracey and rumour had it that he was being groomed for the post of Commander-in-Chief of Pakistan Army. Apart from Khwaja Rahim the only senior civil servant from the centre who attended a meeting before 22 October, was Colonel A.S.B. Shah, secretary to a Minister at the centre. I cannot state with certainty as to who had deputed him to come to our meeting. After the Bharati government accepted the well planned accession by the Maharaja and sent its troops into Kashmir, other officers from the centre began to come to

Rawalpindi and to attend our meetings. I vividly recollect one such meeting at which Khwaja Rahim, Iskander Mirza, A.S.B. Shah, AKbar Khan and I were present. During the course of the discussion a heated argument started between A.S.B. Shah and Akbar Khan. It built up until A.S.B. Shah literally exploded. He addressed Akbar Khan with some unprintable epithets. His already large eyes bulged out of his head, red in a furious rage. Everyone sat, agog. Akbar Khan dropped his head and went mum. I moved close to Colonel Shah and held his hand. I talked to him gently between his outbursts. The others sat stunned for a while and then fidgeted. It was an extremely tense moment and even I thought that Colonel Shah might whip out something and attack Akbar Khan with it. He made a gesture to leap forward to get his hands around Akbar's throat. I held him firmly and continued to talk to him. In a few minutes, which seemed like so many days, he began to calm down. His fury subsided. But Akbar Khan left and we went on with the discussion. Khwaja Rahim later thanked me for preventing an even uglier scene.

Bharati writers have written on the matter of the Pakistani government's complicity in the 'invasion' of Kashmir. They call action taken by the volunteers an 'invasion', as opposed to that taken by the Bharati government on Junagadh, Hyderabad, Goa and other states, which was named 'police action'. In fact, the volunteers went in the aid of an oppressed Muslim majority in Kashmir, which is legitimate in any similar revolutionary situation. It is a tragedy that the Pakistani government failed to fully support the volunteers and the people of Kashmir, with the consequential failure of the revolution as a whole. The Bharati government sent a regular army, in accordance with a planned militarily operation, to invade Junagadh, and smaller states around it, which had acceded to Pakistan. It invaded with full military force the state of Nizam's Hyderabad which was independent, yet deemed to be Bharati, a deception bolstered by the 'most faithful ally the British'. It invaded Goa, a Portuguese territory, legally no more a part of Bharat than Burma. The Bharati government never paused to consider bilateral negotiations. Whenever and wherever the situation permitted Bharat to annexe territory she did so without hesitation. Apart from the perverse Boundary Award, which handed over a whole Muslim majority district and some other sub-divisions to India, the latter did not permit any Hindu majority areas, no matter how small, to go to Pakistan. On the one hand the Indians were determined to ensure that no Hindu majority areas ever went to Pakistan but on the other hand she embarked on occupying, under a pretext and by force of arms, a Muslim majority area. She did not pause long enough to consider the consequences of her invasion of Kashmir. She was unable to swallow the whole of Kashmir. No other territories annexed by her had such serious implications for Pakistan, as did Kashmir. Even more serious were the consequences for the people of Kashmir. Regardless of the Tashkent Agreement[5], Bharati presence in Kashmir will remain a source of acute anxiety for the people of Pakistan. Regardless of the strength of Bharati forces and the duration of their stay, the spirits of Kashmiri Muslims will remain alight. There cannot be and never will be peace, while the immoral and unjust occupation of Kashmir by Bharat remains. The people of Kashmir, with the fullest support from the people of Pakistan, will ultimately rid themselves of all oppressive yokes.

Bharati writers indulge in much fantasy in their efforts to prove the Pakistani government's complicity. They go into absurd arguments in trying to prove that senior British officers prepared the plan for the 'invasion' of Kashmir. In his book 'Political Conspiracies in Pakistan", Jamna Das Akhtar makes two contradictory statements on one page alone. He makes Akbar Khan say that that the Pakistani invasion fizzled out because of the faulty plan prepared by the British officers. Then he states that Akbar Khan was to all purposes Commander-in-Chief of the

---

[5] **Tashkent Agreement,** (Jan. 10, 1966), accord signed by India's prime minister Lal Bahadur Shastri (who died the next day) and Pakistan's president Ayub Khan, ending the 17-day war between Pakistan and India of August–September 1965. A cease-fire had been secured by the United Nations Security Council on Sept. 22, 1965.

invading forces and he invaded the state under the instructions of his Defence Minister, Liquat Ali Khan.

The Indian writers and the British make much of General Gracey's refusal to send troops into Kashmir. It is inconceivable that the British officer, the C-in-C no less, who refused to obey the orders of the Head of State, would have prepared plans for the invasion of the same territory which he himself declined to invade.

It is my personal knowledge that the C-in-C of Pakistan Air Force was not at all aware of the developments for Kashmir. It is also my personal knowledge that no senior British officer attended any of the meetings held for the purpose of organising the volunteers. No senior Pakistani officers, other than Sher Khan and Akbar Khan, participated in the original organisation. There is no evidence anywhere to prove that senior British officers took part in the 'plans'.

It is my belief that Jamna Das Akhtar has confused the elderly Major General Mohammed Akbar Khan with Major General Akbar Khan, about whom we are concerned here. The former commanded 8 Army Division in Quetta and took part in operations in Kalat, in late 1947, and early 1948. The latter was Brigade Commander in Kohat. The former has written several books and articles; the latter has not. In another part of his book Jamna Das Akhtar confuses Nasim, Akbar Khan's wife, with her elder sister Mumtaz. He presents the latter as being Akbar Khan's wife.

Akhtar alleges that the senior British officer allowed officers and men to go on leave and fight as volunteers. The fact that many officers and men of Pakistan army absented themselves from their units to go into Kashmir does not at all prove British complicity. The Pakistan air force C-in-C was not aware of our activities. Yet many of us, officers and men, absented ourselves to go into Kashmir. Under such emotionally charged conditions many officers were prepared to be and were absent, and allowed their men to absent themselves. When unit commanders adopted such an attitude, it was not possible for any superior commander, let alone the C-in-C, to prevent it. Once again, it is a matter for regret that such tactics had to be adopted.

Bharati writers confuse themselves and their readers with this misinformation. Their arguments are based on false premises and not on fact or evidence. They have tried to prove that the British officers prepared plans for the volunteers' organisations. There is no truth in this. Indeed, the senior British officers created obstacles, one example being General Gracey's instructions to Brigadier Iftikhar Khan not to provide assistance.

I am not aware of any meeting between Akbar Khan and Liaquat Ali Khan on the subject of volunteers for Kashmir, at least not prior to 22 October 1947. Thereafter I believe Sher Khan was closer to the Defence Minister and the Defence Secretary than was Akbar Khan.

After the invasion of Kashmir by Bharat many government officials, including ministers, took greater interest. It is possible that Akbar Khan also met officials from the Ministry of Defence. But this is quite different from the allegation that the Defence Minister had been a party to the plans for volunteers and that he, prior to 22 October, had instructed Akbar Khan to carry out an invasion.

It is also my personal knowledge that Akbar Khan did not lead the so-called invasion of 22 October. The volunteers were led by Major Khurshid Anwar and he was not accustomed to taking orders from officers of the regular army. He had many other tribal leaders and others with him. Akbar Khan was on the administrative staff when the volunteers entered Kashmir. It was only after the Bharati army invaded Kashmir that Akbar Khan went to the front. Ultimately regular units of Pakistan army were thrown in and Akbar Khan and others fought a valiant rear guard action, stemmed the tide of Bharati advance and created a stalemate which has lasted to this day – except for a temporary break in 1965. Akbar Khan was a gallant officer. He was the last to leave. A short time prior to his withdrawal, Colonel Gul Nawaz visited him. Akbar Khan invited him to share his last cup of tea. All supplies and rations had been withdrawn. Akbar was left with the most meagre rations.

There were numerous gallant men who took part and innumerable deeds of valour displayed in that unequal combat. I hope with all my heart that some if not all of them, will record their experiences and thus plug the huge gaping holes in the history of our people. Every effort has been made to prevent the correct presentation of events. This tradition must be broken.

India committed an open aggression with her armed force, led under the guise of 'legal accession' and under the umbrella of the august international body – the United Nations. The Pakistani government, having failed to support a people's revolution, played an underhand role. It tried to conceal its military activities after having been compelled to adopt them; it had to keep looking over its shoulder. Pakistan's soldiers were at every possible disadvantage, the worst being their government's peculiar attitude. Although it was an open and all out fight, it was also secret as far as our men were concerned, this encouraged adventurers and we had some foreign mercenaries and agents offering to fight for us and to lead us to victory! They offered to teach their granny how to suck eggs! There is one matter in which we need no lessons and that is the art of fighting. Despite the most inappropriate attitudes of the governments, our men fought the Indian army to a standstill in 1947-48. Nearly eighteen years later they repeated the performance against overwhelming odds and retrieved the situation created by the most disastrous plans of a person, Ayub Khan, seeking glory for himself. However, in the early days of the Indian invasion of Kashmir many men performed great deeds. In the absence of being given any firm directions, many used their own initiative and attacked the Indians wherever possible. In one incident Brigadier Masud took his armoured vehicles deep into Indian occupied territory, inflicted damage on them and returned to his station. In another incident an artillery unit shelled an Indian bridgehead and destroyed it, thus denying the enemy a valuable crossing point.

Not everyone however, covered himself with glory. A senior army officer who had a clear directive to fight and stop the Indian forces in the Mendhar Valley, abandoned the whole valley, when faced with the enemy. He took flight back to the warmth of the club fire in Rawalpindi. Because of his actions the granary of Kashmir was left in enemy hands. But that officer rose to the rank of Lieutenant General, provincial governor and the post of Minister in Ayub Khan's military government. It was the only exception to the normal rule of dauntless courage which otherwise prevailed.

But again all this was in no way in accordance with any plan prepared either by the Defence Minister, Nawabzada Liaquat Ali Khan, or by the British officers. Of course, we had many British senior officials and it is quite possible that some of them came to know about some movements of the volunteers and later of the Pakistan army. Of course, when the problem of Kashmir had been firmly established between Pakistan and India and mutual bitterness aggravated and assured, then the British C-in-C of Pakistan army showed no great reluctance to move troops into Kashmir against the Indians. The Indian army fought against the Pakistani army, but no British personnel were withdrawn from either side. Only days earlier, the Pakistani government had been threatened by the British Commander in Chief, when he said that all British personnel would be withdrawn if fighting broke out between the armies of the two dominions. Prior to the invasion by India, however, no British officer of senior rank helped in any way.

The volunteers crossed into Kashmir at Garni Habibullah on 22 October, 1947. The state troops, already harassed and demoralised, retreated rapidly. Muzzafrabad was soon taken and the volunteers crossed the Jhelum River at Domel. By 24 October they had reached Baramulla. On that day I left Peshawar in the morning alone in a Humber Pullman car.

It was a very large vehicle with a large interior. I went to Risalpur and met Asghar Khan. We loaded the car to capacity with small arms and ammunition and went to Rawalpindi.

From Chaklala we picked up Nur Khan and proceeded to Abbottabad. After a brief halt we went on to Garni Habibullah. There we saw for the first time, non-Muslim refugees. In the compound of the local civil headquarters there were a hundred or more men, women and children. They seemed to have been well cared for. But I confess that the looks of uncertainty on their faces made my heart weep inwardly. They, like millions of Muslims in camps farther east, were the victims of a holocaust created by the most evil forces of vested interests; the exploiters who do not know the meaning of mercy or humanity; the British imperialists, the Indian expansionist government, the oppressive Maharaja retaining power at the cost of millions of lives, the weak Pakistani leadership, encouraging aggression at home and abroad.

The sun was setting over the mountains when we passed through Muzzafarabad, over the bridge and into Domel. In the twilight we walked into a beehive. There were hundreds upon hundreds of people around the Rest House. We met Major Aslam Khan, younger brother of Asghar Khan, who was engaged in organising the volunteers. He informed us that the forward elements, led by Khurshid Anwar, had reached the outskirts of Baramulla and were probably in the town then, as he spoke to us. Not much later it was confirmed that Baramulla had been taken.

At night we were accommodated in a room in the Rest House. We lay on the floor with a score or more people crowded around us. The spirits were high. Hardly anyone pondered over the matter of a continuing revolution, which can only be sustained by the local people with support from other friendly people. Since the advance had been exceptionally rapid no one had doubts about the fact that the Maharaja would submit. In fact he fled to Jammu with all his precious belongings.

He was secure there as a virtual genocide had taken place and the Muslims had been exterminated.

In the Rest House most of us kept awake. Asghar Khan, Nur Khan and I were huddled together and discussed the situation. The volunteers had made speedy progress and if they kept the pace they would clean up the valley of the Maharaja's troops in a matter of another day. While we were all preoccupied in operational matters two persons near us were engaged in what seemed to be a matter of the administration of Kashmir. They talked about setting up Octroi posts, collecting revenue and other similar subjects. They anticipated the liberation of the Valley. We discovered later that one of them was Sirdar Ibrahim.

The night was well advanced when a message was received purporting to have come from Abdul Qayyum Khan, the Chief Minister of the Frontier Province. It was to the effect that the Hindus and Sikhs in areas south of Domal had killed their women and children and were now moving north to outflank the column and rear headquarters at Domal. Their intention was to destroy the main bridge over the Jhelum and isolate the entire force. Under the conditions then prevailing anything was possible. The message indicated a desperate mood. I would have advocated such a manoeuvre under similar circumstances except that I would have evacuated the women and children to safer areas. We came out of the room and joined the crowds outside. Aslam Khan repeated the message to us. Some of those who seemed to be in charge discussed the situation. We began to scan the skyline for signs of movement. Being blessed with exceptionally good sight I soon spotted some silhouettes. Someone else had also noticed them. I became agitated. We had a tribesman, apparently of some standing, near us. He had the largest, roundest and the most closely shaven head I had ever seen. It was the size and shape of an enormously oversized watermelon and with as much hair. His eyes were sunk deep into his head – two large holes cut into the watermelon. His coolness resembled that of another proverbial vegetable, the cucumber. My agitation left him quite cold. He did not turn a hair! I explained that I could see some figures moving on the hill. He looked in the direction I indicated and nodded slowly – agonisingly so – as if he were afraid his head might fall off. He just boomed a couple of monosyllables. Almost in exasperation we left him and spoke to Aslam Khan. The three of us were in full air force uniform. We had the most senior staff car with us. The Government's intention, if not order, was that regular personnel were not to be implicated. We were of no value to anyone as we stood. We had not come equipped to join in ground combat. Therefore we should not take the risk of falling into enemy hands. I, more than anyone else, decided that we, the three force officers, should go back to the other side of the bridge. We managed to extricate the large unwieldy car and drove out. We went back a few miles, to a point from which we could see Domal. We were up all night and saw a few flashes in the distance, south of Domal, followed by sounds of explosions. We were too far to be able to hear or see the activity in Domal. At daybreak we drove back towards Domal. The bridge was intact and when we reached the camp there was greater calm.

Aslam Khan explained that the message was from Peshawar but the information was incorrect. The silhouettes we had seen were those of men on picket duty. At night this detail had been overlooked. However, there was much mirth, at least on Aslam's part, at out rather hurried departure. Many years later we still discussed this incident. Aslam thought we should have stayed on. I maintained that under the circumstances we were right to have gone back over the bridge.

Later that morning we went out to look around. We passed through fields and along the left bank of the Jhelum. I experienced my first shock at the sight of three or four bodies scattered in the fields. They seemed to have fallen to rifle or other small arms fire. There were no signs of mutilation. The bodies were fully clad but had dried up. Further down several bodies could be seen in the river. The clothes on some of them ballooned as air locks formed, the water rushing rapidly past and around them. The countenance on those I could see were chalk white and puffed. While those in the fields were in different postures, betraying the ways in which their lives had ended, those in the river lay straight, the fast flowing water having turned them to conform to its course. They were either near the bank where the current was too weak to carry them forward or were held between boulders in the bed of the river. They looked so innocent and peaceful as opposed to those in the fields, who showed signs of convulsion. I felt exceedingly sad at the sight. I cannot say how the others felt, but outwardly they appeared to be unconcerned. I also assumed an air of calm. It would not be unnatural for Asghar Khan to show indifference to the spectacle. He had had more than one man's share of tragedy and atrocious treatment meted out to some of his family in the Maharaja's state.

I had been given eye witness accounts of indescribable bestiality and brutality inflicted on the Muslims in East Punjab and Jummu. I could not forget and have not forgotten the nightmare scenes described to me by the I.N.A. General Shah Nawaz, which he had witnessed in Bihar and Garhmukteshwar in the first half of 1947. The people of the sub-continent had been caught up in an orgy of killings, slaughter and counter slaughter. Given those circumstances, what I saw near Domal was indeed a minor incident. But more than once I had been disgusted and sickened at the obviously deliberate and planned genocide carried out by fascist Hindu organisations such as R.S.S.S. Again more than once I was infuriated by a peculiar double role of the political leaders and bureaucrats of Pakistan. On the one hand they failed to prevent the massacre of their own people since 1966; on the other hand they displayed sadistic traits when dealing with the problems of the refugees of both sides. At Domal one bureaucrat had seriously suggested that refugees should be disposed of, taking advantage of the darkness and the river, his reason being that there were too many to be accommodated and fed! He was a police officer. It was with difficulty that that terrible plan was prevented. The refugees were moved to the camps and then sent to India, as should have been done without question or hesitation. But a more senior bureaucrat in Rawalpindi, referring to the Muslim refugees from East Punjab and other parts of India, displayed even greater callousness when he said,

"Let them be slaughtered there. We cannot take any more." I was not able to ascertain if he reflected the thoughts and the policy of those at higher levels. In any case it was beyond their power to stop the floods of refugees moving in both directions. That millions of Muslims managed to escape was not on account of the lack of effort to eliminate them, but because genocide cannot be achieved in such a short space of time. Man's will to survive is enormous and enables him to do so in the face of the greatest adversities.

We returned to Rawalpindi and then dispersed. We had expected the volunteers to maintain the advance to join the people of the valley and to lend support to the latter to overthrow the tyranny. We were, therefore, deeply disappointed when we heard on the early morning of 26 October that the volunteers had not moved beyond Baramulla for nearly 36 hours. Various reasons have been given for the fateful delay at Baramulla. Indian writers, understandably, attribute it to looting and arson. Incidents of this nature cannot be ruled out. In a holocaust of that magnitude, even some professional army personnel may deviate from their aim and indulge in irregularities. But the Indians must necessarily exaggerate those incidents, firstly to discredit the volunteer organisation as a whole and secondly to minimise the magnitude of the well planned savageries committed by the Maharaja and the R.S.S.S., in Jammu and East Punjab.

Even though some volunteers most probably did get out of control having learnt of the atrocities further east, Major Khurshid Anwar gave me two reasons for the delay which rang true. He categorically denied that the alleged lawlessness was the cause of delay at that crucial time. If booty were to be the object, than far greater temptation lay ahead in Srinagar. In fact according to him, it was necessary to halt briefly in any event. The advance had been exceptionally rapid and supplies were unable to keep abreast with needs. Secondly, a lengthy discussion took place as to whether the column should remain intact and move to Srinagar, or to the airstrip, or whether it should divide into two and move on both objectives simultaneously. Ultimately the majority view that they should move on Srinagar, prevailed.

At that time, however, our distress at the delay was acute. It was further aggravated when we learnt on the same day that the Maharaja had acceded to India. This was always his intention. He had already threatened on 18 October, that he would seek 'friendly assistance' if his allegation concerning violation of the stand still agreement were not impartially investigated. On 20 October, despite the Quad-i-Azam's own assurance that this would be acceptable to Pakistan, the Maharaja of Kashmir informed the Governor General of Pakistan that he, the Maharaja, was justified in asking for 'friendly assistance'. It was too obvious as to who would provide that 'friendly assistance'. But more significant is the fact that the threat was followed five days later, by the much maligned 'tribal invasion'.

The volunteers had moved forward into the valley when the accession took place. But the delay had cost them time which could not be retrieved. The Indians soon began to land at Srinagar airstrip. It was to prevent such a contingency that we had asked for the airstrip and Kathua bridge to be occupied and denied to the enemy. Now it was too late. Less than a dozen volunteers led by Latif Afghani, tried desperately to reach the airstrip. They arrived within sight of it only to see Indian troops disembarking from the transport aircraft. They withdrew in despair.

A great case had been made by and for the Indians, that the Maharaja of Kashmir came suddenly and that hurried preparations had to be made to assemble and despatch troops, to save the state from the 'invaders'. This is an absurd stand. The Maharaja's threat on 18

October clearly indicates that behind the scenes talks had already taken place. The Maharaja's plan to exterminate the Muslims in Poonch and Mirpur had been successfully resisted. His troops were on the run when he seems to have sought 'friendly assistance'. Had this assistance not been promised and had it not been forthcoming, the domain outside Jammu which belonged to the Maharaja, would have collapsed. The rebellion would in all probability have spread to Jammu where the Muslims may have again tried to return. This would have spelt the doom of the Dogra rule. But in their excessively belligerent mood, the Hindu fascist groups like R.S.S.S. and the expansionist Indian government could not allow this to happen. The preparations, therefore, must have been well advanced when the Maharaja delivered his first threat to Pakistan. Indian troops had to be put on an alert for them to be ready to move in at speed. In order to be able to land on 26 October, they had to be on 24-hour standby. In order to reach the stage of 24-hour notice all arrangements had to be in hand about a week earlier. This coincides with the Maharaja's threat. The Indian government's aggression against the people of Kashmir was as well and as deliberately planned, as that against Junagadh and later against Hyderabad and Goa. The wily capitalist clique in India played a deception on the people of the world, by putting forth utterly false pretexts in the case of all the territories they occupied. A series of police actions reminiscent of Hitler's annexation methods, led to the fall of independent states to India. While morally completely wrong, the annexation of Junagadh, Hyderabad and Goa could be sustained. They were all Hindu majority territories and relatively remote from other countries. Not so the state of Kashmir. It was not a Hindu majority state and its situation is vitally important to Pakistan. The annexation of the three former states is complete and forgotten. The question of the rights of the people of Kashmir has yet to be settled. The world has not yet witnessed the final outcome. It must not and will not be allowed to forget the pledges given to the people of Kashmir.

In the last week of October 1947, the Indian government invaded

Kashmir. The volunteers who had reached the outskirts of Srinagar were now faced by a heavily equipped and mechanised army. They had perforce, to withdraw. But they took a heavy toll on the enemy. In the valley several senior Indian army officers were killed. In the south the first to fall was Brigadier Usman, who led an Indian brigade towards Poonch. U.P. Menon in his book on the accession of states, especially of Junagadh and Kashmir, writes tributes in the most glowing terms, to the Hindu officers, who were killed during their aggression, but fails to even mention Usmanm, a Muslim. So deep rooted is the prejudice of the exploiters of people's sentiments. In the much lauded secular India, a Muslim had to be denied the status of a military hero, while his Hindu colleagues were being extolled to the high heavens.

A regular army had little difficulty in overcoming irregular forces, if the latter were to join battle with them in formation and places, suited for conventional warfare. The Indian army met such a situation on entering Kashmir. The ease with which they were able to advance through the Valley, admirably suited for mechanised and armoured units, did not warrant the countless volumes written in their praise. They do not deserve all the glory bestowed on them as liberators and conquerors. As soon as they encountered Pakistani army regular units, infinitely smaller in size and numbers than they were, they came to a grinding halt. With the exception of the relief of their Poonch garrison, they were unable to make progress on any front where Pakistani army units or even the semi-military militia units opposed them.

But treachery had already taken place; blunders had already been committed; weakness had already been displayed. The Maharaja having failed to exterminate the Muslims of Poonch, Mirpur and Gilgit, entered a treacherous understanding with the Indian government whose Governor General was Lord Mountbatten. Mountbatten was already suspected of being a party to an 'award' which deprived millions of Muslims of East Punjab, Bengal and Assam of their homes. The British C-in-C of Pakistan army had refused to place the smallest possible independent units at Kathua and the airstrip near Srinagar. The volunteers were given help in arms and ammunition in large quantities but direct support in war material was not given in sufficient quantity to the people of Kashmir. The volunteers were expected to carry out a quick operation in a conventional manner but the organisers failed to take into account the worst case scenario. This proved disastrous for them, as it would for any commander who left the worst possible scenario out of his appreciation of the situation. The government of Pakistan displayed humiliating weakness and lack of courage. It failed to give open and all out support to the people of Kashmir. The people of Kashmir and Pakistan paid a heavy price for its weakness and blunders. The former had freedom from tyranny snatched from them and the latter were left to be ever vigilant to meet and to remove the threat posed from the north and northeast.

Sheikh Abdullah, having been resurrected, made highly emotional statements concerning the 'invasion' engineered by Pakistan. He waxed eloquent about the brutalities committed in his beautiful land. He forgot the extermination of Muslims in Jammu; his own imprisonment and the reasons for it; the extermination of Muslims from their majority districts and states in East Punjab. He forgot these and all the other injustices against the Muslims of India and against Pakistan. He forgot the Indian annexation of states which had acceded to Pakistan. He only remembered that he had been put into the chair of Prime Minister of Kashmir, a long cherished dream. He forgot to look down and see that the legs of that chair were inches deep in blood of his brethren in Jammu. He also failed to see the scorched arms of his chair from the fire that had consumed entire villages in Jammu and Poonch. He conveniently closed his eyes to all these, because, if he saw all those realities he would not be able to sit comfortably in the all-important chair. Instead he had eyes only for the atrocities committed by the 'invaders'. He made his accusation that the "tribal Pathan' were not merely armed bandits but a centrally advised force with the avowed object of subjugating our land to the vassalage of Pakistan". Indeed, it was possible that Pakistan would have annexed Kashmir. That, according to Sheikh Abdullah, would have been subjugation. But the continuing tyranny of the Maharaja, with the help of Indian arms, was not considered by him to be vassalage. He could have been the most effective leader of his people at that crucial period and may even have dictated the terms for the freedom of his people. Instead he fell into the trap; agreed to Indian occupation of his beautiful land; later, having been used, he was grossly abused by the very forces he had helped to suppress the revolution of his own people. He was given abundant time to reflect – over 14 years in prison and confinement. Had he exhorted his people to resist the Maharaja and join the revolution begun by the people of Poonch and Mirpur, the entire people of Kashmir may well have been free today. Above all, the problem which has bitterly poisoned the relations between Pakistan and India would not have been created. But such analysis, conclusions and actions are for a revolutionary. Despite his 'constitutional', admirable and highly commendable struggle for the Kashmir Muslims, Sheikh Abdullah was not a revolutionary.

On the other side the British C-in-C of Pakistan refused to obey orders to move into Kashmir and against the Indian army. Three reasons were advanced for this mutinous behaviour. Firstly, that the Pakistan army was not yet organised; secondly, that in the event of a direct conflict between the two armies the British personnel would be withdrawn; thirdly, that he would have to refer the matter to the so-called Supreme Commander, Field Marshal Sir Claude Auchinleck. None of these excuses bears scrutiny.

The Pakistani army was as well organised as the Indian army. Indeed, very shortly after his direct disobedience of the Quad-i-Azam's command, units of the Pakistan army were moved into Kashmir and were amply and admirably able to halt the Indian advance. The withdrawal of all British personnel would not have made the slightest difference to our fighting ability or capacity. They comprised but a minute and negligible portion of our armed forces personnel. Not one of them was indispensable. Indeed, we would have been much better off without them. There would have been much less intrigue, betrayals and treachery. As for consulting the supreme commander; the latter seemed to have either become utterly ineffective, as the Indian government found no need to consult him, or he consciously agreed with its policy. He also threatened the Quad-i-Azam, that should the armies of the two 'dominions' come to blows, all British officers on both sides would immediately resign. Ultimately the two armies did come to blows, in Kashmir – much too late and at the wrong time for the army of Pakistan – yet not a single British officer resigned. Did the British C-in-C of the Indian army consult the supreme commander before marching on Junagadh or invading Kashmir? If he did, obviously the supreme commander's advice must have been exactly opposite to that which he gave his British subordinate in Pakistan and to Quad-i-Azam. On the other hand if he was not consulted by the C-in-C Indian army, then why was he consulted by the C-in-C Pakistan army? If the Indian government did not consider it necessary to consult him, or perhaps their own C-in-C, then why did our government find it necessary to consult him? If the British C-in-C of the Indian army carried out the orders of the Indian government, why did the British C-in-C of Pakistan army refuse to carry out the orders of Pakistan government? It needs no genius to imagine the consequences to a Pakistani officer if he were to have disobeyed a direct command.

If the Indian government were able to order troops into Junagadh and Kashmir, the Pakistan government should have been able to do likewise. But there was a great difference between the two governments: one fully confident of its strength, completely dedicated to its policy of annexation and expansion and ready to occupy as much territory of the sub-continent as possible by fair means or foul: the other fully conscious of its weakness, having already lost vast areas of land and millions of lives, fearful of losing even more; having placed the fate of a hundred million people in the hands which betrayed them without hesitation, our government was terrified of further betrayals. So it succumbed to threats from those who had known well how to deliver them, little realising that submitting to such threats led to yet greater betrayals of a larger number of people. They put themselves at the mercy of the most astute operators in modern history. And the people of Pakistan and Kashmir have paid with blood and suffering.

The foregoing factors led to aggression by the Indian government and withdrawal of the volunteers to the mountains west of Baramulla. Since the volunteer force, comprising of people from distant places, could not be sustained, it gradually dispersed. Later, at least having learnt some lessons, regular camps were set up by the volunteer organisation. Better arrangements were made for accommodation, rations and other supplies. The emphasis shifted to arming the indigenous people of Kashmir. As the people armed and the Pakistan army units moved to the front, the volunteers carried out a fluid rearguard action. I returned once again to the road to Domal. However, I met Akbar Khan in Abbotabad. He had with him two Masud leaders, Ghulab Khan and Khoney Khan. The former was a remarkable man. He had sharp aquiline features and even sharper eyes. His men had ambushed an Indian convoy south of Uri the day before. They had destroyed the transport, captured supplies of diverse types and routed the Indian troops, inflicting some fatalities. The tribesmen from Waziristan are among the finest guerrilla fighters in the world. They have fought ceaselessly for centuries, in their mountainous homeland, against successive rulers of India and Afghanistan. During their occupation of India the British kept them in excellent form. They are, indeed, superb mountain fighters and that is where they should have been placed. Even in small numbers, strategically replaced, they are capable of containing large regular units.

I had brought some pilot jackets with me. I selected the best two and presented them to Gulab Khan and Khoney Khan. I returned to Rawalpindi and attended a meeting at the Commissioner's house. Akbar Khan having gone forward, Sher Khan attended the conference. Among others present there were the sisters Mumtaz Shanawaz and Nasim Akbar Khan. They were almost hysterical as they related their experiences, especially those of Mumtaz, in Barala, where the women rendered first aid to the volunteers, the refugees and others. They all but disrupted the meeting with their persistent demands for reinforcements for Akbar Khan, who they said, was exposed to extremely dangerous conditions. There was much heat generated by the discussion, but little progress made. After the meeting I told Sher Khan and Khwaja Rahim that I would not be able to attend meetings of this nature unless they were properly conducted. Sher Khan later promised that the Headquarters would be moved from the Commissioner's house. All meetings thereafter were held in an organised operations room and were attended by those concerned with the operations.

From the air all we could do was drop supplies to the outposts in the Indus valley as far as Shardu. In the winter especially, the land routes were closed. The young men of the air force performed this hazardous task in a splendid manner. By late November, the Indian army had reached the points at which the people of Azad Kashmir, the volunteers and elements of Pakistan army held them. Of course, in their own way, the Indians claimed the air space over the entire state of Jammu and Kashmir, which included Gilgit. Air Vice Marshal Mukerjee came over the radio telephone to me.

"Look, Janj, your aircraft are violating our air space." He said, "Would you please order them not to do so."

"Which air space are you referring to?" I asked.

"Air space over Kashmir" He replied.

"That is vast territory." I said. "We are dropping supplies at several points and they are vitally important. I cannot stop them."

"Well, I have to inform you that the air space I am talking about should not be violated." He said.

"Thank you for the information." I said, and the conversation ended.

Of course, under no circumstances were we prepared to abandon dropping supplies to those isolated areas. Most of the loads contained food, clothing and stores for the civilian population. However, I passed down the information to the units concerned and instructed them to exercise greater caution on their sorties. Not many days later Flying officer Dogar decided to use the quicker route to the upper reaches of the Indus valley. He was flying a DC3. On his way back to the base, he encountered two tempests. At first he took them for our own. But they came closer and he was able to identify them as belonging to the Indian air force. They signalled him to follow them. He maintained his course for home. After another unsuccessful attempt to persuade Dogar to follow them, they broke off and carried out a warning attack, firing bursts of tracer bullets ahead of the DC3. While they flew out to position themselves for another attack, Doga dived to lose height rapidly. He took evasive action on his way down. He was completely unarmed and under normal circumstances would have been a sitting target. By the time the Tempests swooped back he had lost considerable height but was not yet at a safe level. The Indian Tempests fired at the DC3 which was like a clay pigeon, and hit it. One army officer was killed and another injured. Soog Doga had reached a safe level, tree top, and flew at the bottom of the valley, following its contours. The Indian Tempests made a couple of passes and when they felt uncomfortably close to our base, they broke off and returned to their base. Doga returned to his. I made no complaint to AVM Mukerjee. He made no apology to me. That was the only incident during that period.

In order not to expose our transport aircraft to avoidable risk of enemy air attack, we decided to drop supplies to some posts at night. The pilots of Pakistan air force and some civilian pilots carried out the most hazardous operational sorties that any air force has ever been called upon to undertake. They followed the Indus valley all the way to the posts. This route is difficult enough during the day, at night it required superb flying and navigational skills and nerve. The young men of our air force had an abundance of all of these. Asghar Khan accompanied the young transport pilots on some of the sorties. He went with the first pilot ever to undertake a night flight on that route. It was an excellent gesture and undoubtedly did immense good to the morale of the pilots and other personnel.

A stale mate in the fighting was soon reached along almost all fronts. The Indian army knew that the people of Azad Kashmir and the volunteers had the solid support of Pakistan army as such. While it may have been possible for them to have taken towns from the former, thus leaving them the mountains from where to wage guerrilla warfare, Pakistan army would not permit them to occupy important strategic towns. The Indian army had made substantial advances when the volunteers and the people of Kashmir had been forced to fight conventional rather than guerrilla battles. They had advanced as far as Uri in the north and Poonch in the south. They held this shaky line. However, Poonch was later besieged by a combination of our regular and irregular forces.

There was reference made to this siege by A.V.M. Mukerjee when he visited Karachi, with the Indian Defence Secretary, towards the end of 1948. They had come in connection with beginning cease-fire talks.

As they alighted at Drigh Road I went out to meet my Indian counter part, Mukerjee. He looked at the Pakistan ensign and asked me when we had made it. I told him that it had been flying since 14 August 1947, and that the first P.A.F. ensign was made in New Delhi. He was astonished because the Indian air force still flew a flag of a British dominion air force. That was the R.A.F. flag with the 'star of India' superimposed on it. They had been strictly constitutional in a minor matter. We had been quite unconstitutional.

As we proceeded to their place of residence, A.V.M. Mukerjee briefly discussed the situation with me. Since Pakistan air force as a whole was not involved in the war and he was aware of the activities of our transport aircraft, there was little we could say to each other on that matter. But he broached the subject of Poonch. Their garrison had been besieged for some time. They brought in supplies by air. Their aircraft were harassed while landing and taking off. Some had been damaged and at least one destroyed by a direct hit from our artillery.

"This is a matter of prestige." He proceeded. "We cannot agree to a cease-fire until we have relieved our garrison in Poonch."

"This is a matter on which I am unable to comment" I said.

"We have known each other so well, indeed intimately. I wanted you to know that this is the thinking in Delhi." He said.

"Thank you for the confidence placed in me." I acknowledged. "But this is a matter for the government. While you represent your government, I do not represent mine."

I informed A.T. Naqui about my conversation with Mukerjee. He confirmed later that he had conveyed the information to the Prime Minister. However, it is a matter of record that the Indians were able to relieve Poonch and that the cease-fire followed soon after.

A few weeks after the Indian government had taken aggressive action in Kashmir, my own direct association with the operations at the front began to diminish, although whatever help was possible, continued to be rendered. In May 1948, the Air Headquarters moved to Mawnipur (Karachi) and the front became rather remote.

At that time I flew frequently between Peshawar and Karachi. One day as I was about to embark on a transport aircraft at Peshawar, Ghulam Ishaq, Private Secretary to Abdul Qayyum, came with a message containing a request from the latter. I was asked to take a civilian on board and fly him to Karachi. When I enquired as to who he was, I was informed that he was a Public Relations man who was working for us on Kashmir. Shortly after that I was given a copy of the Blitz Weekly of Bombay. It had a supplement on Kashmir, the author was Reddy. I gathered that this was the man that I had been asked to take with me to Karachi.

The supplement contained a venomous attack on the Prime Minister and others. It was replete with inaccuracies. It referred to Pakistan air force as "Janjua and his hot heads." It made absurd suggestions that we had carried out operational flights with Tiger Moth aircraft, the lightest, the oldest and no more aggressive than a dove. It could not carry a peashooter. Nor is it of any value for carrying or dropping supplies. The Tiger Moth serves no purpose for an air force, except in the most elementary form of training. That is the only use to which we put it. We all laughed at the ludicrous article. The Indian air force officers must have laughed at it too, unless they had lost their sense of humour, or had come to believe in fantasy.

I have often wondered how Reddy had been able to throw the proverbial dust in the eyes of as shrewd a person as Abdul Qayyum Khan, Chief Minister of the Frontier Province, if we are to believe that that was what actually happened. We were all too busy and I did not broach the subject with Qayyum Khan.

Some months after the Indian invasion of Kashmir and the involvement of Pakistan army, I was shown a letter by A.V.M. Perry-Keene in his office in Manipur. It was from the Inspector General of Special Police, Nawabzada Aitizaz-ud-Din. It contained information about some of the items supplied by us to the volunteers. It named Wing Commander

Rashid Malik as the officer who was alleged to have given some air force equipment to 'unauthorised' persons. Perry-Keene was being asked to inquire into the matter. After he saw that I had finished reading, Perry-Keene asked,

"Do you know anything about this?"

"Yes, I know all about it," I replied. "I shall deal with this."

I kept the letter.

I was furious that such a communication should have been addressed to Perry-Keene. I went to the Ministry of Defence and saw A.T. Naqui. I explained the situation to him. We then asked Nawabzada Aitizaz-ud-Din to join us. When he came I repeated what I had already told Naqui.

"I am personally responsible for what is contained in your letter," I said. "There is much more involved and whatever was done by any officer or airman, in the matter of supplying equipment to the volunteers for Kashmir, was carried out under my direct orders. Therefore, if any proceedings have to be taken, they must be against me and no other person in the air force." Aitizaz looked dazed.

"Also Aitizaz I think your letter should have been addressed to me." I said.

"I am extremely sorry that this letter was written at all." He said.

He took the letter from me and tore it into small pieces and threw them into the waste paper basket. Aitizaz was a soft spoken and exceptionally polite man. When we rose to go, he embraced me with warmth and apologised profusely once again. In the air force we heard no more about it. Perry-Keene did not revert to the subject. He probably sensed that I would not be communicative on the matter. Again, it is possible that he obtained all the relevant information from the senior British officers in the army. The latter did not have to look far for informers.

Shortly after this incident Khwaja Rahim came to me and told me that he had been accused of misappropriating and misusing equipment put at his disposal for the use of volunteers. He especially mentioned that the accusation claimed that he had kept a kerosene oil refrigerator for his own purpose. In fact he used it for the vaccines he had stored at his house. He asked me if I would testify that he had not indulged in the alleged malpractices. I told him that I had witnessed no malpractices on his part and was prepared to say so. No misuse had taken place in my presence. I oversaw the actual distribution of some of the equipment among the volunteers.

I heard no more on this subject also. But Khwaja Rahim retired from his post with his mouth firmly shut, in case he was ever to think of uttering facts about the roles of various persons in the early days of volunteer activities. I believe he was the first high-ranking casualty in the confused intrigues which have accompanied the Kashmir problem.

Having failed to occupy the vast northern territories in general and Poonch and Mirpur districts in particular, the Indian government took the case of Kashmir to the United Nations. It was placed before the Security Council on 1 January, 1948 and there it has remained ever since. It has been presented and re-presented ad nauseum. The most important undertaking given by the Indian government was that 'when order had been restored' a plebiscite would be held to ascertain the wishes of the people of Kashmir. This undertaking had already been given when the Indian government accepted the Maharaja's offer of accession. However, every time thereafter that the case was taken to the Security Council, generally by Pakistan, the Indian government moved further away from its original undertaking, until it refused to even discuss the matter, refused to consider it to be a problem at all, refused to admit Pakistan's right to discuss Kashmir and now dismisses the entire burning question by saying that Kashmir is an integral part of

India. The Indian government not only feels no shame or remorse at having broken its pledge to the world and above all to the people of Kashmir, but it displays arrogance and has the temerity to show irritation at the very mention of the Kashmir problem. While India progressively and deliberately tore its own pledge to shreds, the so-called Big Powers helped her to maintain her hold on Kashmir and make permanent the subjugation of the Kashmiri people.

The highest international organisation, going under the misnomer of the 'United Nations' went deaf, dumb and mute. No voice of or on behalf of the people of Kashmir does it hear, except the crack of the gun when the people of Kashmir resort to it. The world will recognise that they have the right to decide their own destiny. Freedom loving people all over the world will come to their aid, to be rid of a suffocating subjugation.

I have had occasion to discuss the problem of Kashmir with various persons throughout these years. It is a problem which has always been discussed and will always be discussed while it remains a problem. And it will remain a problem so long as the Indian government remains in occupation of Kashmir, in utter disregard of its own pledges and the wishes of the people of Kashmir.

In 1950 Nawabzada Liaquat Ali Khan visited the United States. It was a state visit. He, with his entourage, came to London before returning to Pakistan. I was at the Imperial Defence College. I knew Agha Shahi very well. He was a pre-partition civil servant. He had accompanied the Prime Minister to America. He came to our flat and we discussed the inevitable question of Kashmir.

"The Prime Minister has done a wonderful job for Pakistan in America." He said, very excited.

I was attentive and waited for him to continue.

"The Americans gave him a tremendous welcome."

"Why is that considered to be good?" I asked.

"He has got the Americans supporting us on the question of Kashmir." He said.

"How do you make that out?" I asked.

He began to get irritated

"Hundreds of thousands of Americans came to cheer him wherever he went."

His voice rose as he continued.

"The American newspapers carried banner headlines about him. 'He has conquered America, as his forefathers had conquered India' and other such captions appeared."

He looked triumphant and paused, as if for applause.

"Do you really believe that all that was sincere?" I asked. I had asked questions and that was making Agha Shahi angry.

"Yes, I do" He said emphatically and loudly. "Why do you doubt it?"

"It is the oldest public relations trick in the world." I said. "It's called bluffing the public. It is not and cannot be sincere. It is puerile to believe that our Prime Minister's visit, successful as it may be, can be seriously compared with any conquest."

"I am sure that the Prime Minister has won American support for us over Kashmir. It is impossible to satisfy you." He said with some vehemence, sadness and disappointment. He seemed to sincerely believe that the object of securing American support for Kashmir had been achieved. I was unable to see it that way and saw the whole American campaign, of making the Prime Minister's welcome so warm, as a transparent exercise in public relations.

"I am sorry that I am unable to swallow all this." I told him. "I cannot see the support which you believe we will have from America."

He was really angry now. He thought I was deliberately belittling the Prime Minister's achievement.

"What do you think is the solution to the Kashmir problem?" He threw the question at me.

"We allowed the problem to be created. It need never have been a problem." I said, "However, now that it is there, I do not see it being solved by the so-called support of the Security Council. There is no reason known to me as to why the Big Powers should support us in preference to India. But let us examine various possibilities, remote as they may be. First, that we become so strong that we are able to drive the Indian army out of occupied Kashmir. This is highly unlikely in the foreseeable future. Secondly, that the Indians become strong enough to force us out of Azad Kashmir and other areas which at one time were a part of Kashmir. This is equally unlikely. Thirdly, that in a wider conflict between major powers, we find ourselves on the side which occupies or enables us to take Kashmir. This could apply equally to India. But this is beyond our control and the decision would have to lie elsewhere. Fourthly, that the cease-fire line becomes frozen and we and the Indians stay in the areas where we are now. This is the most likely outcome for some considerable time." I paused.

"But we have so far not taken the Kashmir people into account. They are the most vital element as they happen to be the inhabitants of that country. And the problem applies more to them in an extremely acute way. I believe that this problem cannot be solved at the United Nations, at least not in the manner now being adopted. The best and indeed, the only way to achieve a permanent solution to the problem for the people of Kashmir, would be for them to wage an armed struggle against the Indian army and physically remove them from the land of Kashmir, which they have occupied by force of arms. No other solution can be final or permanent."

Agha Shahi was not satisfied but he became pensive. We were unable to see eye to eye on the subject so we drifted to other matters. That was the last time he and I exchanged ideas on the problem of Kashmir. Many years later he became Pakistan's permanent representative at the United Nations. The question of Kashmir was undoubtedly brought to the U.N. during his tenure. I wonder if he ever recalled the talk we had in the middle of 1950!

It is difficult to imagine that any other problem has been taken to the Security Council more often, and perhaps, more frequently and over a longer period than the problem of Kashmir. No other question has aroused emotions of the people of Pakistan more intensely and more frequently than the one of Kashmir. No other question has been used by the successive leaders of Pakistan, to deceive the people of Pakistan. Each government up to the regime of Ayub Khan promised to solve the problem of Kashmir and, of course, always without delay. In 1952 a statement by Dr. Mahmud Hussain, a Minister in the central government has ever remained vivid in my memory. It was completely without justification and was so absurd that I laughed out loud in my prison cell in Hyderabad (Sind) when I read it. As was customary for statements of those in power, the caption was in banner headlines.

"Solution to the Kashmir problem is around the corner."

These were almost the exact words. There was no basis for this optimism. There was not the slightest indication that the problem was near a solution of any kind. Time has proved it to have been as false a statement as all the other myriad statements, on this most delicate matter, by hundreds of so-called leaders of Pakistan. This deception was and remains typical of the Pakistani leadership. It was a most cruel deception. It raised the hopes of people in Kashmir and Pakistan. It kept them tense but did not prepare them for any action. I had laughed out because I had heard similar statements on countless occasions and on scores of other problems facing the people of Pakistan. The words 'around the corner' brought to my mind the Great Wall of China. And when I discussed it with my colleagues, that is what I referred to. "That corner must be at the other end of the Great Wall of China."

While statements continued to be made in Pakistan and India; while threats of war went back and forth across the border, faster than a ping pong ball; while Skeikh Abdullah went into prison for longer periods than a criminal does for manslaughter or rape; while the Indian domination of Kashmir progressively solidified; the Security Council made sham attempts to honour its pledge to the people of Kashmir, but looked down with disdain on the representatives from Pakistan, who indulged in rhetoric which did not add up to a row of beans. Seemingly neutral, the Security Council invariably leaned heavily towards India from its lofty Himalayan heights. The great powers pushed it that way. And the UN being their hand-maid had to do their bidding. The great powers played their own game according to the situation. The Soviet Union, having been shunned by Pakistan, befriended India and took upon herself the blame for non-settlement of the Kashmir problem. She forgot her principle of upholding the people's rights. Of course, the other major powers pretended that the Soviet veto stood in the way of a solution. This suited them but it was an absurd stand. The Soviet veto has ceased to be applied for many years, yet no solution has been found by other powers. They were as much in favour of a status quo as the Soviet Union. And when war broke out between India and Pakistan in 1965, the members of that august body wanted Pakistan and the people of Kashmir to forget the past and deal with the situation as it was then. In other words, they were not prepared to discuss the pledge they had themselves given to the people of Kashmir, but wanted merely to talk about the fight between India and Pakistan and the plans to stop it. This is precisely what they did, completely disregarding the problem of the Kashmir people. They dealt with the symptom, the war, but not with the causes. The cease fire was followed by the ostensibly laudable but in fact the disgraceful, anti-people role of Mr. Kosygin at Tashkent. This was intended to bury the problem of Kashmir together with the pledges and volumes of representations placed before the Security Council for 18 years. The Tashkent agreement was intended to gag the people of Pakistan through their ruling cliques, who would be only too willing to be gagged. They would bow to this unjust and cruel command but would not compel the Security Council to honour its own resolutions in respect of Kashmir.

The Tashkent agreement was as ignominious as the attempt by Ayub Khan to solve the Kashmir problem by means of a commando force was absurd. While his predecessors had been content with bombast, Ayub Khan decided to try his hand at exporting a revolution. His entire background was one of anti-revolution. It was absolutely impossible for him to be aware of and to apply revolutionary methods. He had no conception of the basic and elementary requirements of a revolution. He started a hazardous campaign which was based on assumptions, misconceptions and worst of all, misinformation. This is a disastrous combination and the participants found it to be so. However, it was the latest endeavour to prove to the people of Pakistan how genuine and earnest the rulers were to solve the problem of Kashmir. Ayub Khan went out to cut the Gordian knot, but he was no Alexander. The most puzzling part of the whole affair was that Ayub Khan was the one who made the attempt. He was not only reputed to be less than lukewarm over the Kashmir problem, but while in power he had actually told some people around him to forget about it.

"That issue is dead", he was reported to have said. He had offered defence pacts to India which Nehru turned down with contempt and without hesitation. Nothing in his entire career, military or political, gave the remotest indication of his interest, let alone desire, to solve the Kashmir problem. Yet he embarked on an adventure that was in no way in keeping with his character. It brought about the invasion of

Pakistan by India. In spite of a host of miscalculations on the part of the high command the local initiative superbly and gloriously applied by the young officers and men of Pakistan army and, their peerless valour, brought the Indian juggernaut to a halt. The people of Pakistan gave their armed forces the support which only an immensely patriotic, dedicated and revolutionary people can give.

At a most inappropriate time he agreed to a ceasefire and then submitted abjectly at Tashkent. If it were not so fantastic one would draw the conclusion that Ayub Khan went through all the motions of a war in order to agree, ultimately, to bury the issue of Kashmir. That he deliberately manipulated the whole gruesome affair to achieve a humiliating agreement such as at Tashkent, which he could not have succeeded in obtaining in normal circumstances. This type of treachery, whereby a whole nation is exposed to fatal danger, is not unknown. However, I would put this speculation in the realm of fantasy. That brief war needs to be scrutinised as closely as possible even though the information available is far from adequate. Up to the present era, war is still an exceptionally important part of the history of nations. The only war Pakistan had had to fight openly as a country, against foreign aggression, is the war of 1965. That it was brought about by a most ill considered project by Ayub Khan does not make the impact any less important than a war fought for more solid reasons. The people of Pakistan underwent a baptism of fire. No foreign power should be permitted to compel us to forego a part of our history. Right or wrong a war was fought. Let history give its verdict on that war, but silence must not be imposed on us by those who measure their history in terms of wars; before the war, during the war, after the war, between the wars. These and similar statements are part of the daily conversation of the foreign powers. They refer to them with pride, even when most of them were wars of aggression, waged by imperialism. There are countless volumes concerning their colonial and other aggressive exploits. They shout about them from rooftops. But they choke us when we even whisper about our struggle against oppression and aggression.

While the system of wars for national defence is current our people must not be denied the right to refer to their supreme sacrifices. When the final people's war against predatory, exploiting classes has been won, there will be no need to refer to the national wars in the present manner. The peoples of the world will then look back on them as an unfortunate part of their evolution. Such wars will belong to the bygone ages, interesting albeit painful and cruel experiences of humanity. Until that time comes, all peoples fighting against aggression must record it for posterity. The people of Pakistan must not submit to any foreign pressures or local dictation in respect of recording their history. They should use every conceivable method to reduce to words the events of which they are aware. I know only a fragment of that vast event of 1965. I shall relate it here with the fervent hope that others will reveal that which is within their knowledge, so that the different pieces may be put together. Rumour has it that most, if not all, records relating to that prominent milestone in our national life, have been destroyed. Let those who are able to pick up those pieces and lay as complete a picture as possible before the people of Pakistan and of the world. The origin of that war may be absurd, the motive may be shameful, the outcome may be humiliating, but the part played by the armed forces and the people of Pakistan was glorious. The glory lies with them. The shame and humiliation lie elsewhere.

I went to Karachi at the end of July 1965 and was there for the entire month of August. In the first week of that month the news began to appear in the newspapers and over radio Pakistan, that incidents had taken place in Kashmir. Small bridges, culverts and other lines of communication had been attacked. Soon, 'The voice of Kashmir' radio began to blare out the news of the successes of those attacks and of some others, on the State and Indian troop positions. The attacks were attributed to 'Mujahidin' freedom fighters, from Azad Kashmir and other parts of Kashmir. The volume of successes, hence the news and radio broadcasts, increased with every passing day.

I noticed a peculiar feature of those days. Although privately the development in Kashmir was discussed excitedly and enthusiastically, there was no such open or collective expression emotion. The newspapers carried exceptionally bold headlines, but there was neither an excessive demand for them, nor did people crowd around to read or have the papers read to them. The crowds did not gather in any large numbers around the radio sets in the streets to hear the news. The most emotional problem was not the subject for national discussion. There were no demonstrations in favour of the people of Kashmir. The political leaders, who normally took every opportunity to deliver their rhetoric, ultimatums and to threaten dire consequences for all and sundry, did not come forth with these favoured responses. Ostensibly, events were taking place for which the people of Pakistan had been prepared for eighteen years. They had already shed their blood more than once on the soil of Kashmir. They had held mammoth meetings and demonstrations in support of the rights of the people of Kashmir. Now that an apparently revolutionary liberation armed struggle was being waged there were no fiery speeches or statements by the political leaders. There were no demands of support for the people of Kashmir. The reaction of the people to the news was not much different from that to events in remote places, although their carried their own excitement. One reason could be that Ayub Khan had waged a private war of his own and taken neither the political leaders nor the people into his confidence. But even in that case the people would have shown greater interest. My view was that in the seven years that he wielded power he had deliberately and progressively demolished all semblance of political or people's organisations. The people had been deprived of every conceivable liberty by him. They lived in terror, in misery, in contempt. Since he had destroyed collective action by the people, he could not mobilise them for his own purpose. Of course, he presented the farcical reason that the rebellion was by the indigenous people, therefore, he could not himself ask the people of Pakistan to demonstrate support for Kashmiri people. But he could have managed, in the traditionally deceptive manner, by getting someone else to arouse the masses. The masses were not aroused and the communiqués from the 'front' left them only mildly interested.

I was told that he did not want the masses to be aroused. If this was his intention, then he was admirably successful. But an armed struggle by Kashmir people would be meaningless without active support from the people of Pakistan. They were not receiving help from any other source known to us. What were Ayub Khan's intentions and aims in launching a commando operation in territory for which he had displayed utter lack of sympathy? Why did he not want the people of Pakistan to go to the aid of Kashmiri people? They had always done so before and they would be only too eager to do so again. These questions are, perhaps, difficult to answer. But Ayub Khan can answer them himself. He should be compelled to do so. If not, then the officers who helped him to prepare that disastrous campaign should record their respective roles and experiences. In the meantime let me proceed to relate what came to my knowledge. This is by no means the entire story. It does, however, provide a framework for those events. A great deal may be learnt from it.

In the later part of the third week, or early in the fourth week of August 1965, I had occasion to meet the most senior Pakistan Police officer in Karachi. I had known him for many years when he was a relatively junior officer in the Frontier Province. In 1965 he was Inspector General of Police and was head of a vital department. He had been told that I was in Karachi. When he came on a short visit from Rawalpindi he contacted me. We were able to meet at the Civil Airport where we had lunch, prior to his departure for the North. The so-called struggle in Kashmir was in full swing.

"What do you think of it?" He asked me.

"If you ask me a specific question I may be able to give you a more precise answer." I said.

"Do you think we have done well?" He asked.

"If your intention is to tell the world that the Kashmir issue is not dead, then you have done well. It is obviously not dead now because fighting is in progress." I replied. "To this extent it is good. But please tell me more about it."

He then told me that preparations, under direct orders of the president, had been made for some months. He said that he had no part in the operational training of personnel. His one obvious role was to provide information and keep contacts in Kashmir. The initial arrangements had gone very smoothly.

"We assembled supplies and stores right under their noses and the damn fellows never knew." He said.

"Can you tell me what has happened according to your assessment and what has gone contrary to it?" I asked.

"There has been no large scale or appreciable betrayal of our presence by the local people. We have had food supplied to our men but we have invariably paid for it. This is to offset the bad publicity of 1947 when it is alleged that, no payment was made." He said. "But we had expected some form of civil disobedience; demonstrations and public meetings, to disrupt the day to day administration. This had not taken place."

"That is bad. Without the direct involvement of Kashmiri people themselves, the project cannot succeed." I said.

"Have any Kashmiri persons, no matter how few, been in action against the Indians?" I asked.

"No" He replied, "Only those from Azad Kashmir."

"That is even worse." I said. "How long are you prepared to go on?"

"For six months, one year, two years" He said. "We want to bleed them. Already some police reinforcements had been brought in from India."

"If you are prepared in this manner, then there is a chance that the people of Kashmir will mobilise themselves in due course and join in the struggle for their liberation." I said.

"We are confident of being able to go on for an indefinite period." He said.

"I wish you the best of luck." I said.

He left for Rawalpindi or Lahore. I left for London on 31 August. When I landed at Heathrow airport on the morning of 1 September, the first news I was given was that the Pakistan army had launched an attack towards Jammu. I was more than surprised. I was literally stunned. I had been told only a few days earlier that the 'mujahid' campaign was designed to go on not for days, not weeks, but for years. Then the army had been thrown in within four weeks commencement of that operation. Apart from incidents which were in violation of the ceasefire, Pakistan army had not openly clashed with the Indian army in Kashmir. Now an independent brigade, mainly armoured, had been committed. It was not possible to assess the reasons immediately.

The Pakistan army attack was successful and rapid. Major Akhtar Hussain was in command. He advanced Panzer fashion. His armoured brigade commander put up a magnificent performance. However, it seems that they were too successful too soon. In the midst of an advance, in pursuit of a virtually routed enemy, Ayub Khan changed commanders. Akhtar Malik was withdrawn. Major General Yahya Khan replaced him. The pace of Pakistan army slackened.

While Ayub Khan pondered over the utter chaos his ill-considered commando operation had created. The Indian army launched an attack over the international border between the two countries. Their obvious objective was to take Lahore. Indeed, the Indian army C-in-C, General Chaudhry is reported to have said that he would be in Lahore to have his 'chota' (small) peg of whisky in the Lahore Gymkhana on the evening of 6 September. Of course, we know that General Chaudhry was not allowed to enter the Gymkhana, where he may have had his whisky that evening, and even many evenings thereafter, we cannot say. But few Commanders in Chief have less reason to be proud of their performance. With a superiority of 5:1 in every respect and with surprise, perhaps the most important element in war after the calibre of men involved, entirely in his favour, he was unable to advance the necessary 15 odd miles to Lahore. The Lahore garrison was completely unaware of the Indian attack for several hours after it had been launched. Shortly afterwards the Indian army moved towards Sialkot, with their armour. The cantonment of Sialkot is barely 3 miles from the border. The Indian army was unable to reach it in a fortnight of fighting. They launched yet another attack in the south in a bid to take Hyderabad (Sind). Not only were they halted, but were thrown back into their own territory, losing large areas to Pakistan army. In short the Indian army failed to take and hold any territory of importance to Pakistan. It is not possible to believe that it was not India's aim to take the strategic points of Lahore, Sialkot (even deeper in as far as Wazirabad) and Hyderabad and then to dictate the terms of peace to Pakistan. It is said that the Indian aim was to relieve the pressure against Jammu and against their army in Kashmir. Perhaps that was the case, but attacks along the entire front and air attacks deep into West and East Pakistan were hardly necessary for that limited aim. It seems more likely that India had larger aims and so did Britain, which abruptly suspended arms aid to Pakistan.

The Indian Prime Minister and other Ministers had openly declared in May, that India would attack Pakistan at the time and place of her choice, when their army had suffered a humiliating defeat at the local battle in the Rann of Kutch. There was no undue pressure against the Indian army in Kashmir. Indeed, the pressure was elsewhere.

The performance of the Indian air force was even more unimpressive. Again, having 5:1 superiority and surprise on their side, they not only failed to establish air superiority, but were rapidly neutralised by Pakistan air force. Before Ayub Khan agreed to the ceasefire, Pakistan air force enjoyed local air superiority over some areas, Jammu being one of them. Foreign television showed Indian aircraft destroyed at Jammu airfield in a Pakistan air force attack. The destruction was quite complete. It could not have been achieved without local air superiority.

Pakistan navy carried out a superbly daring raid against Dwarka in Kathiawar peninsula. In conjunction with Pakistan air force they destroyed the radar installation and left the warning system for Bombay against P.A.F. attacks, quite blind.

Despite the Himalayan blunders of Ayub Khan; despite utter surprise due firstly to lack of information and secondly to treacherous assurances by American imperialists that India would not violate the international border, the men of Pakistan's defence services blunted the enemy aggression against their people. For the first two or perhaps three vital days of Indian aggression her army was halted by the relatively junior officers and men of Pakistan army. They used their initiative to the maximum. The casualty ratio of men to officers was 8:1. Normally it is about 50:1. This indicates that officers were in the forefront in close combat and hand to hand fighting. It was to all intents and purposes a people's army.

While the men of the defence services of Pakistan halted the aggression by India, the people of Pakistan rose spontaneously to defend their homeland; the organised civil defence which Ayub Khan had not only neglected, but ignored. In the Lahore and Sialkot sectors the people went to the front line to deliver food and other aid to their soldiers. Old men, women and school children participated in these activities. The people of Pakistan, who had almost completely ignored Ayub Khan's private war only a few days earlier, now rose as one in defence of their country. Patriotic songs were composed and reverberated throughout the land, in the remotest corners of the country. Crime, which had become rampant, due to personal corruption, ceased. Unity among the people, which is the deadly enemy of the exploiting classes, emerged in the face of a threat from an external enemy. In the face of such unity, profiteering by exploiters became unthinkable. The prices were brought down. The Indian aggression was repulsed everywhere.

The foreign press began to talk about the possibility of Pakistani tanks running in the plains of the Punjab. They foresaw that soon the heavy weapons and the air forces on both sides would be exhausted and the fighting would assume the character of irregular or guerrilla warfare. The Indian army had committed its reserves to the Western front. They could not withdraw their forces from the north east, where they had tried to strengthen their position after the debacle against the Chinese forces three years earlier. Having repulsed the enemy; having forced him to throw in his reserves without success, the Pakistan army awaited orders for the counter attack. That order never came from the High Command. Once again a cowardly attitude on the part of the leadership deprived the people of Pakistan decisive action. It yielded to pressure and agreed to the ceasefire. Later Ayub Khan submitted completely and agreed to virtually bury the issue of Kashmir at Tashkent.

The war of 1965 is a large and extremely important event. I do not have all the material available. Therefore, I am not qualified to discuss it in detail. Let those who possess the facts come forth and place them on record. Whether we agree with some aspects of it or not, it must be placed before the people. Let the people discuss the matter and come to their own conclusions. It is part of their history. They have the right to know the facts.

After the ceasefire and Tashkent agreement, I met my senior police friend twice in London. We resumed our discussion on the commando campaign, and the ensuing war, from where we had left off in Karachi. He gave me more details concerning both. The entire planning had been done by some army officers under the direct command of Ayub Khan. Only the latter can say with certainty the factors which led him to undertake such a venture. It seems to have occurred to him some time after he had been re-elected President in 1964 and his nominees had been returned to the puppet and sham parliament. He felt secure. He broached the subject of Kashmir with my police friend in early 1965. He asked my friend to remind him about the matter when they were on a foreign tour. My friend duly reminded Ayub Khan and was thanked. The former heard no more about it until he was asked to provide information regarding the conditions in Indian occupied Kashmir. All training and other preparations were in the hands of Generals Yahya Khan, Akhtar Hussain Malik and the Head of Military Intelligence, Inshad. For close liaison and day to day working with the army was Malik Habibullah, a senior police officer, who had been in charge of the Rawalpindi Conspiracy Case fourteen years earlier. The plans were a closely guarded secret and there was no indication of an impending event. This was not surprising nor was it any great achievement, because commando type of training and preparations are almost routine occurrences, in the locations where they were being carried out. However, the build up of men and material within Indian occupied Kashmir, speaks very highly of the men involved. Suddenly a 'mujahid' movement burst into the world. The attack towards Jammu by Pakistan army was almost as much a surprise to my police friend as it was to me.

However, according to my friend, the Indian aggression against Pakistan was not a surprise to him. His intelligence department was accused of having failed to provide information concerning Indian intentions and their troop movements. He categorically denied this accusation. He stated that the relevant information was conveyed to Ayub Khan, but the latter relied more on information and assurances from other sources and did not alert the army to meet the threat to the most obvious objective – Lahore.

"But why was the possibility of an Indian attack on Pakistan not considered right at the outset?" I asked.

"Because it was thought that the Indians would confine the fighting to the disputed territory in Kashmir." He replied.

This type of myopic analysis was typical of Ayub Khan. While being a past master at manipulation at home, especially in consolidating his position of power, he failed to foresee the threat to Pakistan from the only source of danger. He decided that the Indians would agree with his assumption that fighting should be confined to Kashmir. And this despite the fact that the two armies had clashed in the Rann of Kutch less than four months earlier; despite the fact that the Indian leaders had given him an assurance of an attack on Pakistan, at a time and place of their choice. He should have had no doubt whatever that the time would be when he sent an independent brigade towards Jammu and the place would be Lahore. Yet he left that vital place exposed at a crucial time.

My friend had conveyed the correct information. It should have been heeded. He was among the best in his service; man of great personal integrity. Although coming from a feudal background and having a bureaucratic career, he was a nationalist, putting the interests of his country before those of imperialism. I believe he possessed a wealth of information of immense value and interest to the people of Pakistan. I hope he will record it for posterity. Believing his policies to be in the interests of Pakistan, my friend gave his wholehearted support and service to Ayub Khan. The latter abandoned him at the first opportunity after the war. While he helped Ayub Khan to remain in power, and undoubtedly took part in some machinations to that end, he would not indulge in the type of cold-blooded acts which rulers of Pakistan have committed. He was asked by Ayub Khan to 'liquidate' a person in their in the larger interests of the nation. My friend refused to commit a political murder. Perhaps Ayub Khan did not forget nor forgive him for it, because the former presided over the removal of the latter from his post as head of department. My friend was a disappointed and shattered man. He gratefully accepted another post. According to him his service need not have been extended and worse could have happened! It did happen as soon as Ayub Khan's rule came to an end. He was sent on prolonged leave preparatory to retirement. Such are the intrigues which take place in the corridors of power.

From my talks in London with my friend I drew some conclusions. If we were to assume that Ayub Khan had deliberately planned the whole affair in order to arrive at an agreement such as that at Tashkent, then there was nothing more to discuss. In that case he must have been advised and assisted by those well versed in international intrigues. Strange, involved and incredible as it may seem, such an intrigue is not impossible. American imperialism has subjected several nations in the third world to similar machinations. However, I believe this was not the case in 1965, which caused the war between India and Pakistan. The probable cause is the excessive desire for self glory and an obsession for greater power on the part of Ayub Khan. He wanted to climb further up the ladder; to be a hero who solved the problem which seemed well nigh insoluble. His amateurish attempt at creating a situation which would compel India to come to a settlement over Kashmir misfired. It was basically wrong to export revolution to Kashmir. A revolution must be waged by the people of Kashmir from within and undoubtedly with support from friendly people of the world, especially those of Pakistan. The commandos were too regular in their fighting tactics. They could not be sustained long enough to have the desired impact, either on the Indian army, or on the people of Kashmir. Their fate would not be better, indeed, it would be worse, than that of the volunteers in October 1947. The latter had had a safe line of withdrawal. The commandos had to use routes through Indian occupied territory. These could be cut off, depriving them of reinforcements and supplies and denying them the means of escape.

The Indians were taken by surprise. The 'mujahidin' were able to commence their operations. The Indians could not have wittingly allowed a build up of men, arms and supplies. Ayub Khan may have achieved the aim he had hoped for, and the Indians should have feared creating disturbances throughout Kashmir. To that extent Ayub Khan's plan was successful. But he completely failed to realise that a commando force was too small to achieve as large a military success as was required, to force the Indian army out of their positions, or to put it heavily on the defensive. He relied on his ability to continually reinforce the commandos for as long as two years. He assumed that the people of Kashmir would rise in revolt or at least resort to civil disobedience to disrupt the administration. Apart from the initial success of introducing the commandos into occupied Kashmir, building up supplies and commencing the operations, the plan soon began to collapse. The Indians, having recovered from the shock of a possible rebellion on their hands, assessed the situation. They must have obtained the correct information concerning the 'mujahidin'. Before the end of August 1965 the Indian army units occupied all points which were being used for infiltration and reinforcements. They sealed off the most important supply route, the Haji Pir Pass, which was the lifeline for the Pakistan army. The 'mujahidin' were cut off from their base and it showed quite clearly that Ayub Khan had failed to consider what the minimum reaction on the part of the Indians, may be. All the most vulnerable posts to suffer the consequences of the actions of the Indian army were in the disputed area of Kashmir.

As a sequel to the Indian manoeuvres, the 'mujahidin' were isolated in enemy territory. In due course their activity had to cease, whether by piecemeal withdrawal or due to capture. In either event the 'Voice of Kashmir' and the headlines adorning the newspapers would have gradually but surely died away. The people of Pakistan and the world had not been deceived. They knew that the government of Pakistan had sent the commandos into Kashmir. The sudden demise of the operation would have cast the worst reflection on the Field Marshal

President of Pakistan. He, therefore, decided to drown the 'Voice of Kashmir' and the press headlines, by creating a bigger incident. The world may have, but Pakistan has never known a more costly, painful and cruel face saving exercise on the part of one person. As soon as the Pakistan army launched the offensive in the south all eyes turned towards it and all voices were raised about it. The 'mujahidin' were soon forgotten and remain forgotten to this day. Who knows how many were able to make their way back to Azad Kashmir or Pakistan and how many were taken by the enemy? Since Ayub Khan had officially denied association with them, they were left to their fate. They could not be claimed as prisoners of war. Their plight can be imagined. One hopes that the traditional underhand dealings, including the Tashkent agreement, worked in favour of the captured 'mujahidin' and that, as the result of some deal, they were able to return home.

Had a ceasefire not been agreed it is possible that the heavy weapons would have been exhausted and the war, so far as Pakistan was concerned, would have become a people's war. The people without exception were prepared for it. It is inconceivable that the people of Pakistan would tolerate occupation of their country by any foreign army, least of all the Indian army. They would have waged a war of resistance. No army in the world is large enough to occupy Pakistan and hold it in the face of a resistance movement by its people. This is assuming that the Indian army could have succeeded in occupying sizeable territory, which is a far-fetched assumption. The indications were quite contrary to it. However, if the war had been prolonged and become a people's war, then Ayub Khan would have vanished overnight. He was not capable of conducting a people's war. The people did not need him for it. He could at best have conducted a local conventional war. A people's revolution and guerrilla warfare are not waged from Presidential Palaces. With him the main exploiting classes would have vanished. They are incapable of taking part in people's struggles and, with few exceptions, would have abandoned the country in favour of other places where capital would be secured; could be used and increased. At the first opportunity they would have transferred their capital to safer areas.

It was for these reasons that a ceasefire was being accepted when a massive counter attack should have been taking place. The governments of Iran, Indonesia, Saudi Arabia and other Arab nations, Turkey and the Peoples republic of China, had extended the offer of all possible assistance at the most critical time in the history of Pakistan. The United States of America, Britain and the Soviet Union cut off all supplies to Pakistan, when she was fighting for her very existence. The Peoples Republic of China guaranteed continued help for a prolonged war. But after having accepted the offer once, Ayub Khan betrayed their trust and yielded to the pressure from those who had proved to be our enemies. His class interests were better served in submission.

Even from my limited knowledge the discourse on Kashmir has been lengthy. I do advocate however, that all the citizens of Pakistan and Kashmir, who are in possession of the facts on any aspect of the Kashmir issue, should put them on permanent record. For eighteen years large and small skirmishes took place frequently, culminating in full-scale war in 1965. The Tashkent agreement is being adhered to and the frequency and intensity of clashes between the two armies has lessened. This is no reason to believe that the issue of Kashmir is now to be considered settled. The governments of India and Pakistan may be in collusion against the people of Kashmir, but the latter need to decide their own destiny. A people's right to decide their own destiny cannot be denied forever. Feeble as it may be at present the voice of the Kashmir people can be heard, through the sealed wall erected around them and above the din proclaiming that Kashmir is an integral part of Maha Bharat. The people of Kashmir have not accepted this and never will. They will ultimately attain the freedom to exercise their own choice, through their own struggle and with the active help of all freedom loving people of the world.

It is necessary to sum up this vast and vital subject, as briefly as possible. The people of Kashmir have been subjugated for many generations. This is not unlike the fate of many other peoples in the world, throughout the history of mankind. However, the British imperialists did them the gravest injustice and cruelty when they sold them to the Dogra rulers. The latter inflicted the most inhuman oppression and indignities on them.

Leaders like Sheikh Abdullah had begun the political awakening of the Kashmir people earlier, but in 1947 they rose and began to wage an armed struggle against the oppressive Dogra Maharaja, in Poonch, Mirpur and Gilgit. They were successful. The Muslims of Jammu were liquidated in a most successful genocidal campaign under the aegis of the Maharaja. The Muslims of Poonch, Mirpur and Gilgit resisted further attempts at extermination and in fact, routed the Dogra troops from their areas.

The people of Pakistan went to the aid of the Kashmir people on a voluntary basis. The government of Pakistan adopted a most ambiguous and cowardly stance. It would not openly support the Kashmir people. There was no need to think that it was wrong to help in the freedom struggle of a people, especially those as close to us as the people of Kashmir. This abject weakness encouraged the Maharaja to use greater force without fear of intervention by Pakistan. The greater oppression on the Maharaja's part led to a much greater volunteer organisation coming into being, which went in large forces and routed the Dogra troops. The Maharaja, who had already been in close contact with the Indian government, headed by Lord Mountbatten, acceded to India, upon which the Indian forces invaded Kashmir. The volunteers were obliged to withdraw to the mountainous areas to the West. The Pakistan army, after refusal by the C-in-C General Gracey to enter Kashmir earlier, then entered Kashmir. The combined forces of Pakistan army, the Azad Kashmir people and the volunteers, held the Indian army at points which more or less conformed to the cease fire line.

Having failed to take all of Kashmir and advance to the borders of Pakistan, the Indian government took the Kashmir issue to the United Nations in January 1948. The case has remained there ever since. The Indian government gave a pledge to the people of Kashmir and the world, that when 'order had been established in Kashmir', a plebiscite would be held to ascertain the wishes of the people. This is incorporated in the relevant Security Council resolution. But that pledge has not been honoured by India. Indeed, the Indian government has progressively retracted from it and now tells the world that Kashmir is an integral part of India. The Indian government remembers Kashmir but forgets its people and has torn up the pledge she made to them.

The issue of Kashmir has plagued relations between India and Pakistan. They went to war in 1965 even if it was due to an adventure miscalculated on the part of Ayub Khan. Because of Ayub Khan's utter insincerity, the war was inconclusive and he deliberately abandoned the cause of Kashmiri people, which in turn means that he accepted that Kashmir was in fact an integral part of India. Therefore, he became party to the tearing up of the Indian pledge to Kashmiri people and of the Security Council resolution. Of course, the Soviet Union, who initiated and concluded the Tashkent agreement, other major powers and the United Nations itself, all became party to breaking the Indian government's and Security Council's pledge to the Kashmiri people. It is not easy to find instances of a greater and more cruel injustice done to a people.

But the last word rests with the people of Kashmir. They must and they will fight for their right to decide their own destiny. It is not possible to gain freedom through any means other than armed struggle. They will resort to this. And this time the people of Pakistan will compel their government to render all possible help to the doubly oppressed people of Kashmir, in their endeavour to gain freedom. This time the freedom loving people of the world will come to their aid in their liberation movement. No power can stop a people's liberation struggle from succeeding if they have the will to wage it. There is every indication that the people of Kashmir have the will; they have the desire; they will find the means. Their muted demand for emancipation will assume the volume of thunder. It will be the clarion call which the peoples of the world will hear and to which they will respond.

Chapter Nine

Clashes and Intrigues

In May 1948 I assumed the duties of officiating Commander-in-Chief (then known as Air Commander).

During the earlier part of my tenure as the officiating Air Commander it was suggested that the post of Deputy Air Commander be established and that it should be my official designation. It entailed no extra expenditure and no promotion or rank. The case was put to the Defence Ministry. A.T. Naqui informed us that the designation of Deputy Air Commander could be used. At the time we overlooked the fact that it was not confirmed in writing.

Perry-Keene, who had already been ill, took sick leave for at least six months. Several parallel developments, which I have already described, went ahead at a rapid pace. I was free from irritation by the British Commander of P.A.F., but the foreign domination was still generally felt. It was not possible to avoid clashes between the foreign personnel, who were mainly concerned with the interests of their own country, and the nationals who saw it, felt it acutely and resisted it. Those clashes were aggravated due to the subservient attitude of many of the politicians, civil servants and a few senior officers in the armed forces. Their inability to stand up to foreign domination was nauseating, humiliating and infuriating. Generally they leaned heavily on the British military and civil officers, but General Gracey's voice, in particular, was taken as the voice of the oracle. Those gentlemen, who had shouted themselves hoarse in telling the world that they were fit to rule themselves and were over-ripe for independence, would not move a step without consulting foreign persons, concerning the affairs of their own independent nation and that too in matters of vital importance to the country. General Gracey did what he pleased or what pleased his imperialist bosses. He had refused to send Pakistani troops into Kashmir when he was required to and when it was so necessary to do so. Yet he ordered them to march in against the Indian army, in complete contradiction to his earlier arguments. His opinion was sought, and he readily gave it, on political matters not even remotely concerned with the affairs of the army. He expressed opinions on such matters without being asked and it was heeded. His views against Pakistan establishing Diplomatic relations with the Soviet Union led to the postponement of such a move on the part of the Pakistan government. Most officers were terrified of contradicting him. They were terrified of the possibility of all British Officers resigning, and of supplies of British equipment being withheld. Some of us were not terrified. I for one would have been too happy to see the last of them. I was never apprehensive about the availability of British equipment. That was a purely commercial matter. It was inconceivable that the British would not trade with us if we declined to keep their officers, to run our national affairs. It is one thing to be friendly with a foreign country. It is quite another to permit non-nationals to interfere with and dictate on matters of national policy. But general Gracey did virtually dictate and our politicians did often submit to him.

In the third quarter of 1948, we began to sense that India was moving towards aggression against the Nizam's Hyderabad. The customary bombastic statements began to be made by our politicians in favour of

Hyderabad.

"We shall pluck out the eye which casts an evil glance at Hyderabad." Screamed Abdul Qayyum Khan and he almost literally marked out the route he would follow to go to the aid of the Nizam.

Rumours began to go around that the British were providing military aircraft to the Nizam and that training of personnel was taking place 'somewhere in the Middle East'. After all, he was the most faithful ally of the British and had given them a whole air force squadron during their war against Hitler. Of course, the rumours came to nothing. They had less substance than a bubble. The Nizam was their most faithful ally. It did not necessarily follow that the British were his allies! Indeed, they were not. All his pleas were in vain.

The bellicose statements from Pakistani leaders encouraged the formation of a local resistance movement under Qasim Rizvi. Under different conditions it may have been largely successful. But being virtually an island, surrounded by India on all sides, the movement did not stand a chance. The situation was further aggravated by the introduction of the predictable and inevitable gun running. Hyderabad State being land locked, the weapons had to be flown in. In order to avoid interception by the Indian Air Force, a long route had to be used and night flying was resorted to. The airfield at Mauripur and the civil airport were both used. At least one Minister from the Central Cabinet of Pakistan, Malik Ghulam Mohammad, aided and abetted the gun running which was being organised by Sydney Cotton. I referred to him earlier. The Defence Secretary, Iskander Mirza and the Joint Defence Secretary, A.T. Naqui, were closely associated with it. Undoubtedly there were other civil and possibly military persons, involved in that operation. The actual operation was strictly secret and even I was not aware of it, although Pakistan Air Force airfield was being used. I was generally aware that aircraft on charter by Sydney Cotton were engaged in airlifts of arms and ammunition to Hyderabad. But I was not aware of the details of the contents.

I was able to see the load of only one aircraft which crashed at Mauripur. This could not be concealed from me because emergency measures had to be taken to prevent fire and explosion. That load consisted of small arms, mainly automatic, rifles and ammunition. It seemed that the weapons had been placed loosely in the aircraft. As it climbed after take off, the load drifted to the tail end, the aircraft climbed steeply, lost speed rapidly, stalled and crashed on the perimeter of the airfield.

There were extremely strong rumours that the aircraft which went into Hyderabad with guns came back with gold. But it was as closely guarded when it returned, as it was when it flew out and the secret remained with the select few.

The tension built up. The statements became increasingly more bellicose. Matters were moving to a head.

A meeting was called at short notice at the Prime Minister's residence. This was on a day which will remain, for another reason, forever on the pages of the history of Pakistan. It was 11 September, 1948. Quad-i-Azam Ali Jinnah expired on that day.

The meeting was attended by Nawabzada Liaquat Ali Khan in his dual capacity as Prime Minister and Defence Minister, Chaudhry Mohamed Ali, Secretary General to the Cabinet, Iskander Mirza, A.T. Naqvi and perhaps some more civil officers, General Gracey, Major General Cawthorne, Deputy Chief of Staff Pakistan army, Major General Iftikhar Khan, Brigadier Sher Khan from the army and possibly a few more, Admiral Jefford and Rear Admiral H.M.S. Chaudhry from the Pakistan Navy and I represented the Pakistan Air Force. The meeting lasted almost the entire day. The subject of the meeting was Hyderabad. Information had been received that the Indian armed forces had taken up aggressive positions around Hyderabad and were poised to attack. A lengthy analysis and discussion ensued. There seemed to be no doubt that the much proclaimed and threatened 'police action' by India was imminent. The Pakistani government had been belching fire and its leaders had made declarations to the effect, that in the event of Indian aggression, Pakistan would go to the aid of Hyderabad. Now that that eventuality had arisen, the obvious question was "What could Pakistan do?"

The service which could provide the answer was the army. General Gracey replied in the negative: "Nothing" He said. This was an anti-climax. Inwardly I felt nausea at the response. It had been said that "We shall pluck out the eye" of anyone who invaded Hyderabad. When the time came, "Nothing" was the answer. However, although it was a shameful betrayal, the conclusion seemed inevitable. If we had not gone to war over Kashmir it was absurd to think that we would do so over Hyderabad. The decision was final. General Gracey also opined that the Indian army would overcome the Hyderabad armed resistance in about three weeks. This seemed a conservative forecast and proved to be so. The resistance was defeated in about a week.

We then discussed the measures we should adopt for defence should we be compelled to fight. General Gracey gave out his plan for the army. My first skirmish with him came soon after. In his plan he included air support in a sector we had agreed three months earlier would not be provided.

"I am sorry General Gracey, but you cannot have air support there." I interrupted.

"Why not?" He asked. And without waiting for my reply went on to make a categorical statement.

"If I cannot have air support in this sector then I cannot take responsibility for the defence of Pakistan."

This was an astounding statement, coming from the man in whose hands the destiny of Pakistan seemed to have been placed. But it was an absurd statement. However, none of the army or Defence Ministry officers tried to question it.

"Sir Douglas, three months ago you had agreed about the role of the air force in the event of hostilities." I said. "This particular sector was discussed in detail. You were thoroughly satisfied as to our role as well as to the fact the army would function without air support. We were to only provide limited reconnaissance. You were to rely mainly on your own resources for obtaining information about the enemy." I continued.

"What has happened in these three months to change the situation in such a drastic manner?"

"What...what?" He muttered.

The Prime Minister, who had not so far intervened in the purely operational discussion, looked concerned. He shifted his gaze from me to General Gracey.

"General, the Air Commodore is asking you as to what has happened in three months, to make you change your army plans so drastically." He said.

I went on to complete my statement.

"The strength and structure of the air force has not altered in three short months. We are fully prepared to carry out the functions originally allocated to us. I sincerely hope that the army has suffered no set back. If it has, then we have not been informed."

The Prime Minister waited for General Gracey's reaction. The latter pondered for a brief moment.

"Well Sir, if the air force is unable to give me support then I shall readjust my plans." He said.

This was incredible. If there were alternative plans then why make so definitive a pronouncement! I did not pause to try to fathom General Gracey's aim in this respect. We had far too much work to do and could not take time off to puzzle out his motives. We proceeded with the discussion for a while longer and then broke off for lunch. Of course, the conversation among groups continued during lunch. Preparations for defence of the country against aggression, is a matter of the utmost importance. It was quite natural that all conversation should be dominated by it. During this break A.T. Naqvi came over to me and paid me the best professional compliment, even if qualified, I have ever been paid.

"You are the best of the three commanders." He said. "But you want to be the dictator of the air force."

I was embarrassed and overwhelmed.

"Thank you for your kindness." I said. "It is not possible to visualise a more complete dictator than the commander of a defence service. The very nature of his command is dictatorial. But I hope you will never find me unreasonably so."

I was also saddened, because I believed that he indirectly referred to a personal request he had made to me and which I had turned down. It crossed my mind that perhaps in governmental and bureaucratic corridors this was the impression of me that was being circulated. Was this also being strengthened by subtle foreign observations? Perhaps with a hint being dropped at an appropriate time? Our erstwhile imperial masters excelled in the art of creating, sustaining and strengthening such suspicions. They had found fertile ground. Some minds were susceptible and receptive, the ones that suffered from acute inferiority complexes and utter lack of self-confidence. Even at that early date the leaders had started looking over their shoulders. This was a sad commentary on the trend of thought expressed by Naqvi. In such a frame of mind the leaders would feel danger lurking in the darkness – of their own minds – and lash out. Among a host of mediocrities, if one stood out a shade they would try to strike him down. They would indulge in slanging matches among themselves. Those in power would try to retain it by placing the bayonet in the hands of an imbecile. The others aspiring to gain power would employ every stratagem, almost invariably immoral, to attain it. The interminable game of snatching power would go on.

After lunch we resumed discussion. Having decided that Pakistan could not intervene on behalf of the Nizam, the meeting proceeded do consider defence of Pakistan, against the highly unlikely possibility of a direct Indian attack. The three defence services gave their plans for a six-month preparation. The air force presented four major steps to be adopted. The budget was allocated for the same. The Prime Minister ordered that the plans should be implemented immediately and the budgets were deemed to have been approved. However, for the record, the plans were to be reduced to being written down and formal approval appended to them.

At the end of the general discussion the Prime Minister asked a specific question.

"I am a mere politician," he said. "Can you soldiers tell me what the Indians will do after they have occupied Hyderabad?"

I wanted to scream.

"No Sir, this is a purely political question. You tell us what the Indians might attempt and we shall prepare ourselves to meet the situation."

Of course I was unable to say so. General Gracey responded immediately.

"Well Sir! After they have occupied Hyderabad they will keep on throwing us ultimatums. We will keep on accepting them. But the 'bania' will never attack us." He said with assumed confidence.

He looked around as if for applause. This was accorded him in looks of admiration, but met with utter silence. For me, it was too much to swallow.

"Sir Douglas. I am unable to agree with your observation." I said. The silence was shattered by a rustling and creaking of chairs. All heads turned towards me sharply. There was amazement written on many a countenance. The word of General Gracey had been challenged, by the youngest at the meeting. This was unbelievable! The Prime Minister looked puzzled but sat silently as if to wait for the outcome of the most unexpected dialogue. General Gracey was stunned.

"What – what do you mean?" He stammered.

"I do not agree with your analysis." I replied.

He repeated his question, still unable to believe that he had been challenged.

"Give me one reason as to why the Indians would not follow up their ultimatum? Why have they not attacked Hyderabad all these months since partition?" I asked.

"There are many reasons." He replied vaguely.

"Please give me just one." I insisted.

"There are many reasons." He repeated.

This was getting monotonous.

"Alright, General Gracey, I will give you one reason and that is us." I said.

"What do you mean?" He asked, while the other persons looked on, still bewildered.

"The Indians did not attack Hyderabad earlier, because they thought we may intervene and attack them." I said. "But now we have decided we can and will do nothing. This means our bluff will have been called. It will have been proved that we had neither the strength nor the will to fight them. After the conquest of Hyderabad, their tails will be right up. They will have no reason to fear us. And you are implying that they will be afraid of us."

"Then do you think they will attack Pakistan?" He asked.

"No I'm not saying that at all." I said. "There may be a hundred and one reasons as to why they may not attack us. But your analysis that after occupying Hyderabad they will still be afraid of us, is obviously wrong. They will have no reason to be afraid. Their morale will be very high. If they throw us ultimatums then we must take them seriously."

"What do you want us to do?" Asked Major General Iftikhar Khan, his voice booming with anger and indignation. His eyes were fiery and fixed on me. I was able to return his gaze.

"I want you to do nothing." I said. "But if you are thinking of relying on General Gracey's conclusion, then I suggest you do not. Instead of allowing yourselves six months you should allow only three months. As I have said, they may not attack for other reasons. If we believe that, or if in any event we believe General Gracey when he says the Indians will not attack us, then there is no need to adopt any special measures."

No one else spoke during this triangular discussion. I considered it to be a matter of immense importance. But there was no contribution from any quarter except some glares of disapproval in my direction. My thoughts wandered back to the lawns in New Delhi, where about fourteen months earlier, the Quad-I Azam had stressed the supremacy of civil authority. The mere mention of the specialist opinion of the commanders had brought a fierce retort. Now that the Quad-i-Azam lay on his deathbed his Prime Minister had gone a long way from that policy. A foreign national was being allowed to virtually dictate the policy of our nation.

After the meeting I was joined by Asghar Khan, whom I had called from Risalpur, and Haider Raza. We drove to Air Headquarters at Mauripur. The sun glowed red as it set. About half way to Mauripur, as I left the built up area and came into the open, I saw an ambulance parked at the side of the road. I slowed down but was waved on by someone standing beside it. Asghar Khan told me later that he had been able to see inside the ambulance. The rear door was open. He later described to me what he thought he had seen.

In the ambulance lay the founder and father of Pakistan, Quad-i-Azam Mohammed Ali Jinnah, his head resting in the lap of a lady. Asghar Khan said that he thought the Quad-i-Azam was already dead. It was not possible to ascertain this. But in any event he was only minutes away from death. Why was he being transported in an obviously ill maintained civilian ambulance, when well-maintained air force and army ambulances were available in abundance? He was the Head of State and the founder of it. The air force had not been asked to take the Governor General's aircraft to Quetta to fly him to Karachi for his last flight. If any single person had the right to an air force aircraft, it was the Head of State, even if we were to forget the emotional aspect of that person being the father of the nation. Why was he not allowed to exercise his right? If secrecy were to be maintained, then absolute observance of it by the air force would have been possible. In any event, why was it necessary to maintain such secrecy? The Prime Minister should have received his Governor General, especially in that critical condition. It was perhaps necessary to avoid ceremony, but there appeared to be no reason for the utter lack of concern, on the part of the senior members of the cabinet. Indeed, complete indifference was displayed by the Prime Minister. He showed not the slightest concern throughout the day, when we sat discussing, what may be termed a non-event. It is not only in order but necessary to take the members of the cabinet and the heads of the three defence services into confidence. I know that I was not informed. The British heads of the other two Pakistani services may have been told. Since no members of the cabinet accompanied the ambulance, in which their Governor General lay, I can only conclude that they were not informed about his flight from Quetta to Karachi. If, however, they had been told, then they displayed cruelty and callousness. I do not say that most of them were incapable of such callousness, but I believe that on that occasion they were not made aware of the Quad-i-Azam's last flight. The Quad-i-Azam had been abandoned to die in isolation. His last gaze, in all probability, rested perhaps on the most untidy spot in the suburbs of Karachi. Not the multi coloured curtains of the Government House, but the heaps of filth around the slums in which the refugees and fishermen's families dwelt, who were also neglected and abandoned.

At about 2.30am on 12 September, my telephone rang at home. Naqvi's voice came over it as I answered it, woken from an uneasy slumber.

"The Quad-i-Azam has died!" He said.

Despite the fact that I had half expected the tragic news, I was terribly shocked.

"When?" I asked.

"Earlier tonight." He replied. No definite time could be obtained, even later.

It would be superfluous to describe the funeral of the Quad-i-Azam on the following day. The nation mourned the founder, its father. This applies only once in the life of a country. There may be more than one resurgence, but there can be only one birth.

The successor to the Quad-i-Azam in his capacity as Governor General was installed. I had witnessed the first ceremony thirteen months earlier to the day. The contrast was immense. The first ceremony was a solemn occasion in every respect. The second was a mere routine formality. When the Quad-i-Azam entered a room he dominated the situation and a hush fell over those present and there was complete silence. When Khwaja Nazim-u-`din entered the murmuring and shuffling continued. The former occupied the chair; the latter was placed on it. For the former every detail had been worked out meticulously; for the latter hardly any attention was paid to detail. The Military Secretary to the Governor General was still a British officer. I was frustrated and furious at the glaring discrepancies and I told him so. The chair which had been used by the Quad-i-Azam was provided for Khwaja Nazim-u-Din. His feet were suspended about six inches above the floor. One did not expect the legs of the chair to be shortened but a step covered with carpet could have been placed in front of it. I was so angry that I said,

"We have all seen the reaction of the audience in a cinema at the scene of a ritual ceremony of some nineteenth century central African Chieftain. One can imagine what the reaction would be if the film of this ceremony were to be shown. No one would know that an experienced British Colonel had managed the whole affair. It is a Pakistani occasion and people would assume that it has been organised by Pakistanis."

Asghar Khan and other officers helped me prepare the four cases for formal approval. They were submitted to the Defence Ministry within a day. A few days later the entire file was returned to me with provisional and conditional approval.

"Such and such is approved providing no other arrangement can be made."

"Training can be carried out abroad if it cannot be done at home."

I was asked to study the possibility of meeting all the needs in a manner other than had been discussed at length, in detail, at the Prime

Minister's residence. The papers that I had submitted to the Defence Ministry contained no factor which had not been discussed, agreed and approved by the Prime Minister. Now I was being asked to consider a possibility which did not exist. Had it been possible to carry out our programme in a manner other than we had arrived at during the meeting, it would have been incorporated in the case. In view of these factors I was astonished and exceedingly distressed to receive a virtually negative response to a matter of apparently vital national importance. And it was from the Defence Secretary, Iskander Mirza himself.

I had already taken steps to implement the programme. I had asked the British to train twenty-two engineers and the same number of pilots. They were able to undertake the former but not the latter. I therefore, asked the American Air Attache, Major John R. Brown Jr., Bob to his friends, to convey our request for training our pilots, to his government. He had already informed me that although the U.S. air force was unable to take our pilots into their training establishments, a civilian firm would be able to make adequate arrangements. Later the twenty-two pilots were sent to America. The engineer trainees were sent to Hamble in Britain. At home larger numbers began to be taken into the Recruits Training centre for trainee airmen and the Flying Training College for all branches of officers, especially pilot trainees. Also the training periods were shortened. I had deputed Maqbool Rabb to proceed to Britain and interview Polish air force refugees, with a view to offering them rehabilitation in Pakistan. This would provide a home for them and trained personnel for us.

Under conditions of national emergency, when we were taking vigorous action to meet our targets, if possible ahead of time, Iskander Mirza's notes had a shattering and disturbing effect. I wrote back on the lines mentioned here, in very strong words. It was not unnatural in these circumstances and from a person who took the possibility of war seriously. I had been asked to prepare the nation's air force to meet Indian aggression. It is not possible to imagine a matter more serious and urgent than a war of defence.

I had no response in writing from the Ministry of Defence. I was told that Iskander Mirza was very angry. I conveyed a message back that I was very angry too. Although I went ahead with the programme as agreed on 11 September, I was not able to see Iskander Mirza for many weeks. I worked with and through A. T. Naqvi. I sought interviews with the Prime Minister; for which I sought help from Iskander Mirza, when I eventually managed to see him. I was always told the Prime Minister was very busy.

The Indian government occupied Hyderabad in a few days. Pandit Nehru, the disciple of the prophet of non-violence – Mahatma Gandhi – made bellicose and belligerent statements. I sent cuttings of these to Iskander Mirza, to convey the seriousness of the situation. Still there was no response.

In the meantime Perry-Keene returned from leave – which had been a prolonged period of absence. Iskander Mirza lost no time in putting him in the picture, so to speak. I also apprised him of the situation. He almost audibly smacked his lips. He hated my presence. But generations of cunning, which had developed among the ruling class of Britain, always came into play. Perry-Keene kept a calm composure. He put up a remarkable façade. The situation was to his liking. Iskander Mirza, the Defence Secretary, was now my avowed enemy and hence Perry-Keene's ally. The former had an acute case of Anglophilia. He could be counted on to support British personnel and interests as far as and as long as possible. Now if Perry-Keene were to suggest any action to my disadvantage, he would have unhesitating support from Iskander Mirza. The entire file, once again, was returned by Iskander Mirza but this time to Perry-Keene personally. The covering note was to the effect that 'the file was being returned in order to avoid any mischief being created.' Of course, the only mischief on record was that created by him; his reluctance to carry out the programme agreed, indeed ordered, by the Prime Minister himself.

Perry-Keene realised that direct communication between Iskander Mirza and I was severed, even if only temporarily. He was, therefore, able to discuss with Iskander, all subjects pertaining to the air force, with the full knowledge and confidence that they would not be re-discussed with me. On the other hand he assured me that, despite Iskander Mirza's obvious reluctance, he would definitely arrange for me to see the Prime Minister. This was transparently untrue, but I made no comment. In the past, he had told me on occasions when I had a violent disagreement with him, that even at cabinet level there was mutual tearing of hair. He now had occasion to remind me. Iskander Mirza ceased to speak to me, even at social functions. But the implementation of the programme proceeded. He could neither halt nor reverse it.

The collapse of Hyderabad came, as expected by many and as known to the Prime Minister. The so-called leaders of Pakistan had been making promises to the Nizam and to the people of Pakistan, that the independence of Hyderabad would not be allowed to be violated. If words could break bones, the entire aggressive Indian army would have been crushed to a pulp, under the tirade which had emanated for months from the political leaders in Pakistan. Forever ready to shed their last drop of blood for causes, territories and people, they never came within miles of the Kashmir front. They never exposed themselves to the possibility of tripping over a stone in the hills of Kashmir, or to suffer a scratch. Hyderabad was a thousand miles away. Their false promises led the state of Hyderabad to have expectations which could not be fulfilled. There was no justification for aggression by India; the relationship between them should have been settled by means of bilateral negotiation. But equally there was no justification for Pakistani politicians to issue belligerent statements on the subject, but since they had done so and the inevitable collapse had taken place, Pakistan had to resort to a shameful face saving stratagem. The Prime

Minister promptly issued a statement accusing the Nizam of having betrayed his people. One of his close associates called this a masterstroke.

The Nizam, having decided to resist Indian aggression, put up a valiant struggle. The help promised by Pakistan did not come. The State was already besieged even before the first shot was fired. When the Indian army attacked, the blockade was complete. The borders were sealed and so was the fate of the State. A full-scale war cannot be sustained by means of gun running. Lack of reinforcements in men and material had to lead to diminishing resistance and futile, avoidable loss of human life. The Nizam was compelled into submission by Indian action on the one hand and complete absence of action by his allies on the other. He was betrayed. He took the only wise course left open to him. He sued for peace in order to prevent unnecessary destruction and loss of life. He was called a traitor to his people by the Pakistani leaders, when in fact the boot was on the other foot.

As I have stated earlier, I had been profoundly affected by the manner in which Pakistan came into being; truncated and a mere fraction of the Pakistan envisaged in the 1940 Lahore resolution. A possible genocide in the entire sub-continent had been averted, but an enormous price in lives and territory had been paid by the innocent Muslim masses. The wounds that were inflicted had still not healed. In mid 1948, the British delivered yet another blow to the Muslims – this time in the Arab Middle East. They had yielded to Zionism. During the First World War they had promised a homeland to the much and long persecuted Jews. This was to be in Palestine, which was to be divided into Arab and Jewish nations. After the Second World War the demand for it was stepped up. There was violence against the British forces of occupation by Jewish organisations such as the Stern Gang (they seem to have learnt their methods and borrowed their name from the oppressors and exterminators of their people, the Nazis) and Irgun Zvai Luemi. Ordinarily it should not have been necessary for them to resort to armed struggle even against the British. The establishment of their homeland, at the expense of the Arabs, was imminent. But not only were they able to acquire small arms normally used in a resistance movement, they were able to organise regular formations of heavy weapons and armour. As the day for the establishment of Israel approached, the volume and intensity of Zionist aggression against the Arabs increased. Eventually they were able to drive out large numbers of Palestinians from their homes and to occupy areas beyond the boundaries set by the British and acknowledged by the United Nations. The neighbouring Arab countries tried to contain the Zionist forces within their legal borders and to stem their expansion. But their combined, though in no way co-ordinated or united efforts, did not succeed. With the help of British and American imperialism, the Zionists were able to commence their existence as a nation in excess of the land promised them and legally theirs. They took the excess land from the Arab Muslims mainly, if not entirely. In the Indo-Pakistan sub-continent, less than a year earlier, the Muslims had been deprived of land and millions of lives on account of British machinations.

I was so profoundly moved by events in the Middle East that I wrote a lengthy political analysis on the foregoing theme. I sent it to the Prime Minister. Some time later Agha Hamid, his Private Secretary, came to my house. He told me that my paper had been read with great interest. It was considered to be the best political analysis they had ever read.

"But the Prime Minister was very unhappy on one point," said Agha Hamid.

"And what's that?" I asked a little surprised.

"You have used a sentence which he does not like." He said. "You say that India was divided and Pakistan created because it suited the British. The Prime Minister says that you have belittled the great role of the Muslim League in the Independence and Pakistan movements."

"Good gracious! He must not read that sentence out of context." I said, in anger and dismay. "You have read the entire paper. I have given every conceivable reason in justification of Pakistan. But even more I have said that we have been deprived of our legitimate territory. A vast territory had gone to India at our expense, just as Arab territory has been handed over to the Zionists." I continued in exasperation.

"In the end I have given an additional reason; that it also suited the British. But I do not stop there. I say that had the Pakistan of the 1940 resolution been achieved, the sub-continent would have been at peace and strong. Not the British, nor any other power, would have been able to overawe it and interfere with the policies of the two countries at peace and friendly with each other. India would have had no option but to be friendly with us."

"Yes I agree." Agha Hamid said. "I appreciate it, but the Prime Minister was unhappy about it."

I threw up my hands in disgust.

This was towards the end of December 1948. I had already received some anonymous letters accusing me of dictatorial intentions and aspirations. This campaign became intense. Some began to echo A. T. Naqvi's remark that I wanted to become a dictator of the air force. The rumours were extended to dictatorship of the whole country! At least one officer used the word Hitler when he referred to my attitude. Of course, he was a thoroughly inefficient and unintelligent officer and was terrified of action against him. To such officers I would appear to be the worst dictator because their jobs were likely to be in jeopardy. But to the highly efficient professionals like Asghar Khan and Nur Khan, I was too soft and kind. I do admit that I was inclined to overlook lesser human errors, but I believe I was quite firm in matters of discipline. It was the latter which was quoted as an example of my dictatorial severity. The inefficient and the incapable are always apprehensive and nervous. They, therefore, resort to cunning stratagems. To safeguard their interests they betray confidence, form evil alliances and attack the source of danger to them. In a system of exploitation, this type of evil is rampant and informs the greater part of political leadership. Officialdom and bureaucracy spend the greater part of their time, in machinations and manoeuvring to protect their interests, always at the cost of the greater interests of the people. The air force and other services and departments of Pakistan were no exception to the rule of capitalism.

Some time in December 1948, Group Captain M. Rabb came to my office with a type written note. It was from Perry-Keene in his capacity as Air Commander of Pakistan air force. It contained words to the effect that "The unofficial post of Deputy Air Commander was abolished' and that I was to be assigned other duties.

"Take it back to Perry-Keene", I told Maqbool Rabb. "I do not accept this order."

I was quite angry that Perry-Keene should have sent an open note to me through my subordinate. He had shown such contemptible lack of moral courage that I found it necessary to return his written instruction through the same junior officer. I had never known Perry-Keene to be able to stand up to me and look me straight in the eye, but I thought he would have felt strong enough, having Iskander Mirza firmly on his side, to call me and deliver the order personally. A. T. Naqvi had said, on more than one occasion to more than one person, that I had Perry-Keene by the neck and rubbed his nose in the ground. Maybe he had heard that remark. However, he did not have to be told about my temperament. He had abundant opportunity to witness and experience it.

I was also angry that the post of Deputy Air Commander had been declared unofficial by Perry-Keene, while the Joint Secretary, Ministry of Defence had approved it. I went to see Naqvi and asked him whether the post had been abolished.

"No it has not been abolished in writing." He said, "It was a verbal approval. Still I believe you should have the designation of Deputy Air Commander. But another view is that should you have the designation, then there would be demand for it from the army and the navy."

"In other words the post was not confirmed in writing," I said, "and I have been holding a designation without written sanction. I think I should have been told about it and also the argument about the other two services."

"I am sorry about it all." Naqvi said. "Leave it to me."

On the evening of 4 January I attended the Indonesian Independence Anniversary party. The American Air Attache, Major Brown came over to see me. Pointing at Nawabzada Liaquat Ali Khan, who was surrounded by dozens of people, he said,

"Do you see Liaquat there? I will come after ten years and find you similarly surrounded."

Bob Brown was informal with me and occasionally was given to pull my leg.

"God forbid!" I said, "Anyway, why ten years?"

"We diplomats have a way of assessing such matters." He said.

Of course I could not take him seriously and shrugged off his remark. He edged me towards the Prime Minister, who had Altaf Hussain, editor of 'Dawn' standing next to him. He went right up to them.

"I am Major Brown of the U.S. air force, Mr. Prime Minister," He said, "And this is Air Commodore Janjua of Pakistan air force."

"Well that is the long and the short of it" said the Prime Minister. He was referring to our statures. Bob Brown very tall and I very short, especially in comparison. This subtle humour brought an amused response from all of us.

"Do you know the Air Commodore?" Brown asked for some inexplicable reason.

"Does he know him?" Altaf Hussain intervened. "He knows him too well." This was an ambiguous statement and, I thought, not well intended. However, as we drifted from place to place I forgot about it.

On the morning of 5 January, 1949, Rabb again came to me with a note. It was now signed by the Defence Secretary, Iskander Mirza, himself. It repeated that the 'unofficial' post of Deputy Air Commander was abolished, but it added, that I was to retain the rank of Air Commodore. It further stated that I was to proceed abroad on a special mission and should be prepared to stay out for a long period. Even on that occasion Perry-Keene showed utter lack of moral fibre in not telling me himself. He had obviously conspired with Iskander Mirza to remove me from the air force of my own country. They had taken advantage of a technicality to abolish a designation, which I had held for many months and they were fully aware of it. An officer does not have to be removed just because the post he held is abolished. On the other hand an officer may be removed despite the existence of a designation. In this case they employed the usual underhand tactics of abolishing a post in order to remove me. They could not place another P.A.F. officer in that post. They were far too junior to me and the trick would have been exposed.

I considered it futile to protest. The Defence Secretary had signed the orders; technically he was right. The Prime Minister had concurred. Obviously Naqvi had failed in his attempt to restore the situation. I was not able to see the Prime Minister. He was unable to find time. The Governor General Khwaja Nazim-u-Din continued to call me to social functions and was his gentle self. But I was sad beyond description. I had never imagined that I would be victimised on an issue of national importance. Even less had I realised that underhand methods would be used to get rid of me. I had been naïve enough to believe that any disagreement would be openly expressed, as was my wont, and a fight would be openly fought. That the Prime Minister downwards had resorted to surreptitious methods came as a grave shock to me. I was so gloomy that perhaps for the first time in my career it showed on my face. I had to have photographs taken for my passport. When Group captain Fayyaz Mahmood, the Senior Education officer, saw the expression on my face in those photos, he exclaimed sadly, "Oh no! I never expected to see this."

It was indeed a shattering experience for me. I went home early that day. Later on I received a message from Perry-Keene that he would like to see me in the next day or two. I went to his office the following day. I was not going to give him the pleasure of seeing me broken and shattered. I walked in solemn and stern. At first glance he looked pleased and satisfied. He went through his characteristic motions of lighting his pipe and sucking at it. He looked at me over the pipe and around and through the clouds of smoke. He stood up and said,

"Well Jan, I'm afraid the situation is not very good."

"You have always told me that this sort of thing occurs at the highest levels." I said, "I accept it as such."

He was puzzled. He had experienced supplication on the part of some of our relatively senior officers. He expected to see me bend. I was rigid as ever. He soon recomposed himself; his second nature was the quick compromise of an imperialist, and it came to the fore. He then briefly explained my assignment. It was not at all necessary to have any officer go to Britain to speed up the supply of equipment. I had already placed officers of adequate rank and appropriate branches there, to obtain requisite supplies. There was no hold up anywhere. At the end of his talk he informed me that his replacement would be Air Commodore Atcherley.

"You know what David said to the people of Israel!" He enlightened me.

"I chased you with a whip; my son will chase you with scorpions."

I could have laughed at the implication that he, Perry-Keene, had chased us with a whip. I could have cried with the irony that he was able to say so.

"No one will find us lacking in our profession." I told him. "We would like to have someone with life in him."

And then I left him.

The word soon went around about my removal.

"Janjua has gone for a six!" remarked an R.A.F. officer, who ordinarily could not find a small enough hole to hide in when I was in his vicinity. The R.A.F. officers collectively held a party at Drigh Road to celebrate the occasion.

Six of the most senior Pakistan Air Force officers decided to take a petition to the Prime Minister concerning my removal. Two other officers, who had hesitated earlier, joined them. This joint action on the part of so many officers was termed a 'concerted act' and tantamount to mutiny. However, the Prime Minister received them and assured them that my removal from Air H.Q. was only temporary. He also told them that no harm would come to me, and, indeed, it was for my good that I was being sent out of the country. Of course it was not necessary that they should have seen the logic of his statement. One reason given by Iskander Mirza was that it would broaden my outlook and education. Perhaps I had a purely national outlook, hence it was too narrow. I had to be exposed to imperialist education. I thought I had had enough of it, but they considered that it was too little.

I underwent great dismay; even the Prime Minister had declined to face me with his criticism, if any, of my professional conduct or his displeasure, if he were indeed, displeased. He dropped several more notches in my estimation. At the manner of the Quad-i-Azam's arrival from Quetta on the day of his death, the Prime Minister stood exceedingly low in my view. Nothing happened in latter years to restore my respect for him.

Major Bob Brown met me later and said that he thought my C-in-C Perry-Keene should have stood by me. I laughed loudly at his remark. Obviously he had thought that in my tussle with the Defence Secretary, the air force Chief should have been at least neutral and at best on my side. How little he seemed to know!

I began to make preparations for my departure to Britain. There was little to be done in this respect. I discussed my situation with Naqvi. He advised me to meet Air Commodore Atcherley (Air Vice Marshal when he took over command of P.A.F.) and to tell him the whole story.

I left for Britain in the third week of January, 1949. On arrival, I had very little to do. I visited aircraft factories, training establishments, where we had our training and generally occupied myself reading and writing. I helped the High Commissioner, Ibrahim Rahimtoola, to establish better and more effective communications between the High Commission in London and Karachi.

At the first opportunity, I established contact with Air Vice Marshal R.L.R. Atcherley. He had a reputation for being aggressive and energetic. He was unorthodox in his approach. I was delighted to learn this. It was an excellent combination of qualities, much needed in the building of a young air force such as ours. He was an excellent pilot. He had won the Schneider Trophy for Britain. He was literally crazy about flying. He had acquired the nickname of Batchy; not quite right in the head.

We met and exchanged notes. Of course, he had more to learn about his new command from me, than I had to learn from him about equipment and other matters. I took the opportunity to tell him, in detail, the reason for my presence in Britain.

"So they have got you!" He remarked at the end of it all. "It is really the Defence Secretary."

They were all mere names and designations to him. No one was personally known to him. He had vaguely heard of Perry-Keene and knew that he was a retired officer. A.V.M. Atcherley understood the situation quite readily. He had experience enough to know. I was the naïve one. He seemed to sympathise.

A.V.M. Atcherley had occasion to refer to an energetic approach in the building of a young air force. I told him that he would not find us lacking in energy and as for myself, I was very aggressive in the matter.

"Do you think they will let me do what I like?" He asked me shortly before we left for Pakistan.

"They have no option." I replied. "After all, they have sought your services. Perry-Keene was a retired officer. He had to do everything to safeguard and prolong his tenure. He would have had to yield, against his better judgement perhaps. You're a serving officer. You can always come back to your own job. The must need your professional advice. You will be able to do whatever you think necessary for the air force."

He thanked me. At that time little could he have realised that he would be able to do whatever he liked in every field; that he would be able to literally ride rough shod over everyone. And little did I realise that he would replace General Gracey in many ways. Unorthodox and aggressive, in a position of strength, conscious of his power and confident of his ability, he did exceptionally well for his own country, receiving awards for services rendered, and he pursued our expansion programmes, improved upon them, in due course and got through projects which had been held up due to my friction with Iskander Mirza. Atcherley was a splendid professional. He gave his all to Pakistan air force. He was a senior officer of the British Imperial services. He gave even more to Britain.

A few days after his arrival in Pakistan, he wrote to me to the effect that the air force had outgrown its strength and that he wanted me back as soon as possible to help him. It was quite natural for the air force to seem to have outgrown its strength. About four months earlier, on account of the so-called national emergency arising from the Indian aggression against Hyderabad, much equipment had been ordered. Aircraft had been obtained and many transport aircraft had been modified to perform the functions of bombers. While the equipment was readily available and could be seen, the men were still being recruited and trained and could not be seen on the ground.

I was, however, happy to note that A.V.M. Atcherley had found it necessary, desirable and natural to seek the help of the senior-most national of Pakistan, in the air force. I wrote back to tell him that I would return as soon as he sent me a message to that effect. Of course he realised that I had been sent on a false errand. I had been asked by the Defence Secretary to send him progress reports. I did so even if they seemed futile and unnecessary.

In the third week of February 1949, I received a signal from the Ministry of Defence asking me to return to Pakistan as soon as possible after 21 February. I acknowledged the signal and took the flight which landed in Karachi on 22nd. I discovered that the date had been given because Perry-Keene had to sail for his home on 21st.

On arrival I found that A.V.M. Atcherley was on tour of the P.A.F. stations in the north. I stayed a week in Karachi. That day the Governor General was due at Mauripur by air from Dacca. Being the most senior air force officer present I went to receive him. There were several civil and some military officers present. Mauripur being an air force station, I was nearest the steps and the first to meet the Governor General. I saluted and he put his hand into mine. He never shook hands, but invariably placed his hand into the other person's hand, as limp as a piece of mutton. That is precisely how his hand felt when I held it. Then he looked at me. His hand stiffened – a most unusual experience. Obviously he was surprised to see me.

"Oh! You have come back?" He said.

"Yes sir, I have come back." I replied.

"How was your trip and your mission?" He asked, and immediately followed with "Did you enjoy yourself?"

"My trip was fine and I enjoyed it; thank you." I said.

He proceeded to meet the dignitaries who waited anxiously to greet him. When he had met the last of them, he returned to speak to me.

"You must come and see me." He said. "You must tell me all about your mission."

"I have sent my reports to the Defence Secretary. I hope he will pass them to you for your perusal." I said.

"But you must come and see me anyway." He insisted.

"Thank you sir, I shall be glad to." I said and saw him to his car.

What and how much he had been told about my so-called mission and the reason for it, I was unable to discover. Although I met Khwaja Nazim-u-Din on several occasions after that, he never broached the subject.

I joined A.V.M. Atcherley at Risalpur. He greeted me formally, but not quite as cordially as I thought he might have done. He told me that he would like to speak to me privately. We were unable to have our conversation in Risalpur. In Peshawar after lunch at Amlot's residence, I believe, A.V.M. Atcherley spoke to me.

"I have some serious matters to discuss with you." He said. "I have had talks with almost the entire government. The Governor General, the

Prime Minister, the Defence Secretary, General Gracey, General Cawthorne and all senior officials have complained about you. They say you are insolent to your superiors, harsh to your subordinates, aggressive in your approach. In short you are like a bull in a china shop. When I heard all this I thought I would be a fool to work with you. But I met you in England and I liked you. Therefore, I have decided that you can remain at Air H.Q. We shall start with a clean slate."

All this time I looked at him in disbelief. But he proceeded.

"However, all of them say that your attitude is due only to patriotic reasons. You have only one friend – Naqvi. He has said that possibly he has been partly responsible for your attitude."

"It is very nice of them to at least attribute my behaviour to patriotism. As for being insolent, I do not believe that that is the correct word but I have never hesitated to express my views strongly whenever I found it necessary to do so. As to the charge of harshness, I have been accused f excessive softness by the most capable officers in our air force. I cannot disguise the fact that I am dangerously honest; I do not permit dishonest practices when it is possible for me to stop them. In any event, I do not approve of them. I shall try to work with you as best as I can. Of course, you have yet to tell me as to what my duties are to be." I asked in the end. It took me the greatest effort to keep control over my emotions. I had to listen to the harangue of a foreign national, no matter how good he may be in his profession. Foreign persons had been given the right to assess, gauge and pass judgement on my patriotism. Foreign nationals had to decide whether I did one job or another and indeed, whether I should do any work at all in the air force of my own country. As for the slate being clean; it no longer seemed possible.

"We can discuss the details later, but I think you should take charge of the Training and Reserves" Said A.V.M Atcherley. "Amlot will be my Chief of Staff (COS)."

Douglas Amlot had reported to me a few months earlier. His turn out in uniform and his bearing was the most slovenly I had had the misfortune to witness. His uniform was creased and crumpled. He lifted his arm to salute with such effort that I thought he was unwell, or that he had lead tied to his forearm. His hand barely reached his cap and seemed to be made of rubber. I had sent him to Peshawar at the Group Headquarters which he had recently formed.

"Look, we are a young service." I had told Amlot. "The most important factor to remember is the example you are setting to our young men. Therefore, particular attention has to be paid to how you are turned out and to bearing."

When he departed there was little life left in his arm movement.

Now that same officer was to be our COS. He remained number two throughout Atcherley's two-year tenure. Under such conditions it was not possible to work in harmony. During 1949 A.V.M. Atcherley, ably aided and abetted by Amlot, caused me as much anxiety as is humanly possible. They even meddled in my domestic problems. And why not when they had the entire government behind them. A.V.M. Atcherley found that my assessment of his position had been correct. He was able to literally ride rough shod over the highest dignitaries in the land.

We returned from the north and visited Drigh Road for inspection. On our round of the barracks, we saw that several windowpanes needed to be replaced. We came for a post-inspection conference to the Commanding Officer's office. The most important point to be discussed was that of the windowpanes.

"Why are the windowpanes in such a disgraceful condition?" Atcherley asked.

"We cannot get the glass Sir." was the reply. "It is controlled."

"Who controls it?" Atcherley asked again. He was given the

designation of the civilian officer in the Ministry. Atcherley picked up the receiver and asked the operator to get the officer. Someone came on.

"This is the C-in-C Pakistan Air Force here," said Atcherley. "I want to know why it is not possible to get glass for our doors and windows?"

He was told that he was talking to the wrong person.

"Alright, then tell me who the right person is!"

Ultimately he obtained the right person and repeated the question. He was told something about controls and quotas.

"I don't give a damn about controls and quotas." He shouted. "I cannot have one of my stations falling to pieces. Where is the glass at this moment?"

He was told.

"Alright I am sending a vehicle with an officer." He said firmly. "You have your forms ready and the officer will sign whatever you need on my behalf. I must have the glass now. Thank you." And he replaced the receiver with a gesture of anger and triumph.

After the conference we were to go to the officers' mess. A.V.M. Atcherley asked me to sit with him in his car.

"Well what do you think of that?" He asked me as we drove out of the station.

"First class" I replied. "I would have done more or less the same, to obtain results. But I would have been called a dictator. You are only a good, forceful C-in-C."

He went and related the incident and my remark to Naqvi. I believe on Atcherley's part it was more in good humour than malice. However, the word went round as if it was all taken seriously by Atcherley. In order to harass me, Atcherley arranged that I undergo conversion and an intensive flying course at Risalpur. This was firstly to convey the impression that I was otherwise reluctant to fly and secondly to have me away from Air H.Q. Of course, I needed to fly more than I had done in 1948. But there was far too much work to do and flying could be resorted to only occasionally. I was fond of flying and a person like Aspey Engineer had written 'Excellent' twice in my log book, describing my qualities as a pilot. However I completed in one month, the amount of flying I was required to do, this was two months sooner than anticipated by Atcherley.

It was said that I was unrepentant, unyielding and incurable. As for myself, I felt I had done nothing about which to repent, on which to yield, of which to be cured. While at home, this type of thinking was displayed by ones own highly placed persons, outside, others interested in our affairs expressed similar views. I was told, by an army officer that a feature had been written about me in Amrit Bazar Patrika, an English daily newspaper published in Calcutta. The caption was, 'The man to be watched'. Whether the foreign enemy was able to watch me or not I cannot say, but the national friend certainly kept a strict eye on me. Later events proved that the eye saw far more than there was in my activities.

An Urdu periodical in Nizam's Hyderabad had produced a pen sketch of friendly remarks. I was to be watched but not as an enemy. That lies somewhere in our belongings, scattered throughout a dozen different prisons in Pakistan.

During his tenure, A.V.M. Atcherley made it impossible for me to work in peace. And he went around saying that my reputation for vigorous, energetic and aggressive action had no basis. I believe he was fully aware of the falsehood of his statement. I was with him in New Zealand in November and December, 1949. We met Air Chief Marshal Sir Keith

Park in his club in Aukland. During the course of conversation to which I was, perhaps, not supposed to listen, Sir Keith asked Atcherley about me in my capacity as the senior-most Pakistan Air Force Officer.

"He is a first class officer." In a subdued voice, "But he is anti...." He left the blank after the 'anti' for Sir Keith to fill in. The latter could have had no difficulty in finding the missing word. A.V.M. Atcherley had had this view of me drummed into him, between the time he asked me to return from Britain and when I arrived in Pakistan. So not only was I guilty of patriotism – extreme nationalism – But I was also anti-British! Being for my country was seen as synonymous with being against the British. Yet at no time had I sought equipment from sources other than Britain; training in establishments other than British, if the latter were capable of providing it; technical personnel to help us other than British, except in an emergency such as that following Indian aggression against Hyderabad. It would have been silly and chauvinistic on my part to have advocated a complete break with the British. It would have been costly and time consuming to convert to equipment from other countries. There was no need, nor the desire to do so. But the most acute differences existed in attitudes. I and many others were passionately against foreign domination from any quarter. But many were humiliatingly in favour of it. There was the inevitable clash. Since foreign domination in matters of national policy was accepted, there could only be one outcome. Those in favour of it won.

Up to the end of 1948, I had been extremely strict on economy in the PAF and the rigid application of regulations concerning use of all manner of equipment; an ordinary pin, if properly used and looked after, could last a lifetime. The use of transport, especially for the officers, was strictly according to regulations laid down for the purpose. Either, they could have unlimited use of transport by paying on the basis of mileage, or limited use by paying a set amount. This type of discipline was maintained in all departments. When I returned from Britain I noticed that abuse of equipment had begun. Some officers were using staff cars all the time, while paying less under a different rule. Trucks were being diverted from their direct routes to deliver rations at the residences of some of the officers, without a charge being made for the extra mileage. These and a host of other irregularities had crept in. Above all, deliberate sabotage seemed to have begun to be practiced. The officer in charge of the Technical Engineering Branch was Air Commodore Bowditch, 'Honest Bob', to his friends. I saw him driving an imported car, with zero miles on the gauge at full speed on the tarmac at Mauripur. It should have been 'run in', at low speed for one thousand miles. I do not know when the engine and the car were replaced, but it could not have been much later. Our sterling balance had to be reduced rapidly; the British exports had to be boosted. What better way to achieve this than to destroy equipment as speedily as possible. And with no national to watch, it was too easy to do so. What Perry-Keene had failed to achieve by trying to sell us obsolete aircraft, his successors were achieving by destroying our most modern equipment.

Where could I take the complaint? Iskander Mirza had closed his ears to my voice. The Prime Minister had shut his door to me. Naqvi had become ineffective. I decided to see the Secretary General, Chaudhry Mohammed Ali. I met him at his house and related all that I knew. At the end of it he turned to me and said,

"We know what is happening in the Air Force. But in a vast country like Pakistan it is a very small department. In the larger interests of the country we must overlook these malpractices. You have fallen foul of the Defence Secretary, Iskander Mirza. You go and make it up with him. He is a thorough gentleman and you will be alright."

It is not easy to describe my feelings as I heard this observation and advice. It was nauseating and agonising.

"The air force may be a small service." I managed to remark, "but if you were to ask an honest officer from each department, you will be told of similar malpractices. That makes the whole nation corrupt."

I thanked him for his advice and left him. I had no intention of following it. I did not want to be 'alright' personally. Had that been my aim I would have been alright from the outset. I just had to fall in line with Perry-Keene; buy the Spitfires; readily hand over the Tempests to India; keep undesirable and unnecessary British officers, reduce the expansion programme to the capacity of a flying club; and there would have been nothing between me and the Chair of C-in-C after Perry-Keene. But that was not the aim. The attitude was not acceptable to me and was, indeed, sickening. It was impossible for me to agree to the compromise suggested by the Secretary General. I did not know what the consequences of my attitude would be, but I had no doubt whatever, that I would not accept them.

I had two brief unpleasant confrontations with the Prime Minister. Shortly after my return from Britain in February 1949, an exhibition was held in the grounds of the Parsee school in Karachi. The air force had a stall. The Governor General came to visit it and insisted that I accompany him round our stall. I did so. After that I was taken to the first floor of a house where I was told a 'Moghal' room had been arranged. I went with Wing Commander Qasim Hussain, the senior accounts officer. Since he knew the place, he went ahead of me. He entered the room and went straight to a dais on which the Prime Minister, his wife and one or two other persons sat. The Prime Minister was dressed in a suit and his wife was dressed in gold thread 'Moghal' style clothes. A 'hukka' rested several feet from the Prime Minister, but he held the end of the long tube in his hand and sucked at it and puffed. Qasim Hussain walked the length of the most beautiful Persian carpet, which covered the floor, and made his supplication by bending double and almost touching the floor in front of the Prime Minister and his wife. I stood in amazement, framed by the doorway. I could not believe my eyes. This could not be serious; this playing at 'Moghal' emperor! But then the Prime Minister could not be part of a tableau. As I watched another person went past and paid his respects in a similar fashion.

I had already lost respect for the Prime Minister. I was now petrified at the seriousness of the assumptions; this was a 'Moghal darbar' (noble court). I had the same emotions well up inside me as those in childhood, when I saw my father touching the knee of a 'pir', and as I heard the clicking of heels and saw the bowing of heads and bodies, when Lord Mountbatten went round in Government House. I glared at Liaquat Ali Khan. I was in uniform but I could not bear the thought of saluting him in that pantomime – and I did not. He saw me and glared back till he was tired and looked away to pursue his game of playing emperor. Qasim Hussain came back and asked me whether I would like to meet the Prime Minister. I said that I would not. And we went into the next room where the meals were being served. Of course, they were 'Moghalai' dishes.

The C-in-C Pakistan Navy invited the entire cabinet of Pakistan and all civil and military officials to one of his shore establishments. This was soon after the foregoing incident. As I stood talking to an officer, someone pushed past me towards the table laden with food. I looked around and it was the Prime Minister. Now we were a few inches apart and there could be no mistake in gauging expressions on our respective faces. For some reason which I could not understand, I was exceedingly angry and I showed it in my face. He looked at me very seriously for a few seconds, waiting for me to say something to him, or perhaps to talk to me himself. I did not greet or wish him. He turned slowly to the table and I rejoined the group. I had no respect left for him.

In the meantime Atcherley and Amlot continued to persecute me in every possible manner. I was appointed President of a Court Martial to try an officer for corruption. During the proceedings Atcherley took the most unusual step of attending a sitting of the court. No convening officer ever attends the court convened by himself. His reason for attending was that the Prosecuting officer had complained that I had been favouring the defence. Of course, it was lodged in order to cover his own glaring inadequacies. Far from being biased in favour of the defence, I had allowed unlimited and unjust latitude to the prosecution. The main prosecution witness became hostile almost at the opening of his testimony. He was a Belgian attached to SABENA. The prosecuting officer bullied him; threatened to confiscate his passport; asked me to be allowed to see the witness separately. I allowed all this. The witness then changed his testimony in favour of the prosecution. At a later stage he again gave a hostile statement. After further threats he once again came back to the prosecution version. In view of this, how any court could have come to a verdict of 'guilty' is not possible to imagine. The case should have been withdrawn. But I allowed the prosecution to complete their case. The verdict of the court of five members was 'not guilty'. The convening officer, C-in-C P.A.F., called it a perverse verdict. He dismissed the accused officer from the service. That was his right. But he had no right whatsoever to attend the court; to entertain a complaint from the prosecution; to call the verdict perverse.

After the trial I confronted Atcherley on the tarmac behind his office at Mauripur. When I questioned him concerning his most irregular behaviour, he said that the prosecuting officer had complained to him.

"Why did you not ask me to explain?" I asked. "You could have reconvened the court. Instead you decided to take notice of the complaint by my subordinate and to act on it. This is unheard of."

He muttered some unintelligible words and cantered back to his office.

Chapter Ten

Coup de Grace

Time marched on and soon it was the last month of 1949. I had been on a tour of Australia and New Zealand. We had gone there to discuss the possibility of having some of our apprentices trained by the Royal Australian Air Force. I returned to Karachi on 9 December, after an absence of exactly one month. In about the middle of December, Atcherley informed me that I had been selected to attend the Imperial Defence College in London. Vice Admiral Chaudhry from Pakistan Navy and Major General Nasir Ali Khan from Pakistan Army, were also selected. This was the first batch ever from Pakistan to attend the I.D.C. Since the course was to commence in the first week in January 1950, I hurriedly made arrangements for my departure. I left by air about five days after our daughter, Shahidah, was born in the Maternity Ward which had been established at Drigh Road, about a year earlier with the money taken from Sidney Cotton. My wife and child joined me in London a few weeks later.

The course, as such was interesting, but otherwise uneventful. I did, however, become tired of being told by my colleagues, especially Nasir Ali, not to say this or that because 'they won't give us the equipment we need'. It was an instructive course, where we were free to express our views. There was not much controversy. But the over cautiousness of my colleagues cramped ones style in a manner of speaking.

During 1950, Asghar Khan and Haidar Raza came to attend the Staff College. They met me on several occasions and we discussed matters of common interest. Some time before the middle of August, Brigadier Akbar Khan, later Major General and Chief of General Staff, came to attend the Joint Services Staff college. He came to our flat for lunch one day and stayed for several hours. We covered a wide range of subjects in our discussion. Then he steered the conversation to a particular subject.

Akbar Khan told me that on 5 December 1949, he and four other officers had met at Attock in the Dak Bungalow. I told him that on that day I was still in Australia. Then gradually he disclosed the nature of the discussion at that meeting. They had seriously considered the possibility of staging a coup d'état. They had yet another senior army officer in their confidence, as was a junior commissioned officer from the constabulary.

"If we had overthrown the government what would have been your attitude?" He asked me abruptly.

"I don't know," I said. "It is impossible to say precisely what my reaction would have been. It would have depended on the prevailing factors at that time. But if the army had succeeded there is little the air force could have done to oppose it. In that sense I would have been compelled to be in your favour."

We debated the point for a while. In my view it was purely academic. Nothing had happened. Whatever had been thought had been dropped. I was given no details, but merely told of the intentions of the assembled group a few months earlier. I was told no names and I did not ask for any to be given. I believed that I had no right to any information especially when it was not voluntarily forthcoming.

"Now that I have told you about our meeting," Akbar Khan addressed me, looking serious and somewhat apprehensive, "This is not to be repeated. If you do talk about it to anyone, whether I am there or not it will be ….," and he made a gesture with his right hand of firing a pistol, aimed at me.

There are few things I detest more than a threat of that nature. Akbar Khan had spoken to the wrong person in that manner.

"If you had no confidence in me then you should not have spoken to me." I told him, in a serious tone. "You displayed more confidence in a junior commissioned officer. In any event, no one can say who will be quicker at the draw. As for the threat of death; as a Muslim death means eternal life to me: if you were to take it as a materialist, then one is dead, it doesn't matter a damn anyway. So whichever way you want to take it, I do not fear it."

Akbar Khan composed himself. He assured me that he had not really meant it. We then talked about Kashmir and other matters facing the country. He was exceedingly critical of the government's weak policies and resentful of British domination. In both these I agreed with him. We exchanged experiences concerning both the weakness of our political leaders and domination by the British. Before he left, Akbar Khan told me that he would probably take over the duties of Chief of General Staff (CGS). I congratulated him and promised to meet him on my return to Pakistan. There would be other opportunities to meet as both of us would be Principal Staff Officers, at our Headquarters. It was the most natural thing in the world for opposite numbers from the services HQ to meet.

In the latter part of 1950, Lieutenant General M.Ayub Khan, Commander in Chief designate Pakistan Army, came to Britain. He came to our flat to an evening party, to which we had invited several officers from the I.D.C. He had Brigadier Sayad Ghawas, the Senior Military Liaison Officer at the High Commission with him. They were the last to leave. A few days later I was asked to attend a select gathering of about six at the High Commissioner's residence. Ayub Khan was there. He talked about the purpose of his visit. Apart from meeting contacts and acquaintances, he had come to arrange purchase of some special equipment. He mentioned heavy anti-aircraft guns.

"The damn fellows say they can give the guns but not the chassis'!" He said.

"Take them." I said. He swung round to face me.

"What am I going to do with heavy AA guns without the chassis'?" He said irritably.

"Heavy AA guns are not required at the front." I said. "They are for the air defence of large targets like cities, depots, bridges. All these are invariably on the main lines of rail communications. In the first place they do not need to be mobile but should it be necessary to move them, all we need is one good wagon per gun. I think we should modify railway goods wagons to serve as chassis', fix them at the sidings on railway stations, or keep them free to be moved along the railways whenever necessary."

It was just a spontaneous idea and I did not know as to how feasible it would be. But Ayub Khan was unable to refute it and looked uncomfortable. In my view it was worth trying. Such unorthodox methods had to be adopted by a country like ours. We had no means of producing our own heavy weapons.

"I think we should resort to maximum improvisation." I continued, while silence and some interest was being maintained around me.

"Even during the most highly technical Second World War, larger countries than Pakistan applied methods that would appear to be well nigh primitive. Horse carts, mule carts and even bullock carts were used to provide mobility; small and medium automatic weapons were mounted on them. They were very effective. I believe we should not abandon any part of any weapon. We should take whatever we can get and improvise the rest. In the case of AA guns, it seems possible. We have the goods wagons, the railway lines and the sidings."

If I knew a little about AA guns and improvisation, the persons around me knew even less. Ayub Khan made no comment on it, so we did not learn much about the subject. But Ayub Khan looked positively displeased. Anyway, in my view he was at no time a brilliant soldier, circumstances, which were not always clear, had brought him to head the Pakistan Army. From that firm position he was able to fulfil other ambitions.

The course at the Imperial Defence College ended in December 1950. I sailed for Pakistan on 6 January 1951, on an Anchor Line ship, with my wife and daughter. On board were also two army officers, Colonel Hamid, later Lieutenant General, and Lt. Col. Mohamed Jan. The night before we were due to arrive in Karachi we stayed on deck, in order to be able to see the approaching shores of Pakistan. At about dawn we saw the harbour lights in the distance. It was 24 January that day. I had exposed myself to the chill wind and felt cold. So we went to our cabin to have a brief rest before disembarking. When I was woken up by my wife, the ship had already anchored in the port. I dressed hurriedly but felt the symptoms of an impending cold and sore throat. When we disembarked, Asghar Khan and several other PAF officers came to receive us. We were touched at the gesture.

I reported to A.V.M. Atcherley soon after my arrival. He made a formal apology for not having come to see me at the port. He was joined by Amlot in the exercise of hypocrisy. I resumed work at Air HQ as Deputy Chief of Air Staff, Atcherley being the C-in-C and Chief of Air Staff. My designation and post were the equivalent of the Chief of General Staff at General Headquarters. My cold and sore throat worsened and I began to run a low temperature. However, the annual inspection tour of the Air Board had been arranged to commence on 1 February, a week after my return from Britain. By that day I had developed a severe cough and the night before I had run up a temperature of 101. I thought I would not be well enough to undertake the flight to Peshawar, our first station of call. My wife also suggested that I should stay back and join the team later. I wrote a letter to Atcherley to explain my condition and asked to be allowed to rest for a day or so. He replied to the effect that I should commence the inspection tour, but should my condition not improve I could then break off. In this manner I was compelled to accompany the Board to Peshawar, when I should have been under treatment at Karachi. Apart from other reasons, Atcherley wanted to prove that slight indispositions were not to be allowed to stand in the way of hard work. I could have given him a few tips in this respect, but my activities had been drastically curtailed by the imposition of punitive restrictions by the Ministry of Defence. It was an obvious attempt to destroy my initiative. Iskander Mirza had devised a method of, what he termed, deflating officers with positive traits and talent.

During the flight to Peshawar my temperature rose and the cough was aggravated. I had to be put to bed on arrival. I was lodged with Wing Commander Khyber Khan, the station commander, at his house. Squadron Leader Hasnain, the station medical officer, began to treat me with antibiotics. I missed the entire inspection tour.

During my four or five day stay at Khyber Khan's house I had several telephone calls from Brigadier Zaman. He was the head of Army Signals. He was also a Janjua and hailed from Darapur-Chakri, the seat of the senior most Sultan of the Janjua Rajput Clan. Zaman was exceedingly fond of me. Many years older than me, he was very proud and happy that I had maintained the tribal traditions of good soldiering. We had, for generations, served in various imperial armies. Now, according to him and many others in our clan, I had been very successful in the air force. He phoned me repeatedly to ask after my health but primarily to make sure that I went to Rawalpindi by 6 February. He had organised an evening party at the Army Signals for that day, to celebrate some special occasion of the Signals. General Ayub Khan, who had assumed command of Pakistan Army on 17 January, was to be the guest of honour. Zaman had taken for granted that I would be the next C-in-C of the Pakistan Air Force.

"The army C-in-C is coming to the function" he said. "I am honoured. But I would be further honoured by the presence of the C-in-C PAF."

"He is somewhere near Lahore now" I said. He was being too serious and sure about the possibility of my command.

"I mean you!" Zaman said. "I want you to come. I shall be very happy and it's important for me."

I thanked him. I was greatly touched by his affection. I was extremely fond of him. I promised that I would come, providing the doctor did not order me not to go. The doctor allowed me to travel on 6 February. I would have preferred to rest a day or two longer, but I could not refuse Zaman. Before I left I asked Zaman to inform the CGS, Major General Akbar Khan, about my arrival and to tell him that I would meet him if possible. Zaman told me that the CGS was also coming to his party, but that my message would be conveyed to him.

I flew down to Rawalpindi and arrived there at about mid-day. Akbar Khan had been informed. His office was situated near the entrance gate. He had arranged to have me met and taken to his office. When I arrived at his office he was alone. In the room next to his was Brigadier Gulzar Ahmed. I do not recollect what his designation was, but he had a long background in intelligence during the days of the British.

Akbar Khan spoke to me as he worked. He told me that since I had come at very short notice, he was unable to take me to his house for lunch. He had a meeting later and would have to leave me for some time. He offered me the use of his car. I phoned Wing Commander Abdul Hai, Commander PAF Station Chaklala to come and join me. During that time officers came and went quite frequently. I recollect vividly that Colonel Sultan Ali Shah came in. I had known him since 1934, at the Military Academy in Dehra Dun. He had grown a beard since then. We met each other and Akbar Khan looked up and spoke to him.

"Shall we hang them with ropes?"

"Yes, Sir!" replied Sultan Ali Shah, as if he had been asked this question before and had answered it more than once.

"Order some ropes, Sultan" said Akbar.

"Very good Sir" was his monotonous reply as he saluted and left the office.

Akbar Khan was a practical joker and it seemed he had indulged in this type of humour before. Then he spoke critically about the conditions of the country, the political leadership and the continuing foreign domination. I had seen no change for the better in any respect. In the air force the domination was as severe and strong as I had left it, just over a year earlier. Malpractices were rampant. I agreed entirely with Akbar Khan's views. However, I referred to his talk with Sultan semi-humorously.

"But why the ropes?" I asked, "Surely you can do better than that!"

He took me very seriously for a moment.

"No, no. Someone else can do that." He said.

Akbar sat facing the door and could see the road leading to the entrance gate. I sat with my back to it. He suddenly got up and walked hurriedly to the door.

"I have just seen someone." He said. "I want to say hello and you can meet him too."

I turned round and saw a tall man in civilian clothes walk towards the gate.

"Siddique" Akbar called out.

The man who had passed out of my sight came back. He came over to Akbar and greeted him, by coming sharply to attention and then they shook hands. They both came in immediately and Akbar Khan introduced us.

"This is Colonel Siddique Raja, an old stalwart," said Akbar, "And this is Air Commodore Janjua."

We shook hands. Colonel Siddique Raja explained to Akbar Khan that he should have left for Quetta that morning but had missed the train. He had come to the GHQ to see either the Personnel or the Accounts people, for some reason which I cannot recollect.

"I was unfortunate to have missed the train" Said Siddique Raja, "But fortunate to be able to meet you." He addressed us both.

Fortunate indeed! But for me the most unfortunate meeting I have ever had. Many a time after that I have wished that he had caught the train to Quetta. That accidental meeting nearly cost me my life, because Siddique Raja became the 'Approver' in the Rawalpindi Conspiracy Case. His fabricated testimony was the only evidence produced against me at the trial. It was completely uncorroborated.

I had never seen nor heard of Siddique Raja before that day. After he left Akbar Khan's office I completely forgot about him until I was told, about four months later, that he was the 'Approver' in the case against me. I had met many officers of his rank, and lower and higher ranks; I had no special reason to remember him. However, on that day he stayed in CGS's office with me while I waited for Wing Commander Abdul Hai to join me. Before Akbar left to attend his meeting he said to me, "Remember my talk with you in London? Here is something for your information."

He scribbled on a small piece of paper, folded it and gave it to me. I merely glanced at it. It appeared to contain a few names. I did not read it then. When I tried to find it later, I could not. I had misplaced it. I forgot about it and had no occasion to refer to it.

I had nothing in common with Siddique Raja so we talked about random things. While we sat Zaman came to see me. Siddique Raja greeted him in military fashion. Zaman was surprised to see him there.

"What is he doing in the CGS's office?" He asked, taking me aside.

"I don't know." I replied, and explained the circumstances under which he came to be there. The disapproval was clearly visible on his face. I told Zaman that Hai was coming to meet me in Akbar's office. He said he would come later to collect me.

Before Abdul Hai arrived, I do not at all recollect as to what we talked about. But he soon came and the boredom was over.

"I am sorry for being late, Sir." Hai said, as he entered. "I was in the middle of something when you phoned and I thought you wouldn't mind if I finished it before I came."

I introduced Siddique Raja to Hai. It soon transpired that the former's wife had a brother-in-law in the air force. Then Hai told me about the inspection by the Air Board. It had gone off very well. He was a very good officer and I was not surprised to hear the good report. We then discussed several air force matters, among them being the hypothetical subject of conversion of pilots and technical maintenance personnel, to aircraft of entirely different types. Some time during our conversation

Siddique Raja took his leave.

Later in the afternoon, Brigadier Zaman came and took me to his office. We stayed there till the end of office hours and then went to Zaman's house, where I was to stay the night. Since Zaman was the host we went to the Signal's mess early in the evening. Akbar Khan came later and joined us. He was openly and severely critical, even hostile, towards the government. Ayub Khan came, but his arrival in no way affected Akbar's attitude. He hardly did anything to disguise the fact that he advocated a change of government. Whenever Zaman was within earshot he felt uneasy at Akbar's views. He was a mild person and was close to Ayub Khan; they had been in the same regiment. For both these reasons he had been unhappy that one of the most important Principal Staff Officers should indulge in such talk. There was nothing he could do about it, so he bore the agony with a set jaw and a red face. However, not only did any younger officers not object to, or disagree with, Akbar's tirade against the foreign dominated government, but they seemed to heartily approve of it. That was not the first time they had heard such criticism, nor was Akbar the first person from whom they heard it. After the moment of tremendous enthusiasm, following the establishment of Pakistan, had passed; when realisation had set in concerning the weakness which had led to the loss of East Punjab, part of Bengal, Assam and Junagadh, and the greater tragedy of Kashmir; when firebrand statements on Hyderabad had ended in mere cold douches, there came, first muffled and then vocal and widespread criticism of the leadership. That there was no concerted action or cohesive effort did not at all mean that the resentment was less severely felt or expressed. The protest against ineffective leadership and the corrupt practices, which were beginning to take root, was quite universal. But since there was no organised movement to fight against it, the impression may have been gathered that resentment did not prevail. There were three factors which led to the curbing of any movement and silencing of voices against corrupt and immoral practices. Firstly, the leadership wielding power, claimed all credit for having achieved (a truncated) Pakistan and dubbed all persons and voices raised against their inefficient and evil attitudes to be treacherous and declared them to be enemies of Pakistan. They screamed abuse at their opponents. Secondly, the ruling political party began at the outset to employ Gestapo methods to keep themselves in power, to prevent others from legitimately working to gain political power, to acquire unethical immoral gains, in short to feather their nests. Thirdly, the dominant British imperialist element created conditions of pro-British and anti-British sympathies; in fact those who wished the interests of Pakistan to have priority over all else, were singled out for elimination. In political life and officialdom there were few who stood up to the combined British and the subservient but exceedingly self-motivated political leadership. They were soon made ineffective. Since promotions and other gains rested on the approval of the ruling clique, particularly in the armed forces of the British Officers, mutual throat cutting had begun. It was more important to indulge in kowtowing, to please the foregoing forces and to perform humiliating personal chores for purely personal gain. The primary national interest receded into the background. The policy of permitting corrupt practices 'in the larger interests of the country', was producing its bitter fruit. It was two years, almost to the day, since Chaudhry Mohammad Ali had told me that he and consequently the Cabinet had accepted that disastrous manner of safeguarding the interests of our people. They did not merely condone an evil, but actually deliberately advocated it. They had made corruption a necessary prerequisite of an efficient administration. They had allowed foreign nationals to wilfully destroy not only the nation's equipment but also the morals and morale of its people. They had, in short, let the destiny of our country be moulded by foreign hands. They made our national policy subservient to foreign imperialist policies. The people of Pakistan have paid a heavy price for those humiliatingly weak, cowardly, self-seeking and anti-people policies. The yoke, which the original ruling cliques caused to be placed around our necks, has become progressively heavier. It remains around our necks, waiting for the people of Pakistan to remove it, break it and be rid of it forever.

However, the Signals Mess on 6 February hummed and buzzed with the type of conversation which I have mentioned. While there were many eager listeners and participants who had genuine national feelings, undoubtedly there were several making mental, if not written notes, to be conveyed to those who would be pleased to receive 'information'. There is always demand in that low trade, in a corrupt system where personal gain takes priority over all else.

Before the party ended Akbar Khan met me and asked me to have lunch at his house. I had already arranged to go to Lahore the following morning, where I wanted to stay with my sister. She was there with her husband, Major Nur Asif (later Colonel) and her children. A transport aircraft was going there from Chaklala. I had decided to take this short flight to Lahore and rest for a few days before proceeding to Karachi. However, I promised Akbar Khan that I would visit him again, if there was some aircraft movement between Lahore and Chaklala.

On 7 February, I went to Lahore. Wing Commander Salah-ud-Din met me on arrival. I asked him to let me know when and if he had an aircraft going to Chaklala in the next few days. He informed me on the following day that an aircraft was due to go to Chaklala on 9 February morning and to return the same afternoon. This was ideally suited to having lunch with the CGS and then returning the same day. I asked Salah-ud-Din to inform Hai, Major General Akbar Khan and Brigadier Zaman, that I would come as promised and arranged with Akbar.

I flew to Chaklala on 9 February, where Hai received me and took me to GHQ. I went to Zaman's office and informed Akbar that I had arrived. It was Friday and the office closed early. I went with Akbar to his house. There were only the two of us present, along with Akbar's wife, Nasim. During lunch we talked about a host of things. It is not possible to recollect any special subject. After lunch Akbar and I talked mainly about affairs of the army and air force. We also discussed the political situation. We were both aware of the foreign domination, despite Ayub Khan's assumption of command of the army. There was no let up in this respect. The ruling clique was as weak and subservient as ever; corruption was becoming rampant. Akbar was vehement and bitter in his criticism. I was no less so, because the air force was thoroughly dominated and I felt it acutely. I was the prime target for removal, or least to be crushed. I admit that I would have done almost anything to see an end to the type of domination which I had to witness and bear. We discussed matters in this vein. It was possible to foresee continuing foreign domination, increasing corruption, ruthless and mutually destructive struggles for power, misuse of power, in every possible manner. Foreign domination did increase progressively, from British to American, until it became unbearable for the people.

The most ruthless autocratic military President of Pakistan, self-styled Field Marshal M. Ayub Khan, after over eight years as president, had to give his autobiographic book a humiliating title 'Friends, not masters.' He had to justify the American domination of Pakistan, for which his predecessors and he were responsible, to his own people and the world at large. He found it necessary to explain that the foreign power was a friend and not a master only because of universal allegations to the contrary. It is shameful that the Head of State of a country of 120 million people should talk in terms of master or not master, when referring to a foreign power. This was the result of the foreign domination accepted at the birth of our nation, which in turn was the outcome of utter submission to the imposition of the most unjust award imaginable. There had been a completely wrong analysis of the situation by the Muslim League leadership, and in particular by those who found it necessary to oppose the establishment of the Muslim homeland Pakistan. Above all, the Muslim League leadership was not revolutionary in any sense of the word. They were not, by background or inclination, capable of leading a revolutionary struggle. And what would have required greater revolutionary effort than to save hundreds of millions of lives and to establish a safe and secure homeland for them. There could be no safety and security in a corner, with one's back to the wall, but the people of Pakistan have stood up to the situation even under the worst possible conditions, which their leaders had allowed to be created. But the leadership itself found safety under a foreign umbrella.

The corruption introduced as a matter of policy, as positively stated by the Secretary General to the Cabinet, Chaudhry Mohammad Ali, has poisoned the social structure and eroded the moral fibre of the nation which only a peoples revolution can now flush out.

The struggle for power and its misuse has continued unabated. While the first Prime Minister maligned and abused all possible opponents or contenders for power, Hussain Shaheed Suhrawardy was called the 'dog' of India, he himself fell to the bullets of conspirators, undoubtedly from within his own clique. There is no other reason for the result of the inquiry into Liaquat Ali's assassination not being made public. Only people who had power could withhold such vital information from the people of Pakistan. Thereafter, there is hardly any other country in the world which has witnessed such naked, shameless and ruthless struggles for power.

It was quite possible to foresee and visualise conditions of the type I have described above, and which the people of Pakistan have had to bear. These were the kind of subjects I discussed with Akbar at his house on 9 February. I was not the only one with whom Akbar discussed such matters, nor was he the only one with whom I discussed them. It was almost a nationwide discussion. I discussed it passionately. I was extremely emotional on national matters and sensitive concerning the poisonous fungus of corruption which was forming rapidly round the life of the people. I was far more emotional and sensitive in respect of the foreign domination, which played the greatest role in creating degenerate conditions. Imperialism is the worst enemy of the people. It must prepare the people for exploitation. It can do so only through the political leaders of otherwise nominally free countries. It was doing so in Pakistan. I detested and resented those conditions. My emotions can be easily understood by those who have an inherent hatred of injustice. I would have gladly joined in a struggle to remove those injustices. But there was no such movement known to me. Akbar used vehement words and expressed nebulous views on how a change may be effected. I had immense desire to see a change and if possible to help bring it about. But no concrete way of doing it could be seen. Akbar's utterances were vague and amateurish, far from being revolutionary. At times they were comical and I put them down to his tendency to indulge in practical jokes. For instance, in the middle of a serious conversation he would suddenly turn and ask,

"How would you make Iskander Mirza ineffective if you were to take over command?"

"Lock him up in his bathroom!" I would say.

"Yes, something like that would do." He would respond.

I never knew whether, how and when, he was being serious. However, the talk was no more serious than this. Akbar had correctly concluded that I was a nationalist, almost to the extent of chauvinism. He therefore laid great stress on this aspect of my feelings, whenever we had occasion to talk about the problems facing Pakistan. Our talk during and after lunch on 9 February 1951, was no different.

Hai came and took me to Chaklala from where I went to Lahore. I stayed with my sister and her family for two days. On one of those days, Colonel Nawsharwan took me to inspect the 8th Punjab Regimental Centre, of which he was the Commandant. He was a very good officer albeit quite unorthodox. This irritated some of his superiors, but was most effective with his subordinates. We had known each other from boyhood. He was also a Janjua, from Watli, near

Khewra, in the salt range. Watli was another seat of the Janjua Sultans.

I returned to Karachi on 11 February. I had been away from Pakistan for a whole year and I therefore visited as many units of the air force as I could. Throughout my service I had visited airmen's and sergeant's messes, their barracks and quarters, family quarters and children's schools. I did so now. It was the most natural thing for me to do. I mention this because, like my visit to Akbar's office and his house, the visits to all air force institutions were given a sinister meaning by those who had to prove sinister motives on my part.

On 19 February, an air force aircraft brought General Ayub Khan down to Karachi to attend a meeting at the Defence Ministry. I met him on arrival. When he returned a few hours later I went to the tarmac to see him off.

"This is what I call hard work." He said to me. "I came this morning and I am off to 'Pindi' to do my work there."

"That's good." I said, "But we are not sitting idle. Apart from other things, you are flying in our aircraft!"

I often wonder whether he knew about the events which took place within three weeks of his visit. It was being widely said that when General Gracey handed over charge to Ayub Khan, he had warned him about the existence of a 'Young Turk Party' in the army. If he had said this much it could be safely assumed that Akbar Khan had been named as head of the 'Young Turks'. I also have no doubt that General Gracey had been fully aware of the meeting Akbar and his colleagues had held in Attock on 5 December, 1949, nearly fourteen months before he handed over to Ayub Khan. But General Gracey had taken no action against those officers in all those months. He had also not found it necessary to inform the Prime Minister about a meeting of army officers, which could easily have led to a coup d'état. All officers present at that meeting had troops under their command. Collectively they had enough military force and the structure to capture power, had they decided to do so. They would have preceded Ayub Khan by nine years. He would never have had the opportunity to command the army, let alone rule the nation ruthlessly for ten years, after coming to the top through political manoeuvring.

The Prime Minister of Pakistan remained unconcerned or unaware of a potentially dangerous meeting of participants who could have overthrown him with ease. Yet he became alarmed and hysterical when informed of a meeting of relatively junior officers, with the exception of Akbar Khan, who had virtually no troops under their direct command. They could not have carried out a military coup d'état at all. The conditions for a coup were entirely favourable in December 1949, in so far as military strength was concerned. They were completely unfavourable in this respect in February or March 1951. The dangerous situation and possibilities in 1949 were either not reported on, or were not acted upon, by the Prime Minister. General Gracey, a powerful instrument of British imperialism, was then in command. Had the fact of a conspiratorial meeting and intention been made known during his tenure, it would have aroused emotions against the British. He, therefore, either kept silent on the matter, or advised the Prime Minister to adopt a milder course. The officers who were at the meeting in Attock were gradually dispersed and given assignments which excluded direct command of troops. But he took the most drastic action when the relatively innocuous meeting on 23 February was reported to him. He dismissed and arrested officers who participated in the previous meeting and also one officer who had not taken part in either of the meetings. This was me. I have no doubt that the Prime Minister was still being advised by the British and of course, their stooges such as Iskander Mirza. They put the fear of god in him. He lashed ~~out~~ ~~in~~out in all directions at the assumed danger. It suited the British, it suited Ayub Khan and it suited the party in power, to stage a stunning drama and eliminate some of those who were considered to be security risks to long-term British interests. That the British imperialists were able to express poisonous views concerning us – the nationals of Pakistan – was ample proof of their power and influence. Someone came and told me in Hyderabad Central Prison that Field Marshal Auchinleck, who was ostensibly setting up a carpet industry in Pakistan, had said that in another country we would have been shot. I told him to tell the Field Marshal, if he ever met him, that in his own country no one would even have been arrested for criticising the government. It was only here, in Pakistan, that they could bamboozle the people, advise the Prime Minister to adopt policies contrary to our own interests, and use people like Ayub Khan to carry out those policies.

It was impossible for me to say what exactly went through Ayub Khan's mind as I saw him enter the aircraft. I did not see him for over nine years after that. I did, however, believe that he had every intention of clinging to the chair which he had acquired through much intrigue on his own part and on the part of others. And this he did, improved upon it, wielded it and abused it, for eighteen years.

The Air Staff at Air HQ had arranged to hold an indoor exercise on 1st and 2nd March, 1951. The General HQ had deputed the Chief of General Staff, Major General Akbar Khan, to attend it. I was asked by AVM Atcherley to keep in contact with Akbar Khan, and make arrangements for him to fly down from Rawalpindi. I spoke to Akbar Khan on the telephone on several occasions on this and other matters of common interest to the operational staff of the army, of which he was head, and of the air force, of which I was in charge.

I was told on 25 February, 1951, that Iskander Mirza and Ayub Khan had flown to Sargodha to meet the Prime Minister. The latter was on his election campaign tour of the Punjab. That he should ask the Defence Secretary and the C-in-C to meet him in the midst of an intensive tour aroused great interest. Wing Commander Mukhtar Cheema, a staff officer at Air HQ came to me and said,

"This is most unusual! Why should the Prime Minister ask these two to meet him in the middle of an election campaign?"

"Perhaps he is jittery about the elections and wants to use pressure tactics in predominantly military recruiting areas." I said, without giving the matter much thought.

"There is something fishy about it" Said Cheema.

"Maybe" I said, "Good luck to him and his tactics."

I really gave it no importance at the time. I had learnt that such unusual methods were employed by those in power. However, we learnt later, and Ayub Khan has described in his book, that the Prime Minister had been apprised of a meeting in Rawalpindi and was in a state of panic. Of course, it has been said that he was calm, albeit rather unusually agitated. This is believed by the kind of action he took on the eve of the elections. He shook the country to its foundations by his announcement of a conspiracy to overthrow the government, by suggesting that wholesale massacre was to have taken place; by stating that a foreign power was involved in the plot and then by stating yet another falsehood; that the conspiracy was nipped in the bud. How gullible our people were to swallow it all! The meeting had taken place on 23 February; the arrests were made on 9 March. No one, not even Ayub Khan, had told people as to what date had been fixed for the overthrow of the government. Was it to be soon after 23 February and before 9 March? Obviously not. Nothing took place. No action on the part of the conspirators. No action by the Prime Minister. Was it to be on 9 March, or after the elections? The Prime Minister never said so. There has never been any proof or indication that any steps were taken by any of the accused after 23 February, which suggested that a coup d'état was in the offing. But it did suit the Prime Minister to make the announcement on the eve of the elections.

Akbar Khan arrived on 28 February. I met him at Mauripur airfield. He was to stay with a relative of his wife and I drove him there. He gave me no indication whatever about the Prime Minister's call to Iskander Mirza, and Ayub Khan. He asked me to try to get Brigadier M.M. Latif from Quetta, if an aircraft happened to be coming that way. The next day I was informed that an aircraft was due to come from Chaklala. I asked that it be diverted to pick up Brigadier Latif from Quetta. It was a request from CGS. All concerned were informed. Akbar Khan told me nothing at all about the meeting on 23 February. He merely said that there had been an interesting discussion. I did not ask him anything about the nature of that discussion.

Latif came into my office during a break in the exercise. We had some light refreshment. After that, while I worked at my desk they talked. Latif was hard of hearing in one ear but he had a hearing aid. I was too busy to join them in their discussion and I do not know what they talked about. There was an unusual occurrence while they were in my office. The door, which had never been used by me and opened into another office, was thrown open after a few hard knocks. A person looked in, waited a few minutes and then closed it again. I looked at him slightly amazed, because I had never seen that man before. Since he had retreated rapidly I put it down to an error on the part of a civilian member of staff.

In the evening I asked them Latif and Akbar Khan to dinner at my house. I also invited Brigadier Zaman, who had come to Karachi for a few days and some other officers. After dinner Akbar and Latif went out and sat in the garden, where coffee was served. Zaman and I sat inside and talked about our family matters. Of course, he would not tire of saying how happy he was that I had attended the Imperial Defence College, the highest professional course any officer in the 'Commonwealth' could attend. He had always advised me to try to make up with Iskander Mirza. At times he was joined in this by Colonel Nausherwan, who was much more forceful and adamant. They both wanted me to be the C-in-C of Pakistan Air Force. I was not prepared to pay such a heavy price to attain that post – the price of compromise of moral, patriotic and national ideas. I told them that I had not gone out, nor would go out of my way, to quarrel personally with Iskander Mirza nor anyone else. But my temperament could not and would not tolerate or accept compromise on matters of national importance. Zaman again talked about the relationship between Iskander Mirza and myself. I told him that as far as I could gather they were as cordial as they could be under the circumstances. Zaman seemed agitated at our being inside With Akbar while Latif was sitting outside.

"What are they doing outside?" He asked irritably.

"I don't know and I can't question my guests." I replied.

Zaman left a little later and I took Akbar and Latif to where the former was staying. Akbar asked me to stay for a cup of tea, which I did. During those few minutes we discussed the situation, as was now the vogue. Some strong words were used by all of us. Latif was also emotional, sensitive and patriotic. Akbar asked some usual practical joke type questions.

"What armed men does the air force have on the ground?" He asked me.

"Hardly any," I replied, "But the air force police do have small arms."

The Provost Marshal was Flt Lt. M.M. Said. Out of the junior officers he was one of the closest to me and I had visited his small unit several times, on some occasions with my wife, because Said's family was with him.

"What would you do to Ayub Khan if a change were to be effected in the national interest?" He asked.

Both Latif and I replied in similar words. We believed he was not a patriot and, therefore, he would be replaced.

I had become accustomed to hearing such questions and observations from Akbar. Only a few days earlier when I had asked him concerning his views on Ayub Khan his remarks were favourable. He had said that Ayub Khan had a good personality and bearing and was a reasonably good officer. But one hardly ever knew when to take Akbar seriously.

I left Akbar and Latif and went home. During the trial some months later, Latif told me that he had seen a car following us that night. He did not want to mention the fact, in case we thought he was letting his imagination run away with him. I had no reason to suspect that I was being watched.

I spoke to Akbar Khan, once at night, after he had returned to Rawalpindi. There was no special purpose except to keep in touch with him. However, when I phoned him at night, the operator said that his number was not available. I replaced the receiver. But the phone rang in two or three minutes and I was told that the CGS was on the line. I spoke to Akbar and asked him whether he had been engaged or out of the house. He replied in the negative. I was surprised. I asked him as to how he was. He replied in a cautious apprehensive tone. I could not guess the reason for this. Then I told him that after Iskander Mirza and Ayub Khan had visited the Prime Minister at Sargodha, the former had been going up and down in PAF aircraft like a shuttle cock. I could not make out the reason for such hectic activity on his part. I asked Akbar whether he knew. He again replied in a negative and similar manner. He sounded unlike himself. He was normally cool and confident, but not now. Little did I realise that the delay in connecting me to Akbar's house, must have been on account of the fact that his telephone was firmly in the hands of the intelligence service and was being tapped. Indeed, in all probability, the calls were being controlled. It is possible that Akbar had become aware of the fact, or had sufficient evidence, to be suspicious or cautious. I did not at any time in later years question Akbar on any of the matters I have mentioned.

I continued to perform my duties and to attend social functions without the slightest suspicion of the events which were to shatter my life, in so far as the affairs of my country were concerned, in a matter of days. My wife and I attended a garden party at Government House on 25 February. The Governor General was no less friendly than he had been whenever I met him. On 7 March he sent five ducks to our house, from his collection of literally thousands in the cold freeze. He did his duck shooting in the manner of a major military operation. He collected all available guns and indulged in the massacre of ducks. It could easily be termed as genocide!

My wife and I were invited by Iskander Mirza to attend the first birthday of his grand daughter on 5 March. This was an excellent exercise in diplomacy: he smiled at me in a friendly manner, while he sharpened the knife to cut my throat.

We attended dinner at the residence of Brigadier Mirza Hamid Hussain. He was an old colleague from my days at the Indian Military Academy, Dehra Dun. He was originally in the Ordinance, but was now Director of Military Intelligence. I have had many occasions to recollect the discussion at Hamid Hussain's house that night, in the first week of March, 1951. We talked about malpractices and corruption in the armed forces. He knew my temperament and attitude on this subject. He himself had the reputation of being honest. He was impulsive and quarrelled easily. That night he fiercely advocated dishonest practices. He told me that I should not attempt to stop malpractices by our officers.

"At the moment I am unable to stop them anyway." I told him. "The foreign officers are in control and they not only do not stop them, but actually encourage malpractices."

"But they know you would stop them if you could." He said.

"Yes, I would stop them" I said, "And I don't care who knows it."

"Precisely" He said. "They know that you are their senior. You will command them again one day. They will hang you and your children from the nearest lamp posts before they let you stop them. They are backed by higher officials in the government, who also hate you for your honesty."

"That is too bad." I said in despair, feeling exceedingly sad.

Hamid went on to justify dishonesty. He said that he was not going to expose his wife and children to any dangers. He would not hesitate to indulge in malpractices in order to ensure safety for his family. He had left everything behind in India. He had to build his family's fortune in Pakistan. If this could be done only by dishonest means, as the leaders seemed to be doing, he would adopt those means. I had to agree with him that that was not only the trend but a widespread practice. I could not however agree, that it could be justified on any moral or national grounds. I told him that our temperaments, hence attitudes, were far apart. I could not submit to such evil. I believed that it should be eradicated and every effort should be made to that end.

Hamid's talk left me distressed. He was an honest man. His background was such that he had to ensure his family's security. He was related to the ruling family of Loharu. But I had always thought he was basically honest. He should have been content to resort to legitimate means of claiming property in lieu of that which he had left behind. Maybe he had tried this honest method and failed. But his attitude perturbed me. He held a very delicate post – Director of Military Intelligence. Had he already been dishonest in his appointment, or his prior assignment in the Ordnance? Was his approval of malpractices a justification for what he had already done? Was he trying to soothe his conscience for past deeds? Or was he still the honest person I had known of and heard about, but was preparing himself for a dishonest deed? Whichever the case, he could have found no comfort in that discussion with me. Since I believe he was basically honest, I would give him the benefit of doubt.

It is possible that he had not yet indulged in malpractice. He may have been struggling with his conscience, in order to make his family secure in the manner suggested by him. He wanted to resolve the conflict. It is, indeed possible, that he managed to resolve it, after his discussion with me and remained his honest self.

In March, 1951, I had reached the age, and perhaps the status, when regular flying of Bomber or Fighter Bomber aircraft would not be possible. I, therefore, decided to familiarise myself with transport aircraft. I asked Flt. Lt. Dogar to help me convert to flying the twin-engined Dove. I made myself familiar with the controls on the ground for a day or so and then undertook the first flight on 8 March. I recollected later that whenever I did so, either Atcherley or Amlot would be in the vicinity of the aircraft. After the flight I went to my office, where I had called a meeting of several Staff Officers, to discuss a variety of subjects. We were in the middle of our meeting, when Atcherley came up to the door of my office, opened the curtain, looked in and immediately walked away.

On 9 March I went to my office at Air HQ as usual, to be there for 9 o'clock. Shortly after my arrival Atcherley asked me to go to his office. He had Amlot with him. He asked me to take a seat.

"I have a very serious matter to talk to you about," he said, and I frowned.

"I do not want it to be any more unpleasant than it need be," he went on. I waited for him to continue, as I was unable to make any comment on those introductory and cautionary remarks.

"Major Akbar Khan, CGS of the army, and Brigadier Latif have been dismissed and arrested this morning. Mrs. Akbar Khan and Faiz have also been arrested and are now in prison. They were planning a military coup d'état. It is believed that you were an accomplice. Are you prepared to answer my questions?" He asked at the end of the information and accusation.

"Yes, I am," I said.

It was a shock to learn that two senior officers had been summarily dismissed and imprisoned. This was entirely illegal. However, it was naïve of me to have thought, even for a moment, that the ruling clique would worry about the legalities of a case. They never had the moral courage to face those who may have different views from them. All those who differed, whether they were politicians or serving officers, were ostracised and maligned. Their place was the dungeon. The Prime Minister himself had refused to face me, even on a matter on which there was no clash between us. At least that is what I had thought. He could not be expected to call up his CGS of the army and Deputy Chief of Staff and discuss any difference of opinion that may have existed. He could have severely reprimanded them in the presence of their superiors and the Defence Secretary. No, he did not have an iota of courage to do that. He decided to put them away where he would not have to face them. He deputed foreign nationals to see me on his behalf, in a matter of critical importance to the life of the nation.

"I will ask you the questions and Amlot will record them and your answers." He said.

Then he proceeded to ask me questions concerning my movements since my return to Pakistan from Britain; my meetings with Akbar Khan, the reason for diverting an aircraft to carry Brigadier Latif. I told him all that I could remember. There was an omission which I recollected many weeks later. It was so insignificant that I neglected to mention it, it was when Siddique Raja had met me in Akbar's office on 6 February. I remembered this only when I learnt that Siddique was the 'approver'. I was asked to read over the questions and answers and sign the paper. I read them and signed to the effect that it was the gist of my statement. Atcherley then sent for the third senior British officer, Bob Bowditch. He told him to stay with me in Atcherley's office until his return.

"I am taking this to the Governor General," said Atcherley, "I shall come back with his orders."

"What am I to consider myself in the meantime?" I asked, because I had not been formally told that I was under arrest and I had an officer to escort me.

"You are to consider yourself nothing!" said Atcherley.

That was the first and the last time that he ever spoke to me in a harsh tone. I would not have tolerated it in any event, from him or anyone else. I knew that I was in a precarious situation but had he stayed any longer I would probably have exchanged words with him. I was not at all apprehensive about physical mistreatment and there was nothing else they could have done to me.

While Atcherley was away I tried to make conversation with Bowditch. At the best of times he was no brilliant conversationalist. Now he was literally mute. Anyway, I said that our part of the world seemed to be in turmoil. The day before, Razmara had been assassinated in Iran and now these arrests in Pakistan. But, it seemed that Bowditch had a mouthful of potatoes. He barely uttered a word.

Atcherley came back after about an hour, went straight to his desk and pretended to work. He may have been busy, but he seemed more preoccupied mentally than physically. It was perhaps another hour before he spoke to Iskander Mirza on the phone. He asked for information. A few minutes later the phone rang; he picked up the receiver and listened for a considerable time. He then came to where I was.

"You should go to your house with Bowditch. You will have to arrive there at 2 o'clock. You will be confined to your house. You will not be able to leave your house, but your family will be able to come and go as they wish. We will have to take your staff car away and remove the telephone." He concluded.

So I was formally placed under house arrest. It was not yet 2 o'clock. I went to my office, escorted by Bowditch, to collect my briefcase. At about twenty minutes before 2pm, Bowditch drove me in his car to Gizri Road where I lived. We arrived at my house at 2pm. The police guard had not yet arrived, but Bowditch left me at home and drove away.

My wife and children were waiting for me. I had come at the normal time, and therefore, in that respect, there was nothing unusual. My wife laid the table for lunch. However, I had yet to explain the situation to her, and the food choked me. That was the most difficult part. But I worried in vain. When I told my wife, she did not betray one trace of alarm or shock. She was closer to me than ever and we told the children in a perfectly calm manner. They took it in their stride and went about their business.

My wife and I were still talking about the incident when we heard the crunch, crunch, crunch of marching boots on the gravel outside. It was completely reminiscent of the crunching noise of the Nazi Storm Troopers. We often talked about it later, and of the mental condition of those at whose doors the Nazis must have halted. This was, indeed, a police state, and a cowardly fascist regime. A senior police officer and a magistrate came in to see me. They looked sheepish and guilty. I was given a paper to read. It stated that the Governor General was 'pleased' to confine me to the limits of the house, under Section 3 of the Security Act. They had the temerity to confine me in the interests of the security of Pakistan. I would give my life, many times over for the security of my country. And the Governor General and the Prime Minister knew it. Then for whose security was I being restricted? Not only Section 3 but a host of similar black acts and sections have since been used, to deprive hundreds and thousands of people of their liberty, for purely political reasons. The entire people have been gagged by oppression, fascist dictators like Ayub Khan, who threw a drag net around the nation, in the shape of martial law, ordnances and the infamous section 144, which the British imperialists had imposed on the people of the sub-continent, to curb their struggle for independence. But the seeds of oppression were deliberately sown in those early days of Pakistan. The mediocre leadership was completely intolerant of criticism. It would not tolerate difference of opinion. It was fearful of ideas. Being weak it resented strength; being cowardly it abhorred courage; being mediocre it detested talent; being entirely self-motivated, it hated nationalism and patriotism. But, of course, it claimed it had all the positive qualities which it lamentably lacked. Being the embodiment of the foregoing negative qualities, the ruling clique had to resort to intrigue. That phase began soon after Pakistani Independence and has not ceased.

I read the document more than once and wondered how the Governor General could have been 'pleased' to set his seal to that patently unjust order. I signed it and handed it back to the, none too steady hands, of the official.

We settled down to a routine at home. My wife stayed in the house and did not leave it for sixty seven days. That was the duration of my house arrest.

As I sat out and walked in the compound of the house I saw several familiar faces going past and around. Brigadier Zaman went past in a staff car. Such was the terror that had been engendered that he, who would have come a thousand miles to embrace me, threw but a furtive glance in my direction. I have no doubt that his heart bled and ached with grief, but he had not dared to express it. Then I saw Amlot drive past. He took a little longer look, no doubt thoroughly satisfied that my wings had been finally clipped.

One day an inspector of the armed police came to see me. He was in uniform and was armed with a revolver. He had obviously come with some special purpose. He was being informal and talkative.

"I hope you are comfortable," he said. "The armed guard is necessary, but I hope otherwise you are not inconvenienced."

"No, I am not being inconvenienced," I said. "And I am quite well and as happy as can be."

He then began to describe in detail the loading of a rifle, the driving home of the bolt, the closing of the breach and the clicking sound of the trigger being pressed.

"When one hears that click one's heart trembles," he said, looking at me for effect.

I literally glared back at him, angry at the implication that I could be frightened in such a stupid manner.

"My heart does not tremble at the clicking sound of a rifle being loaded," I said, showing my anger.

He looked down and fixed his eyes on the ground, around his own feet.

I then asked him as to why an armed guard had been posted on the roof of the house. Quite shamelessly he said,

"A small aircraft was seen flying near the house. It is to stop one landing here."

"I don't know who has sent you here on this despicable and stupid errand," I said. I was beside myself. "Be it Mr. Liaquat Ali or anyone else, you can tell them firstly, that I do not fear any clicking noises from rifles and secondly, that I am in my own country. I have more right to remain here than he has. He may have to leave the country, not I."

He left soon after. If he told me his name, I do not recollect it. I saw him once again. He was on escort duty when I was being taken to one of the prisons. He was a slim man, about five feet nine inches in height, of fair complexion, very light brown, perhaps green eyes, with a well trimmed brown moustache.

A few weeks after my house arrest I was told that a superintendent of the police wanted to see me. I invited him in. He was Habibullah Malik CID and was accompanied by an older person. The former said that he just wanted to have a general conversation with me. He had brought the other gentleman because he thought we were of the same age group. Habibullah may have been misled by my rank. In fact I was not much older, if at all, than him. I asked them to have tea with me. Habibullah, in particular, was surprised that I should have offered them hospitality and was embarrassed. Throughout the investigation and the trial I recollect hardly any government official who did not look guilty and embarrassed. Anyway, after some reluctance the offer of tea was accepted.

Habibullah talked generally about the case which was being built up. He was assisted occasionally by his companion. I made it clear that I had nothing to hide and that they were free to discuss the matter as they thought necessary. I vividly recollect three matters on which Habibullah spoke to me. He asked me as to what opinion Akbar Khan had of Ayub Khan. I repeated the formers words, which he had uttered a few weeks earlier. He the referred to the 'fateful day of 5 February, when he said I had met someone in Akbar's office at GHQ. I had met Brigadier Zaman and Gulzar Ahmed, Wing Commander Hai, Colonel Sultan Ali Shah and Lt. Col. Siddique Raja. I could not remember having met any other person in Akbar Khan's office on that day. I could not see why my meeting with any one of them should have been considered 'fateful'. I admit that for a while I had suspected that Brigadier Gulzar Ahmed may have lent his services to the British and local intelligence, spied on Akbar and agreed to concoct evidence against me. He was a distant relative, being married to a third cousin of mine, but I disliked his sly ways and his long background of service to British intelligence. We had not been on good terms since 1935. He was capable of betraying me but I knew he would not do so openly, for fear of being ostracised from our part of the family. I dismissed the possibility of his direct involvement against me, although I still considered that he may have given false information about me.

At no time did I think that the reference was to my meeting with Siddique Raja. And yet he was the one who, to save his skin, and at the insistence of other interests, had agreed to give false testimony against me on oath. He had to be made the 'approver' because he was present at the so-called conspiratorial meetings and the only one who could have given evidence against me. The meeting was, indeed, 'fateful'. It enabled the expert fabrication of evidence, to weave a plausible story around that purely accidental encounter.

Habibullah saw that I was denying all charges and accusations.

"If you say you had no part in the plot, then why do you think you are being implicated?" He asked.

"This question would be better put to the Defence Secretary, Iskander Mirza," I replied. "His British masters, who are very much here, may also be asked."

"But you know there is no smoke without fire." He said.

"In modern times this is a false statement," I said. "There is sometimes a mere spark but the smoke screen produced conceals whole army divisions and naval fleets. Metaphorically speaking there is a fire, but the smoke is beyond all proportion to it."

Habibullah Malik and his colleague departed a while later.

In the second week of May, 1951, an English language evening paper in Karachi carried the banner headline 'Janjua to be tried with others'.

So the deceit was complete. It had to come. The reports of my general behaviour and in particular my response to the rifle loading talk, must have gone back to those who had hoped that my spirit had been dampened, if not broken. I think I would not be wrong in assuming that such reports would have led to the intensification of efforts to concoct evidence and the decision to put me on trial. They were left with no option. Having gone so far, they could not have released me from house arrest. I could not be accommodated anywhere in the service nor, indeed, at that time, in the country at large.

On the morning of 15 May a police superintendent in uniform came to our house and showed me the document according to which I was to be placed under formal arrest. I was informed that I would be taken to a prison and that we were to leave as soon as I was ready. My wife packed my clothes and toilet effects. I said 'Khuda Hafiz' (God keep you safe) to her and my children and left with the armed police guard. At the airfield I found one of the PAF transport aircraft waiting for me. Flt. Lt. Dogar was Captain. It took the crew and me all our effort to remain calm and unconcerned. They had been instructed not to communicate with me. It required no great effort on my part to guess that these were the orders given to them. That foreign nationals were able to take me into custody and that they were able to issue orders to isolate me from those who were like my own children, the men of my nation's air force, was extremely painful.

We arrived at Lahore airport where we were met by Habibullah Malik. I stayed with him for a short while at some office and was then taken to the Borstal Institute (Prison). I had my first glimpse of a prison when the heavy double doors shut behind me. The Superintendent was Ghaffer, a doctor and a nice person. The Deputy Superintendent, Shah, took me to my cell or quarter. It was not uncomfortable but it being the first night away from my family and in isolation, I did feel desperately lonely. The ward in which I was lodged was close to the exercise yard and the next day I heard the inmates playing volley ball.

My sister and Major Nur Asif, with whom I had stayed just over three months earlier, came to see me. My sister perhaps the most sensitive in the family, sat completely silent. Without any other expression on her face, except a trembling lower lip, tears rolled down her cheeks. But those were the only tears I ever saw. My whole family kept excellent control over their emotions, at least when they were with me. My wife came to visit me on 19 May. It was my birthday and she had never missed one. She had packed and vacated the house in less than three days. I had been put under house arrest for two days before my wife's birthday and under formal arrest four days before my own.

However, before being lodged in prison, the police had to obtain a remand. No ordinary court would take cognisance of our case. A special act had been passed under the caption 'Rawalpindi Conspiracy Special Tribunal Act', according to which the Special Tribunal had been set up. It consisted of three members. Justice Sir Abdur Rahman as the President, who had a chronic case of high blood pressure; Justice Mohammed Sharif and Justice Amir-ud-Din were the members. Justice Sharif was in Lahore and I was taken to his house. When I arrived there I found seven other officers waiting for the same purpose. I looked round to see if I knew any of them. I had never seen nor heard of six of them. I only knew Brigadier Mohhamed Siddique (later he was to be called Sadiq to avoid confusion with the 'approver'). I recognised the name Arbab because of my family's long association with the Khalil Arbabs of Tehkal Bala, about a mile or so outside Peshawar. He was in fact from the same family, but I had not met him prior to that occasion.

We sat facing a tall chair and desk awaiting the arrival of Justice Sharif. In the meantime they all introduced themselves to me. Sadiq sat next to me. He nudged me with his elbow.

"They tell me that you are the 'approver'," he said.

I was taken aback by this and angry that Sadiq did not have the sense to realise that an 'approver' would not be sitting next to him.

"How can I be the 'approver'? What do I know that I can approve?" I said, irritably.

"Oh, but that is what I was told." He said stupidly.

I discovered later that with two or three exceptions the police interrogators had tried the age old lie of telling each that the other had confessed. This was not practiced on me for the obvious reasons. I had taken part in no allegedly conspiratorial meetings. That I was fiercely critical of the political leadership and foreign domination, I had not denied, nor would I conceal that fact. To this day my attitude has not changed.

In Borstal I was visited by one of the most hideous products of the British imperialist police. His name was Choudhry Mohhamed Hussain, Superintendent CID. He looked and sounded slimy. He had a conscience battered complexion. In the morning I told him all that I could remember. He said that he would commend me to the authorities for my co-operation. I did not find it necessary to thank him. His sly manner was sickening. In the afternoon he returned to cross-examine me. He became irritated when I would not say things he wanted me to say. He tried to misconstrue every simple, normal and quite innocuous incident. Of course, since I could not have imagined in my wildest dreams, that I would have to answer questions on them, I had made no particular note of my movements in the first and second week of February. I, therefore, had to be reminded about some of the routine or natural activities and meetings with individuals. Mohhamed Hussain implied that I was deliberately trying to conceal facts. Apart from this, he took delight in interrogating senior officers. He told me that some Generals in the army had trembled in his presence. I was extremely irritated at his arrogance and the detestable lying manner of his interrogation. He went round and round the same point, trying to prove how clever he was at entrapping the accused person. I have not witnessed an uglier example of imperialist trained police. He made some rough notes, in pencil, on brown foolscap paper. Later he produced a neatly written police diary, running into many pages and stated on oath, that that was my statement taken down by him as I had made it in the Borstal prison in Lahore. Since I was the accused I could not, on oath, repudiate that perjury.

In the first week of June, 1951, all the accused in the north were assembled at Lahore, Hyderbad and Sind. It had been decided to hold our trial in the traditional place of the British imperialists, who had tried the Mirs of Sind and several other political adversaries in that prison.

A special train was arranged to take us to that place. The train was heavily guarded. It had radio communication with the army, the police headquarters and the Ministry of Defence. We each had a first or second class compartment to ourselves. I was escorted by a Superintendent and two constables, all armed, in a first class compartment. The Deputy Inspector General of the armed police, Haq Nawaz Tiwana came to see me at one of the stations. Later I saw some of the accused taking walks on the platform with their escorts alongside. We had a long halt at a large station for the main meal. I saw Akbar Khan walking past my window. He turned round and saw me. He seemed surprised. He came back in front of my window.

"What are you doing here?" he asked seriously, and appeared to be concerned. I had known him as an excellent officer in command and on staff duties. He was courageous. He showed no signs of demoralisation. I found later that he was not, in any way, broken.

Then, however, I smiled at him and shrugged my shoulders.

The train pulled in at Hyderabad the following day. We went to the Central Prison. As the lofty double doors shut behind me, many more were to open, albeit in a closed court.

Afterword

My father, Mohamed Khan Janjua, died in August 1982. His memoir was a labour of love; love for his country, love for its people. It came to light many years after his death, and can be read as a significant account of the turbulent years marking the birth of Pakistan. The memoir ends at the point at which the trial of my father and twelve other men accused of conspiracy, would have begun. It is likely that he chose not to go into the details of the Rawalpindi Conspiracy Case because he perceived that the trial constituted a different chapter in his life. We will never know if it may have been the subject matter for a second book. There is no evidence to suggest that he left any notes or plans for such a book. He was a scrupulously honest and fearless man; it is therefore not surprising to learn that his 'superiors', in the forces and those in government, either felt threatened by him, or did not take kindly to him. Time and again he was thwarted in his efforts to progress and improve conditions in the air force. He tried where he could to make a positive difference to the lives of citizens.

The Rawalpindi Conspiracy Case; the trial and the years in prison, took their toll on my father. He was deeply hurt by them. In the years after his release I remember times when there were certain patterns on a piece of cloth or a pattern that signified the bars on a window, which would make him visibly upset. My mother alluded to the reasons when

I asked her what was wrong. He may have shared the details of his imprisonment and how he was treated, with my mother, but he would have considered me too young for those conversations, and he was too protective of me to have them. As those years faded in significance for him so did the opportunities for talking with me about them, when I was old enough to hear and understand. Although I did ask him on occasion, he only spoke about some of the friends who were on trial with him, Faiz Ahmed Faiz being one of them, and some of the substance of the trial. Modern day commentators have verified that the convictions of the 'conspirators' were based on circumstantial evidence at best. The Rawalpindi Conspiracy Case was a significant moment in the history of Pakistan. Although corruption was already on the rise, as is documented in the memoir, the imprisonment of the men of influence who were honest and most vehemently opposed to it, gave free rein to the leaders to make personal monetary gains in whatever way they deemed fit. The corruption at the top cascaded down into each and every transaction. It became a political reality and a mode of survival. My father was insightful; his words prophetic when we look at the social, political and economic conditions in Pakistan today. The British left behind a legacy of capitalism and corruption. America practically owns Pakistan, particularly given the loans it has poured into the country's armed forces.

In the years that followed his exile my father was as passionate as ever in his struggle to do his best for his country. In some ways it is a testament to his integrity and political ardour that he alone, of all the men who were imprisoned and convicted, was manoeuvred into exile. All the other men were able to remain in Pakistan. Akbar Khan was, some time later, appointed Chief of National Security under Prime Minister Zulfikar Ali Bhutto, an unlikely outcome for someone who had been imprisoned for conspiring to overthrow the government. As my father mentions in his memoir, Zulfikar Ali Bhutto, while in London, also offered him a post in government, which he declined on the basis of their political differences. As a result of my father's refusal Bhutto attempted to take my father's nationality away from him, which he will have known would hurt my father immeasurably, given the strength of his patriotism. In exile my father became a renowned journalist, writing occasionally for the Jang and Akhbar-e-Watan, London based Urdu newspapers. He launched a journal, 'Democratic Pakistan' in which he was openly critical of successive Pakistani governments and those policies which were harmful to the interests of the Pakistani people. The Pakistani Secret Service prohibited the export of the journal into Pakistan. In the late '60's and early '70's he was active in the anti Vietnam War movement. We were on a demonstration together when the mounted police charged us on their horses, as we shouted anti war slogans outside the American Embassy in Grosvenor Square, London. We ran into the small park opposite to escape being trampled on and later wondered how people had not died in all the fear and confusion that was generated by that attack. My father was also a member of the Society for Anglo-Chinese Understanding (SACU) where he sent me for lessons in Mandarin Chinese. A close friend of my father's lived in Beijing and undertook translation work for the government. He had been encouraging my father to join him there.

My father had occasional meetings with other left wing Pakistani activists in the country, including Tariq Ali who was a student activist at the time. One such meeting took place at the Ganges Restaurant in Soho, where a number of Pakistani activists came together to discuss the struggle for independence taking place in East Pakistan, later renamed Bangladesh. I attended the meeting with my father and recollect that there was an open expression of differences between those for and against independence for East Pakistan. My recollection is that having lived through the partition of India he was loathe to support any further division of the land and Muslims, into smaller and smaller groupings or states.

My father remained an activist even after illness overtook him. He continued to write and had connections with journalists working for the Manchester Guardian. He continued to meet with 'fellow travellers', both from within and outside the country.

His wish had been to end his days close to his sister and brother in Birmingham, he therefore moved to that city in his early sixties. Unfortunately certain adverse family circumstances did not allow him to remain there. He returned to London. His health deteriorated over the years through a series of strokes, until he died in August 1982. Our family was not well off. We asked PIA to fly my father's body back to Pakistan for burial, but they refused. The sense I had of their decision was that even after death he posed a threat to the government. I was aware that he would have been considered a martyr by many people, and there may have been an outcry about his having died in exile. This is largely conjecture on my part, although it is based on what I have heard some of his friends and members of our family say.

Had my father lived out his life in his own country, and maintained his position in the air force, my father would have made a huge contribution to the fight against corruption and for a leadership that was accountable and sensitive to the needs of its own people. There are others on the political stage at the moment who may take heart from the outspoken and honest appraisal of events surrounding Pakistan's struggle for independence, which my father has offered in his memoir.

Shahidah Janjua

Printed in Great Britain
by Amazon

21158384R00203